Financial Reporting Framework for Small- and Medium-Sized Entities

With Implementation Resources

Copyright © 2013 by
American Institute of Certified Public Accountants, Inc.
New York, NY 10036-8775

All rights reserved. For information about the procedure for requesting permission to make copies of any part of this work, please e-mail copyright@aicpa.org with your request. Otherwise, requests should be written and mailed to the Permissions Department, AICPA, 220 Leigh Farm Road, Durham, NC 27707-8110.

The Financial Reporting Framework for Small- and Medium-Sized Entities reproduces substantial portions of the CICA Handbook © 2012, published by The Canadian Institute of Chartered Accountants, Toronto, Canada (CICA), used under licence from CICA.

1 2 3 4 5 6 7 8 9 0 AccS 1 9 8 7 6 5 4 3

ISBN 978-1-93735-256-1

Introduction

In June 2013, the AICPA released the Financial Reporting Framework for Small- and Medium-Sized Entities (FRF for SMEs™ accounting framework). The AICPA anticipates that implementation resources may be a helpful accompaniment to the FRF for SMEs accounting framework. As such, the AICPA has developed this product, *Financial Reporting Framework for Small- and Medium-Sized Entities With Implementation Resources*, which includes two separate sections:

1. The FRF for SMEs accounting framework
2. Accompanying implementation resources

The FRF for SMEs accounting framework is a standalone, special purpose framework intended for use by privately-held small- to medium-sized entities when preparing their financial statements. Proper application of the framework in the preparation of financial statements does not require the use of the accompanying implementation resources.

The implementation resources are intended as aids to help CPA practitioners, financial statement preparers, and users and other stakeholders understand and apply the principles and criteria in the FRF for SMEs accounting framework and report on financial statements prepared on the basis of the framework. These resources include illustrative financial statements, a presentation and disclosure checklist, certain illustrative application examples, sample audit, compilation and review reports, and comparisons of the FRF for SMEs accounting framework to other bases of accounting. Although they accompany the FRF for SMEs accounting framework in the same product, the implementation resources are not considered part of the framework and are not to be viewed as requirements of the framework.

Notice to Readers

Financial Reporting Framework for Small- and Medium-Sized Entities was developed by a task force of CPA practitioners and professionals serving and working at small- and medium-sized entities and the staff of the AICPA. *Financial Reporting Framework for Small- and Medium-Sized Entities* has not been approved, disapproved, or otherwise acted upon by any technical committee of the AICPA or the Financial Accounting Standards Board and has no official or authoritative status.

AICPA FRF for SMEs Task Force (2012–2013)

David Morgan, Chair
Theresa Bible
DeAnn Hill
Karen Kerber
Kenneth R. Odom

Marc Parkinson
Pat Piteo
Thomas A. Ratcliffe
Eric P. Wallace

AICPA Staff

Charles E. Landes
Vice President
Professional Standards and Services

Robert Durak
Director, Private Company Financial Reporting
Accounting Standards

Daniel Noll
Director
Accounting Standards

Preface

About *Financial Reporting Framework for Small- and Medium-Sized Entities*

The FRF for SMEs™ accounting framework has been developed by the AICPA FRF for SMEs Task Force (task force) and the staff of the AICPA as a special purpose framework for small- and medium-sized entities. It is a self-contained financial reporting framework not based on accounting principles generally accepted in the United States of America (GAAP). Special purpose frameworks, with the exception of the contractual basis of accounting, are commonly referred to as *other comprehensive bases of accounting* or OCBOA. Special purpose frameworks include cash basis, modified cash basis, tax basis, regulatory basis, contractual basis, and other non-GAAP bases of accounting that utilize a definite set of logical, reasonable criteria that is applied to all material items appearing in the financial statements.

The FRF for SMEs accounting framework draws upon a blend of traditional accounting principles and accrual income tax methods of accounting. It utilizes historical cost as its primary measurement basis. In addition, it provides management with a suitable degree of optionality when choosing accounting policies to better meet the needs of the end users of the financial statements. The framework eschews prescriptive, detailed standards and voluminous disclosure requirements. Being a more intuitive and understandable framework for small business owners and the users of their financial statements, the framework lays out principles that encourage the use of professional judgment in the particular circumstances of a transaction or event.

The FRF for SMEs reporting option is a cost-beneficial solution for management, owners, and others who require financial statements that are prepared in a consistent and reliable manner in accordance with a non-GAAP framework that has undergone public comment and professional scrutiny. The accounting principles comprising it are appropriate for the preparation of small- and medium-sized entity financial statements, based on the needs of the financial statement users and cost and benefit considerations.

The task force that developed the FRF for SMEs accounting framework with AICPA staff consisted of professionals who have an abundance of experience serving smaller- to medium-sized entities.

The task force and staff believe that the FRF for SMEs accounting framework is criteria suitable for the preparation of general use financial statements and external use of the statements in situations that do not require GAAP financial statements. As such, the framework has the following attributes:

- *Objectivity*. The framework is free from bias.
- *Measurability*. The framework permits reasonably consistent measurements.
- *Completeness*. The framework is sufficiently complete so that those relevant factors that would alter a conclusion about the financial statements are not omitted.
- *Relevance*. The framework is relevant to financial statement users.

FRF-SME

Scope and Characteristics of Entities Utilizing the FRF for SMEs Accounting Framework

The FRF for SMEs accounting framework has been developed for small- to medium-sized entities that require reliable non-GAAP financial statements for internal use and external uses. The task force believes that this framework can be used by entities in many industry groups and may also be used by unincorporated, as well as incorporated, entities. The framework is not intended to be a substitute for GAAP when GAAP-based financial statements are necessary, as determined by the management of a private company and its financial statement users.

A standard definition of *small- and medium-sized entities* does not exist in the United States. However, the term is intuitive, widely recognized, and effectively descriptive of the scope of entities for which the FRF for SMEs accounting framework is intended. The task force and staff deliberately did not develop quantified size criteria for determining what is a small- and medium-sized entity because they decided that developing quantified size tests is not feasible and not an effective way of describing the kinds of entities for which the framework is intended. Rather, characteristics of typical entities that may utilize the framework are presented in the following text. These characteristics are not all-inclusive and are not presented as a list of required characteristics an entity must possess in order to utilize the framework. The AICPA has no authority to prevent or require the use of a special purpose framework like the FRF for SMEs accounting framework. These characteristics are presented as helpful guidelines for management and other stakeholders when determining the appropriateness and suitability of the FRF for SMEs accounting framework in the preparation of financial statements. Ultimately, the decision regarding which accounting framework best meets an entity's financial reporting needs rests with management. The FRF for SMEs accounting framework should only be used if the resulting financial statements are intended to be consistent with the concepts, principles, and criteria described in chapter 1, "Financial Statement Concepts," of *Financial Reporting Framework for Small- and Medium-Sized Entities*.

Certain Characteristics of Small- and Medium-Sized Entities Utilizing the FRF for SMEs Accounting Framework

This list presents certain characteristics of typical entities that may utilize the FRF for SMEs accounting framework. As stated previously, these characteristics are not all-inclusive and not presented as a list of required characteristics an entity must possess in order to utilize it:

- The entity does not have regulatory reporting requirements that essentially require it to use GAAP-based financial statements.
- A majority of the owners and management of the entity have no intention of going public.
- The entity is for-profit.
- The entity may be owner-managed, which is a closely held company in which the people who own a controlling ownership interest in the entity are substantially the same set of people who run the company.
- Management and owners of the entity rely on a set of financial statements to confirm their assessments of performance, cash flows, and of what they own and what they owe.

- The entity does not operate in an industry in which the entity is involved in transactions that require highly-specialized accounting guidance, such as financial institutions and governmental entities.
- The entity does not engage in overly complicated transactions.
- The entity does not have significant foreign operations.
- Key users of the entity's financial statements have direct access to the entity's management.
- Users of the entity's financial statements may have greater interest in cash flows, liquidity, statement of financial position strength, and interest coverage.
- The entity's financial statements support applications for bank financing when the banker does not base a lending decision solely on the financial statements but also on available collateral or other evaluation mechanisms not directly related to the financial statements.

Application of FRF for SMEs Accounting Framework Principles, Concepts, and Criteria

The task force and AICPA staff have developed the FRF for SMEs accounting framework to address transactions that are typically encountered by private, for-profit, small-, and medium-sized entities. If the framework does not specifically address a transaction, other event, or condition, management should use its judgment and apply the general principles, concepts, and criteria contained in the framework when developing accounting policies. The development and application of those policies should result in financial information that is intended to be consistent with the financial statement concepts described in chapter 1 of *Financial Reporting Framework for Small- and Medium-Sized Entities*.

Authority and Effective Date of the FRF for SMEs Accounting Framework

The AICPA has no authority to require the use of the FRF for SMEs accounting framework for any entity. Therefore, use of the framework is purely optional. Management that prepares an entity's financial statements in accordance with the framework may represent or assert that such financial statements have been prepared in accordance with the AICPA's FRF for SMEs accounting framework, a special purpose framework.

Because use of the framework is optional, there is no effective date for its implementation.

Maintenance of the FRF for SMEs Accounting Framework

Appreciating the limited accounting resources that typical entities utilizing the FRF for SMEs accounting framework have, as well as the nature of their financial reporting, the framework is intended to be a stable platform that does not undergo frequent amending or updating. At the same time, it is intended to be responsive to the financial reporting needs of small- and medium-sized entities and, therefore, will be modified in response to significant developments in accounting and financial reporting matters affecting those entities.

Accordingly, the task force and AICPA staff intend to monitor and assess input related to the implementation of the framework after its initial release and propose modifications they deem necessary. Afterwards, staff, with assistance from the task force, intends to review and propose amendments to the framework approximately every three or four years. Amendments will be primarily based on input from stakeholders and developments in accounting and financial reporting.

The AICPA's Accounting and Auditing Technical Hotline provides members with free, high-quality technical assistance by phone concerning issues related to accounting and financial reporting, auditing and attestation, compilation, and review standards. Questions and comments about the FRF for SMEs accounting framework can be directed to the technical hotline.

TABLE OF CONTENTS

Chapter		Paragraph
1	Financial Statement Concepts	.01-.46
	Purpose and Scope	.01-.03
	Financial Statements	.04-.07
	Objective of Financial Statements	.08
	Materiality	.09
	Qualitative Characteristics	.10-.16
	Understandability	.11
	Relevance	.12
	Reliability	.13
	Comparability	.14-.15
	Qualitative Characteristics Trade-off	.16
	Elements of Financial Statements	.17-.30
	Assets	.19-.22
	Liabilities	.23-.25
	Equity	.26
	Revenues	.27
	Expenses	.28
	Gains	.29
	Losses	.30
	Recognition Criteria	.31-.42
	Measurement	.43-.46
2	General Principles of Financial Statement Presentation and Accounting Policies	.01-.26
	Purpose and Scope	.01-.02
	Fair Presentation in Accordance With the FRF for SMEs Accounting Framework	.03-.06
	Going Concern	.07-.09
	Financial Statements	.10-.15
	Comparative Information	.16-.17
	Disclosure of Accounting Policies	.18-.19
	Disclosure	.20-.26
3	Transition	.01-.21
	Purpose and Scope	.01-.02
	Opening Statement of Financial Position	.03-.18
	Accounting Policies	.05-.07
	Election of Exemptions From Certain Principles in the FRF for SMEs Accounting Framework Upon Transition	.08-.12
	Exceptions to Retrospective Application of Certain Principles Within the FRF for SMEs Accounting Framework	.13-.18
	Disclosure	.19-.21
4	Statement of Financial Position	.01-.06
	Purpose and Scope	.01
	Presentation	.02-.06

5	**Current Assets and Current Liabilities**	.01-.12
	Purpose and Scope	.01-.02
	Current Assets	.03-.05
	Current Liabilities	.06-.09
	Debt	.10-.12
6	**Special Accounting Considerations for Certain Financial Assets and Liabilities**	.01-.22
	Purpose and Scope	.01
	Recognition	.02
	Measurement	.03
	Presentation	.04-.05
	Liabilities and Equity	.04
	Offsetting of a Financial Asset and a Financial Liability	.05
	Derecognition	.06-.10
	Transfers of Financial Assets, Including Receivables	.06
	Financial Liabilities	.07-.10
	Disclosure	.11-.22
	Financial Assets	.11-.12
	Transfers of Financial Assets (Including Receivables)	.13-.14
	Financial Liabilities	.15-.20
	Derivatives	.21
	Items of Income	.22
7	**Statement of Operations**	.01-.04
	Purpose and Scope	.01
	Presentation	.02-.04
8	**Statement of Cash Flows**	.01-.40
	Purpose and Scope	.01-.04
	Cash and Cash Equivalents	.05-.10
	Classification of Cash Flows	.11-.18
	Operating Activities	.14-.16
	Investing Activities	.17
	Financing Activities	.18
	Cash Flows From Operating Activities	.19-.22
	Cash Flows From Investing and Financing Activities	.23-.24
	Cash Flows on a Net Basis	.25
	Foreign Currency Cash Flows	.26
	Interest and Dividends	.27-.29
	Income Taxes	.30
	Business Combinations and Disposals of Business Units	.31-.33
	Noncash Transactions	.34-.35
	Disclosure	.36
	Cash and Cash Equivalents	.36-.38
	Business Combinations and Disposals of Business Units	.39
	Noncash Transactions	.40

Table of Contents

9	Accounting Changes, Changes in Accounting Estimates, and Correction of Errors	.01-.32
	Purpose and Scope	.01-.03
	Changes in Accounting Policies	.04-.06
	Applying Changes in Accounting Policies	.07-.13
	Retrospective Application	.08
	Limitations on Retrospective Application	.09-.13
	Changes in Accounting Estimates	.14-.20
	Errors	.21-.24
	Impracticability Regarding Retrospective Application	.25-.28
	Disclosure	.29-.32
	Changes in Accounting Policies	.29-.30
	Changes in Accounting Estimates	.31
	Errors	.32
10	Risks and Uncertainties	.01-.07
	Purpose and Scope	.01
	Nature of Operations	.02
	Use of Estimates	.03
	Significant Estimates	.04-.05
	Concentrations	.06-.07
11	Equity, Debt, and Other Investments	.01-.25
	Purpose and Scope	.01-.02
	Accounting for Investments—Recognition and Measurement	.03-.18
	Equity Method	.08-.16
	Cost Method	.17-.18
	Gains and Losses on Sales of Investments	.19
	Presentation	.20-.22
	Disclosure	.23-.25
12	Inventories	.01-.32
	Purpose and Scope	.01-.03
	Measurement of Inventories	.04-.25
	Cost of Inventories	.05-.15
	Cost Formulas	.16-.20
	Net Realizable Value	.21-.25
	Recognition as an Expense	.26-.27
	Disclosure	.28-.32
13	Intangible Assets	.01-.66
	Purpose and Scope	.01-.06
	Intangible Assets	.07-.58
	Identifiability	.09-.10
	Control	.11-.13
	Future Economic Benefits	.14
	Recognition and Measurement	.15-.46
	Recognition of an Expense	.47-.50
	Start-Up Costs	.51
	Past Expenses Not to Be Recognized as Assets	.52
	Subsequent Measurement	.53-.58

	Goodwill	.59-.61
	Presentation	.62-.63
	Disclosure	.64-.66
14	**Property, Plant, and Equipment**	.01-.26
	Purpose and Scope	.01-.02
	Measurement	.03-.20
	Cost	.03-.12
	Depreciation	.13-.19
	Asset Retirement Obligations	.20
	Disclosure	.21-.26
15	**Disposal of Long-Lived Assets and Discontinued Operations**	.01-.25
	Purpose and Scope	.01-.02
	Long-Lived Assets to Be Disposed of by Sale	.03-.16
	Recognition	.03-.08
	Measurement	.09-.10
	Changes to a Plan of Sale	.11-.13
	Statement of Financial Position Presentation	.14-.16
	Long-Lived Assets to Be Disposed of Other Than by Sale	.17-.19
	Discontinued Operations	.20-.23
	Disclosure	.24-.25
16	**Commitments**	.01-.03
	Purpose and Scope	.01
	Disclosure	.02-.03
17	**Contingencies**	.01-.40
	Purpose and Scope	.01-.04
	Measurement of Uncertainty	.05-.06
	Accounting Treatment	.07-.12
	Contingent Losses	.07-.11
	Contingent Gains	.12
	Disclosure	.13-.18
	Contingent Losses	.13-.15
	Contingent Gains	.16-.18
	Asset Retirement Obligations	.19-.37
	Recognition	.21-.23
	Measurement	.24-.30
	Recognition and Allocation of an Asset Retirement Cost	.31-.35
	Effects of Funding and Assurance Provisions	.36
	Disclosure	.37
	Guarantees	.38-.40
18	**Equity**	.01-.40
	Purpose and Scope	.01-.02
	Acquisition or Redemption of Shares	.03-.14
	Acquisition of Shares	.04-.07
	Resale of Acquired Shares	.08-.10
	Retirement or Cancellation of Shares	.11
	Dividends	.12-.14

Table of Contents

	Accounting for Stock and Other Equity Compensation	.15
	Equity Transactions With Nonemployees	.16
	Presentation	.17-.25
	Disclosure	.26-.33
	Limited Liability Entities	.34-.40
	Disclosure	.38-.40
19	**Revenue**	.01-.33
	Purpose and Scope	.01-.02
	Recognition	.03-.24
	Accounting for Contract-Related Claims	.16-.18
	Effect of Uncertainties	.19-.22
	Reporting Revenue Gross or Net	.23-.24
	Presentation	.25
	Disclosure	.26-.33
20	**Retirement and Other Postemployment Benefits**	.01-.51
	Purpose and Scope	.01-.04
	Basic Principles	.05-.07
	Recognition, Measurement, and Disclosure— Defined Contribution Plans	.08-.09
	Recognition and Measurement	.08
	Disclosure	.09
	Recognition, Measurement, and Disclosure— Multiemployer Plans	.10-.11
	Recognition and Measurement	.10
	Disclosure	.11
	Recognition, Measurement, and Disclosure— Individual Deferred Compensation Contracts	.12-.14
	Recognition and Measurement	.12-.13
	Disclosure	.14
	Recognition, Measurement, and Disclosure— Defined Benefit Plans	.15-.48
	Current Contribution Payable Method	.16-.17
	Accrued Benefit Obligation Methods	.18-.48
	Termination Benefits	.49-.51
	Disclosure	.51
21	**Income Taxes**	.01-.63
	Purpose and Scope	.01
	Accounting Policy	.02
	Entities Not Subject to Income Taxes	.03-.04
	Taxes Payable Method	.05-.10
	Recognition	.06-.08
	Measurement	.09
	Intraperiod Allocation	.10
	Deferred Income Taxes Method	.11-.53
	The Basic Principles of Deferred Income Taxes	.11
	Recovery or Settlement of the Carrying Amount of an Asset or Liability	.12-.15
	Unused Tax Losses, Income Tax Reductions, and Certain Other Items	.16
	Business Combinations	.17-.18
	Recognition	.19-.53

	Presentation	.54-.59
	Income Tax Expense	.54
	Income Tax Liabilities and Income Tax Assets	.55-.59
	Disclosure	.60-.63
22	**Subsidiaries**	.01-.14
	Purpose and Scope	.01-.02
	Recognition and Presentation	.03-.11
	Consolidated Financial Statements	.04-.09
	Nonconsolidated Financial Statements	.10-.11
	Disclosure	.12-.14
	Consolidated Financial Statements	.12
	Nonconsolidated Financial Statements	.13-.14
23	**Consolidated Financial Statements and Noncontrolling Interests**	.01-.37
	Purpose and Scope	.01-.02
	Combined Financial Statements	.03-.04
	Preparation of Consolidated Financial Statements	.05-.22
	At the Date of Acquisition	.06-.09
	At Dates Subsequent to an Acquisition	.10-.12
	Intercompany Balances, Gains and Losses, and Transactions	.13
	Depreciation and Amortization	.14-.15
	Shareholders' Equity Transactions With Interests Outside the Consolidated Group	.16-.19
	Miscellaneous	.20-.22
	Noncontrolling Interests	.23-.30
	Procedures	.23-.24
	Change in Ownership Interest in a Consolidated Subsidiary	.25-.26
	Loss of Control of a Consolidated Subsidiary	.27-.30
	Presentation of Consolidated Financial Statements and Noncontrolling Interests	.31-.34
	Statement of Operations Presentation in a Period of an Acquisition or Disposal	.32
	Noncontrolling Interests	.33-.34
	Disclosure	.35-.37
24	**Interests in Joint Ventures**	.01-.27
	Purpose and Scope	.01-.02
	Definitions	.03-.09
	Jointly-Controlled Operations	.10
	Jointly-Controlled Assets	.11
	Jointly-Controlled Entities	.12-.13
	Recognition	.14
	Proportionate Consolidation	.15-.18
	Presentation	.19-.21
	Disclosure	.22-.27

25	Leases	.01-.75
	Purpose and Scope	.01-.02
	Classification	.03-.12
	Accounting Treatment by a Lessee	.13-.26
	Method of Accounting for a Capital Lease	.13-.18
	Presentation of a Capital Lease	.19-.21
	Method of Accounting for an Operating Lease	.22-.26
	Accounting Treatment by a Lessor	.27-.55
	Method of Accounting for a Direct Financing Lease	.27-.33
	Method of Accounting for a Sales-Type Lease	.34-.42
	Collectability and Recoverability Issues	.43-.45
	Presentation of a Direct Financing or Sales-Type Lease	.46-.49
	Method of Accounting for an Operating Lease	.50-.51
	Participation by a Third Party	.52-.55
	Subleases	.56
	Sale-Leaseback Transaction	.57-.64
	Leases Involving Land and Buildings	.65-.67
	Related Party Leases	.68
	Disclosure	.69-.75
	Capital Lease—Lessee	.69-.72
	Operating Lease—Lessee	.73
	Direct Financing or Sales-Type Lease—Lessor	.74
	Operating Lease—Lessor	.75
26	Related Party Transactions	.01-.15
	Purpose and Scope	.01-.02
	Identification of Related Parties	.03-.06
	Measurement	.07
	Disclosure	.08-.15
	Description of Relationship	.10
	Description of Transaction	.11-.12
	Amount of Transactions	.13
	Representations About Market Value	.14
	Additional Disclosures	.15
27	Subsequent Events	.01-.13
	Purpose and Scope	.01-.04
	Accounting Treatment	.05-.09
	Disclosure	.10-.13
28	Business Combinations	.01-.63
	Purpose and Scope	.01-.02
	Identifying a Business Combination	.03
	The Acquisition Method	.04-.27
	Identifying the Acquirer	.06
	Determining the Acquisition Date	.07-.08
	Recognizing and Measuring the Identifiable Assets Acquired, Liabilities Assumed, and Any Noncontrolling Interest in the Acquiree	.09

	Recognition Conditions...............	.10-.12
	Classifying or Designating Identifiable Assets Acquired and Liabilities Assumed in a Business Combination............	.13-.27
	Recognizing and Measuring Goodwill or a Gain From a Bargain Purchase..............	.28-.36
	Bargain Purchases....................	.30-.32
	Consideration Transferred..............	.33-.36
	Additional Guidance for Applying the Acquisition Method to Particular Types of Business Combinations.........................	.37-.40
	A Business Combination Achieved in Stages	.37-.38
	A Business Combination Achieved Without the Transfer of Consideration..........	.39-.40
	Measurement Period......................	.41-.46
	Determining What Is Part of the Business Combination Transaction	.47-.49
	Acquisition-Related Costs	.49
	Subsequent Measurement and Accounting.......	.50-.51
	Indemnification Assets	.51
	Combinations of Entities Under Common Control ..	.52-.58
	Recognition.........................	.53
	Measurement	.54-.55
	Financial Statement Presentation in Period of Transfer.......................	.56-.57
	Comparative Financial Statement Presentation for Prior Years	.58
	Disclosure	.59-.63
	Combinations of Entities Under Common Control	.63
29	New Basis (Push-Down) Accounting	.01-.18
	Purpose and Scope	.01
	Recognition............................	.02-.07
	Acquisition of an Entity—Push-Down Accounting ..	.08-.15
	Measurement	.08-.11
	Retained Earnings and the Revaluation Adjustment	.12-.15
	Income Tax Benefits	.16-.18
	Disclosure..........................	.17-.18
30	Nonmonetary Transactions	.01-.13
	Purpose and Scope	.01-.02
	Measurement...........................	.03-.05
	Measurement Criteria	.06-.10
	Commercial Substance................	.07-.09
	Restructuring or Liquidation.............	.10
	Recognition of Gains and Losses	.11-.12
	Disclosure	.13

31	Foreign Currency Translation	.01-.13
	Purpose and Scope	.01-.03
	Translation of Foreign Currency Transactions and Related Financial Statement Items of the Reporting Entity	.04-.12
	Use of Averages or Other Methods of Approximation	.12
	Disclosure	.13
Glossary		173
Implementation Resources		189

Chapter 1

Financial Statement Concepts

Purpose and Scope

1.01 This chapter describes the concepts underlying the development and use of accounting principles in general purpose financial statements (hereinafter referred to as *financial statements*). Such financial statements are designed to meet the common information needs of *owners*[1] and management that need reliable financial statements for internal use, as well as the needs of external users of financial information, about an entity.

1.02 This chapter may be used by preparers of financial statements and accounting practitioners when exercising their professional judgment about the application of the FRF for SMEs accounting framework.

1.03 This chapter does not establish principles for particular measurement or disclosure issues. Nothing in the chapter overrides any specific principles elsewhere in the framework.

Financial Statements

1.04 Financial statements normally include a statement of financial position, a statement of operations, a statement of changes in *equity* (changes in equity may be disclosed in the notes to the financial statements or as part of another financial statement), and a statement of cash flows. Notes to financial statements are an integral part of such statements, as are the supporting schedules to which the financial statements are referenced. However, nothing precludes the use of this framework when only a single financial statement (for example, a statement of financial position) is prepared. However, if a statement of financial position and a statement of operations are prepared, a statement of cash flows should also be prepared.

1.05 Financial statements are based on representations of past, rather than future, transactions and events, although they often require estimates to be made in anticipation of future transactions and events and include measurements that may, by their nature, be approximations.

1.06 Material presentation items should not be netted in the financial statements, unless specifically allowed by the framework.

1.07 Financial statements are available to be issued when

   a. a complete set (or a single financial statement, if a complete set is not being prepared) of financial statements, including all required note disclosures, has been prepared (see paragraphs 2.10–.13);

   b. all final adjusting journal entries have been reflected in the financial statements (for example, adjustments for income taxes and bonuses);

   c. no changes to the financial statements are planned or expected; and

---

[1] Italicized terms are defined in the glossary.

d. the financial statements meeting the preceding requirements have been approved in accordance with the entity's process to finalize its financial statements.

Objective of Financial Statements

1.08 The objective of financial statements is to communicate information that is useful to management, creditors, and other users (users) when making their resource allocation decisions or assessing management stewardship, or both. Consequently, financial statements provide information about

  a. an entity's economic resources, obligations, and equity;

  b. changes in an entity's economic resources, obligations, and equity; and

  c. the economic performance of the entity.

Materiality

1.09 Users are interested in information that may affect their decision making. *Materiality* is the term used to describe the significance of financial statement information to users. An item of information, or an aggregate of items, is material if it is *probable* that its omission or misstatement would influence or change a decision. Materiality is a matter of professional judgment in the particular circumstances. Materiality is considered when applying the principles in the FRF for SMEs accounting framework and meeting the objectives of financial statements. Items that are immaterial to the financial statements are not required to be separately presented or disclosed.

Qualitative Characteristics

1.10 *Qualitative characteristics* define and describe the attributes of information provided in financial statements that make that information useful to users. The four principal qualitative characteristics are understandability, relevance, reliability, and comparability.

Understandability

1.11 For the information provided in financial statements to be useful, users must be able to understand it. It is assumed that users have a reasonable understanding of business and economic activities and accounting, together with a willingness to study the information with reasonable diligence.

Relevance

1.12 For the information provided in financial statements to be useful, it must be relevant to the users' decisions. Information is relevant by its nature when it can influence the users' decisions by helping them evaluate the financial impact of past, present, or future transactions and events or confirm or correct previous evaluations. Relevance is achieved through information that has predictive value or feedback value and by its timeliness:

a. *Predictive value and feedback value.* Information that helps users to predict an entity's future income and cash flows has predictive value. Although information provided in financial statements will not normally be a prediction in itself, it may be useful for making predictions. For example, the predictive value of the statement of operations is enhanced if abnormal items are separately disclosed. Information that confirms or corrects previous predictions has feedback value. Information often has both predictive value and feedback value.

b. *Timeliness.* For information to be useful for decision making, it must be received by the user before it loses its capacity to influence decisions. The usefulness of information for decision making declines as time elapses.

Reliability

1.13 For the information provided in financial statements to be useful, it must be reliable. Information is reliable when it is in agreement with the actual underlying transactions and events; the agreement is capable of independent verification; and the information is reasonably free from error and bias. Reliability is achieved through representational faithfulness, verifiability, and neutrality. Neutrality is affected by the use of conservatism when making judgments under conditions of uncertainty:

a. *Representational faithfulness.* Representational faithfulness is achieved when transactions and events affecting the entity are presented in financial statements in a manner that is in agreement with the actual underlying transactions and events. Thus, transactions and events are accounted for and presented in a manner that conveys their substance rather than necessarily their legal or other form.

The substance of transactions and events may not always be consistent with the substance apparent from their legal or other form. To determine the substance of a transaction or event, it may be necessary to consider a group of related transactions and events as a whole. The determination of the substance of a transaction or event will be a matter of professional judgment in the circumstances.

b. *Verifiability.* The financial statement representation of a transaction or event is verifiable if knowledgeable and independent observers concur that it is in agreement with the actual underlying transaction or event with a reasonable degree of precision. Verifiability focuses on the correct application of a basis of measurement rather than its appropriateness.

c. *Neutrality.* Information is neutral when it is free from bias that would lead users toward making decisions that are influenced by the way the information is measured or presented. Bias in measurement occurs when a measure tends to consistently overstate or understate the items being measured. In the selection of accounting principles, bias may occur when the selection is made with the interests of particular users or with particular economic or political objectives in mind.

FRF-SME 1.13

Financial statements that do not include everything necessary for faithful representation of transactions, and events affecting the entity would be incomplete and, therefore, potentially biased.

d. *Conservatism.* Use of conservatism in making judgments under conditions of uncertainty affects the neutrality of financial statements in an acceptable manner. When uncertainty exists, estimates of a conservative nature attempt to ensure that assets, revenues, and gains are not overstated and, conversely, that liabilities, expenses, and losses are not understated. However, conservatism does not encompass the deliberate understatement of assets, revenues, and gains or the deliberate overstatement of liabilities, expenses, and losses.

Comparability

1.14 *Comparability* is a characteristic of the relationship between two pieces of information, rather than of a particular piece of information by itself. It enables users to identify similarities in, and differences between, the information provided by two sets of financial statements. Comparability is important when comparing the financial statements of two different entities and when comparing the financial statements of the same entity over multiple periods or at different points in time.

1.15 Comparability in the financial statements of an entity is enhanced when the same accounting policies are used consistently from period to period. Consistency helps prevent misconceptions that might result from the application of different accounting policies in different periods. When a change in accounting policy is deemed to be appropriate, disclosure of the effects of the change may be necessary to maintain comparability.

Qualitative Characteristics Trade-off

1.16 In practice, a trade-off between qualitative characteristics is often necessary, particularly between relevance and reliability. For example, there is often a trade-off between the timeliness of producing financial statements and the reliability of the information reported in the statements. Generally, the aim is to achieve an appropriate balance among the characteristics in order to meet the objective of financial statements. The relative importance of the characteristics in different cases is a matter of professional judgment.

Elements of Financial Statements

1.17 *Elements of financial statements* are the basic categories of items portrayed therein in order to meet the objective of financial statements. Two types of elements are those that describe the economic resources, obligations, and equity of an entity at a point in time and those that describe changes in economic resources, obligations, and equity over a period of time. Notes to financial statements, which are useful for the purpose of clarification or further explanation of the items in financial statements, although an integral part of financial statements, are not considered to be an element.

FRF-SME 1.14

1.18 *Net income* is the residual amount after expenses and losses are deducted from revenues and gains. Net income generally includes all transactions and events increasing or decreasing the equity of the entity, except those that result from equity contributions and distributions.

Assets

1.19 *Assets* are economic resources controlled by an entity as a result of past transactions or events and from which future economic benefits may be obtained.

1.20 Assets have three essential characteristics:

   a. They embody a future benefit that involves a capacity, singly or in combination with other assets, to contribute directly or indirectly to future net cash flows.

   b. The entity can control access to the benefit.

   c. The transaction or event giving rise to the entity's right to, or control of, the benefit has already occurred.

1.21 It is not essential for control of access to the benefit to be legally enforceable for a resource to be an asset, provided the entity can control its use by other means.

1.22 A close association exists between incurring expenditures and generating assets, but the two do not necessarily coincide. Therefore, when an entity incurs an expenditure, this may provide evidence that future economic benefits were sought but is not conclusive proof that an item satisfying the definition of an asset has been obtained. Similarly, the absence of a related expenditure does not preclude an item from satisfying the definition of an asset and, thus, becoming a candidate for recognition in the statement of financial position. For example, items that have been donated to the entity may satisfy the definition of an asset.

Liabilities

1.23 *Liabilities* are obligations of an entity arising from past transactions or events, the settlement of which may result in the transfer or use of assets, provision of services, or other yielding of economic benefits in the future.

1.24 Liabilities have three essential characteristics:

   a. They embody a duty or responsibility to others that entails settlement by future transfer or use of assets, provision of services, or other yielding of economic benefits, at a specified or determinable date, on occurrence of a specified event, or on demand.

   b. The duty or responsibility obligates the entity, leaving it little or no discretion to avoid it.

   c. The transaction or event obligating the entity has already occurred.

1.25 Liabilities do not have to be legally enforceable, provided that they otherwise meet the definition of liabilities; they can be based on equitable or constructive obligations. A constructive obligation is one that can be inferred from the facts in a particular situation, as opposed to a contractually-based obligation.

Equity

1.26 *Equity* is the ownership interest in the assets of an entity after deducting its liabilities. Although equity of an entity in total is a residual, it includes specific categories of items (for example, types of capital stock, additional paid-in capital, and retained earnings). As used in the FRF for SMEs accounting framework, the term *retained earnings* also refers to owners' capital accounts, depending on the nature of the entity.

Revenues

1.27 *Revenues* are increases in economic resources, either by way of inflows or enhancements of assets or reductions of liabilities, resulting from the ordinary activities of an entity. Revenues of entities normally arise from the sale of goods, the rendering of services, or the use by others of entity resources yielding rent, interest, royalties, or dividends.

Expenses

1.28 *Expenses* are decreases in economic resources, either by way of outflows or reductions of assets or incurrence of liabilities, resulting from an entity's ordinary revenue-generating or service delivery activities.

Gains

1.29 *Gains* are increases in equity from peripheral or incidental transactions and events affecting an entity and from all other transactions, events, and circumstances affecting the entity, except those that result from revenues or equity contributions.

Losses

1.30 *Losses* are decreases in equity from peripheral or incidental transactions and events affecting an entity and from all other transactions, events, and circumstances affecting the entity, except those that result from expenses or distributions of equity.

Recognition Criteria

1.31 *Recognition* is the process of including an item in the financial statements of an entity. Recognition consists of the addition of the amount involved into statement totals, together with a narrative description of the item (for example, "inventory" or "sales") in a statement. Similar items may be grouped together in the financial statements for the purpose of presentation.

1.32 Recognition does not mean disclosure in the notes to the financial statements. Notes either provide further details about items recognized in the financial statements or provide information about items that do not meet the criteria for recognition and, thus, are not recognized in the financial statements.

1.33 Whether any particular item is recognized will require the application of professional judgment when considering whether the specific circumstances meet the recognition criteria.

1.34 The recognition criteria are as follows:

a. The item has an appropriate basis of measurement, and a reasonable estimate can be made of the amount involved.

b. For items that involve obtaining or giving up future economic benefits, it is probable that such benefits will be obtained or given up.

1.35 It is possible that an item will meet the definition of an element but still not be recognized in the financial statements because it is not probable that future economic benefits will be obtained or given up or because a reasonable estimate cannot be made of the amount involved. It may be appropriate to provide information about items that do not meet the recognition criteria in notes to the financial statements. Not recognizing an expenditure as an asset does not imply either that the intention of management when incurring the expenditure was other than to generate future economic benefits for the entity or that management was misguided. The only implication is that the degree of certainty that economic benefits will flow to the entity beyond the current accounting period is insufficient to warrant the recognition of an asset.

1.36 Items recognized in financial statements are accounted for in accordance with the accrual basis of accounting. The accrual basis of accounting recognizes the effect of transactions and events in the period in which the transactions and events occur, regardless of whether there has been a receipt or payment of cash or its equivalent.

1.37 Revenues are generally recognized when performance is achieved or partially achieved in the context of contracts in process, and there is reasonable assurance regarding measurement and collectability of the consideration.

1.38 Gains are generally recognized when realized.

1.39 Expenses and losses are generally recognized when an expenditure or previously recognized asset does not have future economic benefit. Expenses are related to a period on the basis of transactions or events occurring in that period or by allocation.

1.40 Expenses are recognized in the statement of operations on the basis of a direct association between the costs incurred and the earning of specific items of income. This process, commonly referred to as the *matching of costs with revenues*, involves the simultaneous or combined recognition of revenues and expenses that result directly and jointly from the same transactions or other events. For example, the various components of expense making up the cost of goods sold are recognized at the same time as the income derived from the sale of the goods.

1.41 When economic benefits are expected to arise over several accounting periods and the association with income can only be broadly or indirectly determined, expenses are recognized in the statement of operations on the basis of systematic and rational allocation procedures. This is often necessary when recognizing the expenses associated with the using up of assets such as property, plant, and equipment; patents; and trademarks. In such cases, the expense is referred to as *depreciation* or *amortization*. These allocation procedures are intended to recognize expenses in the accounting periods in which the economic benefits associated with these items are consumed or expire.

1.42 An expense is recognized immediately when an expenditure produces no future economic benefits or when, and to the extent that, future economic benefits do not qualify, or cease to qualify, for recognition as an asset.

Measurement

1.43 *Measurement* is the process of determining the amount at which an item is recognized in the financial statements. An amount can be measured on a number of bases. However, financial statements are prepared primarily using the historical cost basis of measurement whereby transactions and events are recognized in financial statements at the amount of cash or cash equivalents paid or received or at the market value ascribed to them when they took place.

1.44 Other bases of measurement are also used but only in limited circumstances. They include the following:

a. *Replacement cost.* The amount that would be needed currently to acquire an equivalent asset.

b. *Realizable value.* The amount that would be received by selling an asset in the ordinary course of business. Market value may be used to estimate realizable value when a market for an asset exists.

c. *Present value.* The discounted amount of future cash flows expected to be received from an asset or required to settle a liability.

d. *Market value.* The amount of the consideration that would be agreed upon in an arm's length transaction between knowledgeable, willing parties who are under no compulsion to act.

1.45 Financial statements are prepared with no adjustment being made for the effect on capital of a change in the general purchasing power of the currency during the period (in other words, inflation or deflation).

1.46 Financial statements are prepared on the assumption that the entity is a going concern, meaning it will continue in operation for the foreseeable future and will be able to realize assets and discharge liabilities in the normal course of operations. Different bases of measurement may be appropriate when the entity is not expected to continue in operation for the foreseeable future. The FRF for SMEs accounting framework should be used only by an entity that is a going concern (see chapter 2, "General Principles of Financial Statement Presentation and Accounting Policies").

Chapter 2

General Principles of Financial Statement Presentation and Accounting Policies

Purpose and Scope

2.01 Financial reporting is, essentially, a process of communication of information. Although the success of this communication depends upon the appropriateness of the accounting principles followed and, ultimately, the degree of understanding by the readers of the financial statements, it also depends upon the extent and clarity of presentation and disclosure in the financial statements. This chapter establishes general principles of financial statement presentation.

2.02 Decisions about presentation and disclosure in specific situations require the exercise of professional judgment, consideration of the FRF for SMEs accounting framework, and recognition of specific provisions in governing statutes or regulations. Effective reporting also gives recognition to new problems as they arise and changes in the requirements of investors, creditors, governments, and other applicable stakeholders.

Fair Presentation in Accordance With the FRF for SMEs Accounting Framework

2.03 Financial statements should present fairly in accordance with the FRF for SMEs accounting framework, the financial position, results of operations, and cash flows of an entity (that is, represent faithfully the substance of transactions and other events in accordance with the elements of financial statements and the recognition and measurement criteria set out in chapter 1, "Financial Statement Concepts").

2.04 A fair presentation in accordance with the framework is achieved by

   a. applying the framework;
   b. providing sufficient information about transactions or events having an effect on the entity's financial position, results of operations, and cash flows for the periods presented that are of such size, nature, and incidence that their disclosure is necessary to understand that effect; and
   c. providing information in a manner that is clear and understandable.

2.05 Management exercises professional judgment to provide sufficient information about the extent and nature of transactions or events having an effect on the entity's financial position, results of operations, and cash flows for the periods presented that are of such size, nature, and incidence that their disclosure is necessary to understand that effect. This information should include the significant terms and conditions of such transactions, as well as the nature of such events and their financial effects on the periods presented.

FRF-SME 2.05

2.06 Management provides information in a manner that clearly conveys the nature and extent, and significant terms and conditions, of the related transactions. Financial statements are prepared in such form and use such terminology and classification of items that significant information is readily understandable. Items not significant in themselves are grouped with other items closest to their nature.

Going Concern

2.07 When preparing financial statements, management should make an assessment of whether the going concern basis of accounting is appropriate. The going concern basis of accounting presumes that an entity will be able to realize its assets and meet its obligations in the ordinary course of business. The going concern basis of accounting is appropriate unless management either intends to liquidate the entity or has no realistic alternative but to do so. The FRF for SMEs accounting framework should be used only by an entity that is a going concern. An entity that is not a going concern should prepare its financial statements on the liquidation basis of accounting.

2.08 When making its assessment about whether the going concern basis is appropriate, management should take into account all known and available information about the future, which is limited to 12 months from the statement of financial position date. When management becomes aware of material uncertainties relating to events or conditions and concludes that a known event or condition is probable of having a *severe impact*[1] on the entity's ability to realize its assets and discharge its liabilities in the ordinary course of business, the entity should disclose those uncertainties along with its plans for dealing with the adverse effects of the conditions and events.

2.09 The degree of consideration, and management's assessment, depends on the facts in each case. When an entity has a history of profitable operations and ready access to financial resources, a conclusion that the going concern basis of accounting is appropriate may be reached without detailed analysis. In other cases, management may need to consider a wide range of factors relating to current and expected profitability, debt repayment schedules, and potential sources of replacement financing before it can satisfy itself that the going concern basis is appropriate.

Financial Statements

2.10 Financial statements, including notes to such statements and supporting schedules, should include all information required for a fair presentation in accordance with the FRF for SMEs accounting framework.

2.11 Financial statements include the statement of financial position, statement of operations, statement of changes in equity (changes in equity may be disclosed in the notes to the financial statements or as part of another financial statement), and statement of cash flows. The selection of specific financial statement titles is a matter of judgment, and the preceding titles are not the only acceptable titles (for example, the statement of financial position may be titled the statement of assets, liabilities, and equity, and the statement of operations may be titled the statement

---

[1] Italicized terms are defined in the glossary.

of revenue and expenses.) Notes to financial statements, and supporting schedules to which the financial statements are cross-referenced, are an integral part of such statements.

2.12 Supplementary information set out in other material attached to, or submitted with, financial statements are not an integral part of the financial statements.

2.13 Nothing in the FRF for SMEs accounting framework precludes management from using it to prepare a single financial statement, rather than a complete set of financial statements.

2.14 Notes to financial statements, and supporting schedules to which the financial statements are cross-referenced, are often essential to clarify or further explain the items in the financial statements. They have the same significance as if the information or explanations were set out in the body of the statements themselves. However, they are not to be used as a substitute for proper accounting treatment. Accounting treatments that are not in accordance with the FRF for SMEs accounting framework are not rectified either by disclosure of the *accounting policies* used or by information provided in notes or supporting schedules. The information conveyed by every note or supporting schedule is consistent with the accounting treatment given to the specific item to which it relates.

2.15 Management should select only one set of accounting policies for purposes of preparing financial statements for general use in accordance with the framework. See chapter 9, "Accounting Changes, Changes in Accounting Estimates, and Correction of Errors," for criteria about changing accounting policies, together with the accounting treatment and disclosure of changes in accounting policies.

Comparative Information

2.16 Financial statements may be prepared on a comparative basis. Comparative information is normally meaningful. However, this may not be the case in some circumstances, such as when the financial structure of an entity has significantly changed or when a comprehensive revaluation of assets and liabilities has been made in accordance with chapter 29, "New Basis (Push-Down) Accounting."

2.17 The classification of an item in the financial statements of the current period may be different from its classification in the financial statements of prior periods as a result of a change in the allocation or grouping of items within or among relevant categories. Such a change in classification is a matter of presentation and is not, in itself, a change in an accounting policy. However, to enhance comparability with the financial statements of the current period, the item should be reclassified in the financial statements of the prior period to conform with the new presentation.

Disclosure of Accounting Policies

2.18 *Accounting policies* are the specific principles, bases, conventions, rules, and practices applied by an entity when preparing and presenting financial statements. The accounting policies adopted by an entity affect the financial position, results of operations, and cash flows, as shown by its financial statements. Accordingly, the usefulness of financial statements is enhanced by disclosure of the accounting policies followed by an entity.

2.19 In addition to this chapter, other chapters provide details of certain specific disclosure requirements relating to accounting policies. Disclosure of the accounting policies followed by an entity is not a substitute for proper accounting treatment.

Disclosure

2.20 An entity that prepares its financial statements in accordance with the FRF for SMEs accounting framework should state this basis of presentation prominently in the notes to its financial statements. Because some reporting standards (for example AU-C section 800, *Special Considerations—Audits of Financial Statements Prepared in Accordance With Special Purpose Frameworks* [AICPA, *Professional Standards*]) also require an auditor or practitioner to evaluate whether the financial statements adequately describe how the special purpose framework differs from accounting principles generally accepted in the United States of America, an entity may want to include a brief description of those primary differences. The effects of the differences need not be quantified. If the differences are described, the description should be tailored to the unique circumstances of an entity, taking into account materiality and relevancy. An illustrative disclosure follows in which the primary difference is that the taxes payable method is used:

> The accompanying financial statements have been prepared in accordance with the *Financial Reporting Framework for Small- and Medium-Sized Entities* issued by the American Institute of Certified Public Accountants. This special purpose framework, unlike generally accepted accounting principles (GAAP) in the United States of America, does not require the recognition of deferred taxes. We have chosen the option to recognize only current income tax assets and liabilities.

Other primary differences would be described as necessary.

2.21 If its operating cycle is less than or greater than one year, an entity should disclose that fact, along with the length of the operating cycle.

2.22 Details about reclassifications of financial statement items to conform to the present year's presentation, as described in paragraph 2.17, should be disclosed.

2.23 An entity should identify and describe those accounting policies that are significant to its operations. At a minimum, disclosure should include information on areas in which judgment has been exercised (that is, when there is a choice between alternatives). Accounting principles, and the methods used in their application, may differ from one industry to another, and it cannot be assumed that a user of the financial statements is familiar with these differences.

2.24 At a minimum, disclosure of information on accounting policies should be provided in the following situations:

  a. When a selection has been made from alternative acceptable accounting principles and methods

  b. When accounting principles and methods used are specific to an industry in which an entity operates, even if such accounting principles and methods are predominantly followed in that industry (Examples of items requiring disclosure of accounting

Principles of Financial Statement Presentation

policies include the recognition of revenue from long-term contracts and franchising and leasing operations.)

2.25 In order to provide an overview of the accounting policies of an entity, it is particularly useful that these be disclosed together in the form of a summary rather than in individual notes to the financial statements. Therefore, the disclosure of a summary of accounting policies should generally be the first note to the financial statements. Suitable titles include "Summary of Significant Accounting Policies" or "Accounting Policies."

2.26 The FRF for SMEs accounting framework addresses what the task force and staff believe to be the most important disclosures needed for most users of small- and medium-sized entity financial statements. Other users, depending on the industry, may request additional information to be included as part of the basic financial statements or as supplemental information. For example, bonding agencies may request a schedule of contracts in progress as additional supplemental information.

Chapter 3

Transition

Purpose and Scope

3.01 The purpose of this chapter is to ensure that when an entity transitions to the FRF for SMEs accounting framework its financial statements provide a suitable starting point for accounting under the framework and contains high-quality, transparent, and comparable information over all periods presented.

3.02 An entity should apply this chapter to its financial statements upon transitioning to the framework. If an entity using the framework stops using it for one or more reporting periods and then decides to again prepare its financial statements under the framework, the exemptions from certain principles allowed by this chapter do not apply.

Opening Statement of Financial Position

3.03 An entity should prepare an opening statement of financial position at the *date of transition to the FRF for SMEs accounting framework*.[1] This opening statement of financial position is the starting point for the entity's accounting under the framework.

3.04 Except as noted in paragraphs 3.08 and 3.13, an entity, in its opening statement of financial position prepared using the framework

    a. recognizes all assets and liabilities whose recognition is required by the framework;

    b. does not recognize items as assets or liabilities if the framework does not permit such recognition;

    c. reclassifies items that it recognized previously as one type of asset, liability, or component of equity but are now recognized as a different type of asset, liability, or component of equity under the framework; and

    d. applies the framework when measuring all recognized assets and liabilities.

Accounting Policies

3.05 Management should use the same accounting policies in its opening statement of financial position and throughout all periods presented in its first financial statements prepared using the framework. Those accounting policies should comply with the accounting policies effective at the end of the year the entity adopts the framework, except as otherwise specified in this chapter.

3.06 The accounting policies that management uses in its opening statement of financial position prepared in accordance with the FRF for SMEs accounting framework may differ from those that it used for the same date under its previous accounting policies. For example, an entity

---

[1] Italicized terms are defined in the glossary.

may have previously reported other comprehensive income, whereas there is no such concept in the framework. Any resulting adjustments arise from events and transactions before the date of transition to the framework. An entity should recognize such adjustments directly in equity at the date of transition to the FRF for SMEs accounting framework.

3.07 In some cases, management may elect to use certain exemptions to the principle that an entity's opening statement of financial position should comply with the framework. Those exemptions relate to the application of certain chapters within *Financial Reporting Framework for Small- and Medium-Sized Entities,* as set out in paragraph 3.08. In addition, principles in certain chapters are prohibited from being applied retrospectively to the opening statement of financial position. See paragraph 3.13.

Election of Exemptions From Certain Principles in the FRF for SMEs Accounting Framework Upon Transition

3.08 Management may elect to use exemptions related to one or more of the following:

   a. Business combinations (see paragraphs 3.09–.10)

   b. Financial assets and liabilities (see paragraphs 3.11)

   c. Asset retirement obligations (see paragraph 3.12)

Business Combinations

3.09 When transitioning to the framework, management may elect not to apply chapter 28, "Business Combinations," retrospectively to past business combinations (business combinations that occurred before the date of transition to the FRF for SMEs accounting framework). However, when transitioning to the framework, if management restates any business combination to comply with chapter 28, it restates all subsequent business combinations and also should apply chapter 23, "Consolidated Financial Statements and Noncontrolling Interests," from that same date.

3.10 When transitioning to the framework, if management does not apply chapter 28 retrospectively to a past business combination, it has the following consequences for that business combination:

   a. The entity retains the same classification as in its previous financial statements.

   b. At the date of transition to the FRF for SMEs accounting framework, the entity recognizes all its assets and liabilities that were acquired or assumed in a past business combination, except for financial assets and liabilities derecognized in prior periods (see paragraph 3.14). Any resulting change is accounted for by adjusting equity, unless the change results from the recognition of an intangible asset that was previously included within goodwill.

   c. The entity excludes from its opening statement of financial position any item recognized under previous financial reporting principles that does not qualify for recognition as an asset or liability under the FRF for SMEs accounting framework. Any resulting change is accounted for by adjusting opening equity,

FRF-SME 3.10

unless the change results from an intangible asset that is reclassified as part of goodwill.

d. If an asset acquired, or liability assumed, in a past business combination was not recognized under the previous basis of accounting but should be under the framework, the acquirer recognizes and measures the item in its statement of financial position on the basis that the principles would require in the statement of financial position of the acquiree.

Financial Assets and Liabilities

3.11 Chapter 6, "Special Accounting Considerations for Certain Financial Assets and Liabilities," requires an entity to classify separately the component parts of a financial instrument that contains both a liability and an equity component. However, under this chapter, an entity transitioning to the framework need not separate the components if the liability component is no longer outstanding at the date of transition to the FRF for SMEs accounting framework.

Asset Retirement Obligations

3.12 An entity that has not previously recognized asset retirement obligations on a basis consistent with the section, "Asset Retirement Obligations," in chapter 17, "Contingencies," may measure the obligation at the date of transition to the FRF for SMEs accounting framework and estimate the amount that should be included in the carrying amount of the related asset based on the original and remaining life of the asset. The difference between the change in the obligation and the change to the carrying amount of the asset is charged to opening equity at the date of transition to the FRF for SMEs accounting framework.

Exceptions to Retrospective Application of Certain Principles Within the FRF for SMEs Accounting Framework

3.13 This chapter prohibits retrospective application of some aspects of other principles relating to

a. derecognition of financial assets and financial liabilities (see paragraph 3.14);

b. estimates (see paragraphs 3.16–.17); and

c. noncontrolling interests (see paragraph 3.18).

Derecognition of Financial Assets and Financial Liabilities

3.14 Except as permitted by paragraph 3.15, an entity transitioning to the FRF for SMEs accounting framework should apply the derecognition requirements in chapter 6 prospectively for transactions occurring on or after the date of transition to the FRF for SMEs accounting framework.

3.15 Management may apply the derecognition requirements in chapter 6 retrospectively from a date of the entity's choosing, provided that the information needed to apply chapter 6 to financial assets and financial liabilities derecognized as a result of past transactions was obtained at the time of initially accounting for those transactions.

Estimates

3.16 Management's estimates in its opening statement of financial position prepared using the FRF for SMEs accounting framework should be consistent with estimates in its statement of financial position for the same date prepared using its previous accounting policies (after adjustments to reflect any difference in accounting policies), unless objective evidence exists that those estimates were in error.

3.17 Management may need to make estimates for purposes of its opening statement of financial position prepared using the framework that were not required for the statement of financial position for that date using its previous accounting policies. Those estimates should reflect conditions that existed at the date of the opening statement of financial position prepared using the framework.

Noncontrolling Interests

3.18 An entity transitioning to the framework should apply the following requirements of chapter 23 prospectively from the date of transition to the FRF for SMEs accounting framework:

a. The requirements in paragraphs 23.25–.26 for accounting for changes in the parent's ownership interest in a subsidiary that do not result in a loss of control

b. The requirements in paragraphs 23.27–.30 for accounting for a loss of control over a subsidiary

c. The requirement in paragraph 23.34 that income is attributed to the *owners* of the parent and the noncontrolling interests, even if this results in the noncontrolling interests having a deficit balance

However, if an entity transitioning to the framework elects to apply chapter 28 retrospectively to past business combinations, it also should apply chapter 23, in accordance with paragraphs 3.09–.10.

Disclosure

3.19 A entity should disclose the amount of each charge or credit to equity at the date of transition to the FRF for SMEs accounting framework resulting from the adoption of these principles and the reasons therefor. If the date of transition is earlier than the current period so that prior period financial statements can be presented, those prior year financial statements need to be restated to conform to the framework.

3.20 When an entity elects to use one or more of the exemptions in paragraphs 3.08–.12, it should disclose the exemptions used.

3.21 Entities should also comply with the disclosure requirements of paragraph 9.29 of chapter 9, "Accounting Changes, Changes in Accounting Estimates, and Correction of Errors."

Chapter 4

Statement of Financial Position

Purpose and Scope

4.01 This chapter establishes the line items to be separately presented in the statement of financial position. In accordance with chapter 2, "General Principles of Financial Statement Presentation and Accounting Policies," management also considers whether additional line items should be presented in order to provide a fair presentation in accordance with the FRF for SMEs accounting framework.

Presentation

4.02 The statement of financial position should present fairly, in accordance with the FRF for SMEs accounting framework, the financial position at the period end.

4.03 If a classified statement of financial position is presented, management should distinguish the following:

 a. Current assets (see chapter 5, "Current Assets and Current Liabilities")

 b. Long-term assets

 c. Total assets

 d. Current liabilities (see chapter 5)

 e. Long-term liabilities

 f. Total liabilities

 g. Equity

 h. Total liabilities and equity

4.04 Ordinarily, the following assets are separately presented. Some of these items may be set out more readily in notes to the financial statements or attached schedules. When this approach is used, the statement of financial position caption that contains these items should be identified. More detailed information about the following assets is presented in the chapters referenced:

 a. Cash and cash equivalents (see chapter 5)

 b. Trade and other receivables (see chapter 5)

 c. Prepaid expenses (see chapter 5)

 d. Other financial assets (see chapter 6, "Special Accounting Considerations for Certain Financial Assets and Liabilities")

 e. Inventories (see chapter 12, "Inventories")

 f. Investments in nonconsolidated subsidiaries and nonproportionately consolidated joint ventures (see chapter 22, "Subsidiaries" and chapter 24, "Interests in Joint Ventures")

 g. All other investments showing separately

Statement of Financial Position

      i. investments measured using the cost method (see chapter 11, "Equity, Debt, and Other Investments")

      ii. investments measured using the equity method (see chapter 11)

      iii. investments measured at market value (see chapter 11)

  h. Property, plant, and equipment (see chapter 14, "Property, Plant, and Equipment")

  i. Intangible assets (see chapter 13, "Intangible Assets")

  j. Assets for current income taxes (see chapter 21, "Income Taxes")

  k. Assets for deferred income taxes (see chapter 21)

  l. Long-lived assets and disposal groups classified as held for sale (see chapter 15, "Disposal of Long-Lived Assets and Discontinued Operations")

  m. Accrued benefit assets (see chapter 20, "Retirement and Other Postemployment Benefits")

4.05 Ordinarily, the following liabilities should be separately presented:

  a. Main classes of current liabilities in accordance with paragraph 5.09

  b. Liabilities for deferred income taxes (see chapter 21)

  c. Liabilities of disposal groups classified as held for sale (see chapter 15)

  d. Obligations under capital leases (see chapter 25, "Leases")

  e. Accrued benefit liability (see chapter 20)

  f. Long-term debt (see chapter 6)

  g. Asset retirement obligations (see chapter 17)

  h. Other financial liabilities

4.06 Equity should be presented in accordance with the requirements of chapter 18, "Equity."

Chapter 5

Current Assets and Current Liabilities

Purpose and Scope

5.01 This chapter establishes presentation and disclosure principles for current assets and current liabilities. Other chapters provide additional presentation and disclosure requirements for specific current assets and liabilities.

5.02 Assets and liabilities are normally segregated between current and noncurrent. However, the segregation of assets and liabilities between current and noncurrent may not be appropriate in financial statements of entities in certain industries.

Current Assets

5.03 As a statement of financial position classification, current assets should include those assets ordinarily realizable within one year from the date of the statement of financial position or within the normal operating cycle, when the normal operating cycle is longer than a year.

5.04 Current assets should be segregated among the major classes, such as cash, investments, accounts and notes receivable, inventories, prepaid expenses, costs and estimated earnings in excess of billings on uncompleted contracts, and deferred income tax assets (see chapter 4, "Statement of Financial Position").

5.05 The cash surrender value of life insurance, unless converted to cash prior to the date the financial statements are available to be issued, should be excluded from current assets.

Current Liabilities

5.06 As a statement of financial position classification, current liabilities should include amounts payable within one year from the date of the statement of financial position or within the normal operating cycle, when the normal operating cycle is longer than a year. The normal operating cycle should correspond with that used for current assets.

5.07 The current liability classification should also include amounts received or due from customers or clients with respect to goods to be delivered or services to be performed within one year from the date of the statement of financial position (that is, deferred revenue).

5.08 Obligations that would otherwise be classified as current liabilities should be excluded from the current liability classification to the extent that contractual arrangements have been made for settlement from other than current assets.

5.09 Current liabilities should be segregated among the major classes, such as bank loans, trade creditors and accrued liabilities, loans payable, billings in excess of costs and estimated earnings on uncompleted contracts, taxes payable, dividends payable, deferred revenues, current payments on long-term debt, and deferred income tax liabilities (see chapter 4). Amounts owing on loans from directors, officers, and shareholders and amounts owing to parent and other affiliated companies, whether on account of a loan or otherwise, should be shown separately.

Debt

5.10 The current liability classification should include only that portion of long-term debt obligations, including sinking-fund requirements, payable within one year from the date of the statement of financial position.

5.11 Noncurrent classification of debt is based on facts existing at the statement of financial position date, rather than on expectations regarding future refinancing or renegotiation. If the creditor has, at that date, or will have within one year (or operating cycle, if longer) from that date, the unilateral right to demand immediate repayment of any portion or all the debt under any provision of the debt agreement, the obligation (or a portion thereof, as appropriate) is classified as a current liability unless

   a. the creditor has waived, in writing, or subsequently lost, the right to demand payment for more than one year (or operating cycle, if longer) from the statement of financial position date;

   b. the obligation has been refinanced on a long-term basis before the financial statements are available to be issued; or

   c. the debtor has entered into a noncancellable agreement to refinance the short-term obligation on a long-term basis before the financial statements are available to be issued, and there is no impediment to the completion of the refinancing.

5.12 Long-term debt with a covenant violation is classified as a current liability unless

   a. as of the date the financial statements are available to be issued, the creditor has waived, in writing, or subsequently lost, the right, arising from violation of the covenant at the statement of financial position date, to demand repayment for a period of more than one year from the statement of financial position date or

   b. the debt agreement contains a grace period during which the debtor may cure the violation, and contractual arrangements have been made that ensure the violation will be cured within the grace period

and a violation of the debt covenant giving the creditor the right to demand repayment at a future compliance date within one year of the statement of financial position date is remote.

Chapter 6

Special Accounting Considerations for Certain Financial Assets and Liabilities

Purpose and Scope

6.01 This chapter establishes principles for

   a. recognizing and measuring *financial assets*[1] (except for equity investments and debt investments held for sale, which are addressed in chapter 11, "Equity, Debt, and Other Investments," and financial liabilities;

   b. the presentation of liabilities and equity;

   c. the circumstances in which financial assets and financial liabilities are offset;

   d. the *derecognition* of certain financial assets and liabilities; and

   e. disclosures about financial assets and financial liabilities.

Recognition

6.02 Except for *derivatives*, an entity should recognize a financial asset or a financial liability when the entity becomes a party to the contract. Derivatives are accounted for by recognizing the net cash paid or received at settlement.

Measurement

6.03 Except for derivatives, when a financial asset is originated or acquired or a financial liability is issued or assumed in an arm's length transaction, an entity should measure it at its transaction amount adjusted by *financing fees and transaction costs* that are directly attributable to its origination, acquisition, issuance, or assumption.

Presentation

Liabilities and Equity

6.04 The issuer of a financial instrument should classify the instrument, or its component parts, as a liability or as equity in accordance with the substance of the contractual arrangement on initial recognition and the definitions of a *financial liability* and an *equity instrument*.

Offsetting of a Financial Asset and a Financial Liability

6.05 A financial asset and a financial liability should be offset, and the net amount should be reported in the statement of financial position, only when an entity

---

[1] Italicized terms are defined in the glossary.

a. currently has a legally enforceable right to set off the recognized amounts and

b. intends either to settle on a net basis or realize the asset and settle the liability simultaneously.

Derecognition

Transfers of Financial Assets, Including Receivables

6.06 An entity should derecognize financial assets transferred to another entity only when control has been surrendered.

Financial Liabilities

6.07 An entity should remove a financial liability (or a part of a financial liability) from its statement of financial position when it is extinguished (that is, when the obligation is discharged or cancelled or expires).

6.08 A transaction between a borrower and lender to replace a debt instrument with another instrument having substantially different terms is accounted for as an extinguishment of the original financial liability and the recognition of a new financial liability. Similarly, a substantial modification of the terms of an existing financial liability or a part of it (regardless of whether attributable to the financial difficulty of the debtor) is accounted for as an extinguishment of the original financial liability and the recognition of a new financial liability.

6.09 The difference between the carrying amount of a financial liability (or part of a financial liability) extinguished or transferred to another party and the market value of the consideration paid, including any noncash assets transferred, liabilities assumed, or equity instruments issued, should be recognized in net income for the period. Extinguishment transactions between related entities may be, in essence, capital transactions.

6.10 When an issuer of a debt instrument repays or settles that instrument, the debt is extinguished. If an entity repays a part of a financial liability, the entity allocates the carrying amount of the financial liability at the date of repayment based on their relative market values between the part that continues to be recognized and the part that is derecognized. The difference between the carrying amount allocated to the part derecognized and the consideration paid to extinguish that part, including any noncash assets transferred, liabilities assumed, or equity instruments issued, is recognized in net income.

Disclosure

Financial Assets

6.11 An entity should disclose the carrying amounts of financial assets either on the face of the statement of financial position or in the notes.

6.12 Accounts and notes receivable should be segregated to show separately trade accounts, amounts owing by related parties, and other unusual items of significant amount. The amounts, and, when practicable, maturity dates of accounts maturing beyond one year should be disclosed separately.

Transfers of Financial Assets (Including Receivables)

6.13 If an entity transfers financial assets during the period and accounts for the transfer as a sale, it should disclose

    a. the gain or loss from all sales during the period;

    b. the accounting policies for

        i. initially measuring any retained interest (including the methodology used when determining its market value) and

        ii. subsequently measuring the retained interest; and

    c. a description of the transferor's continuing involvement with the transferred assets, including, but not limited to, servicing, recourse, and restrictions on retained interests.

6.14 If an entity has transferred financial assets in a way that does not qualify for derecognition, it should disclose

    a. the nature and carrying amount of the assets;

    b. the nature of the risks and rewards of ownership to which the entity remains exposed; and

    c. the carrying amount of the liabilities assumed in the transfer.

Financial Liabilities

6.15 For bonds, debentures, and similar securities, mortgages, and other long-term debt, an entity should disclose

    a. the title or description of the liability;

    b. the interest rate;

    c. the maturity date;

    d. significant terms (for example, covenant details);

    e. the amount outstanding, separated between principal and accrued interest;

    f. the currency in which the debt is payable, if it is not repayable in the currency in which the entity measures items in its financial statements; and

    g. the repayment terms, including the existence of sinking fund, redemption, and conversion provisions.

6.16 An entity should disclose the carrying amount of any financial liabilities that are secured. An entity should also disclose

    a. the carrying amount of assets it has pledged as collateral for liabilities and

    b. the terms and conditions relating to its pledge.

6.17 An entity should disclose the aggregate amount of payments estimated to be required in each of the next five years to meet repayment, sinking fund, or retirement provisions of financial liabilities.

6.18 For financial liabilities recognized at the statement of financial position date, an entity should disclose

Accounting Considerations for Certain Financial Assets and Liabilities

    a. whether any financial liabilities were in default or in breach of any term or covenant during the period that would permit a lender to demand accelerated repayment and

    b. whether the default was remedied or the terms of the liability were renegotiated before the financial statements were available to be issued.

6.19 An entity should disclose the following items:

    a. Interest capitalized

    b. Unused letters of credit

    c. Long-term debt agreements subject to subjective acceleration clauses, unless the likelihood of the acceleration of the due date is remote

6.20 An entity that issues any of the following financial liabilities or equity instruments should disclose information to enable users of the financial statements to understand the effects of features of the instrument, as follows:

    a. For a financial liability that contains both a liability and an equity element (see paragraph 6.04), an entity should disclose the following information about the equity element including, when relevant

        i. the exercise date or dates of the conversion option;

        ii. the maturity or expiry date of the option;

        iii. the conversion ratio or the strike price;

        iv. conditions precedent to exercising the option; and

        v. any other terms that could affect the exercise of the option, such as the existence of covenants that, if contravened, would alter the timing or price of the option.

For an instrument that is indexed to the entity's equity or an identified factor, an entity should disclose information that enables users of the financial statements to understand the nature, terms, and effects of the indexing feature; the conditions under which a payment will be made; and the expected timing of any payment.

Derivatives

6.21 For derivatives, an entity should disclose the following:

    a. The face or contract amount (or notional principal amount, if there is no face or contract amount)

    b. The nature and terms, including a discussion of the credit and market risk and the cash requirements of those derivatives

    c. A description of the entity's objectives for holding the derivatives

    d. The net settlement amount of the derivative at the statement of financial position date

Items of Income

6.22 An entity should disclose the following items of income, expense, gains, or losses either on the face of the statements or in the notes to the financial statements:

    a. Net gains or net losses recognized on financial assets and liabilities

    b. Total interest income

    c. Total interest expense, separately identifying amortization of premiums, discounts, transaction costs, and financing fees

Chapter 7

Statement of Operations

Purpose and Scope

7.01 This chapter establishes the line items to be separately presented in the statement of operations. In accordance with chapter 2, "General Principles of Financial Statement Presentation and Accounting Policies," management also considers whether additional line items should be presented in order to provide a fair presentation in accordance with the FRF for SMEs accounting framework.

Presentation

7.02 The statement of operations should present fairly, in accordance with the FRF for SMEs accounting framework, the results of operations for the period.

7.03 The statement of operations should distinguish the following:

 a. Income or loss before discontinued operations

 b. Results of discontinued operations (see chapter 15, "Disposal of Long-Lived Assets and Discontinued Operations")

 c. Net income or loss for the period

When arriving at the income or loss before discontinued operations, the statement of operations should present major elements, such as revenue, cost of goods sold, operating expenses, other revenues and gains, and other expenses and losses.

7.04 Typical items that are distinguished in the statement of operations are presented in the following text. Some of these items may be set out more readily in notes to the financial statements or attached schedules. When this is done, the statement of operations caption that contains these items should be identified in the notes:

 a. Revenue recognized (see chapter 19, "Revenue").

 b. Income from investments, disclosing income from

   i. nonconsolidated subsidiaries and nonproportionately consolidated joint ventures (see chapter 22, "Subsidiaries" and chapter 24, "Interests in Joint Ventures")

   ii. all other investments showing separately

     (1) investments measured using the cost method (see chapter 11, "Equity, Debt, and Other Investments")

     (2) investments measured using the equity method (see chapter 11)

     (3) investments measured at market value (see chapter 11)

 c. The amount charged for depreciation of property, plant, and equipment (see chapter 14, "Property, Plant, and Equipment").

 d. The amount charged for amortization of intangible assets (see chapter 13, "Intangible Assets").

e. The amount of exchange gain or loss included in net income (see chapter 31, "Foreign Currency Translation").

f. Revenue, expenses, gains, or losses resulting from transactions or events that are not expected to occur frequently over several years or do not typify normal business activities of the entity (see chapter 2).

g. Income taxes. Income tax expense or benefit included in the determination of income or loss before discontinued operations should be presented separately in the statement of operations (see chapter 21, "Income Taxes").

Chapter 8

Statement of Cash Flows

Purpose and Scope

8.01 Information about an entity's *cash flows*[1] enables users of financial statements to assess the capability of the entity to generate *cash and cash equivalents* and the needs of the entity for cash resources. The adequacy of expected cash inflows, taking into consideration their timing and certainty of generation, is evaluated against cash resources required to repay maturing financial obligations, finance the growth of productive assets, and make distributions to owners. Historical cash flow information is often used as an indicator of the amount, timing, and certainty of future cash flows. The purpose of this chapter is to require the provision of information about the historical changes in cash and cash equivalents of an entity by means of a statement of cash flows that classifies cash flows during the period arising from operating, investing, and *financing activities*.

8.02 A statement of cash flows is required as an integral part of a complete set of financial statements for each period for which financial statements are presented. Nothing in the FRF for SMEs accounting framework precludes management from using it to prepare a single financial statement, rather than a complete set of financial statements. However, if a statement of financial position and a statement of operations are prepared, a statement of cash flows should also be prepared.

8.03 Users of an entity's financial statements are interested in how the entity generates and uses cash and cash equivalents. This is the case regardless of the nature of the entity's activities.

8.04 An entity that presents consolidated financial statements includes a consolidated statement of cash flows in which cash flows within the consolidated entity, such as intercompany loans, repayments, and other cash transfers, are eliminated.

Cash and Cash Equivalents

8.05 Cash subject to restrictions that prevent its use for current purposes, such as compensating balances required in accordance with lending arrangements, should not be included among cash and cash equivalents. Cash subject to restrictions should be classified on the statement of financial position in accordance with chapter 5, "Current Assets and Current Liabilities," and increases and decreases should be reflected in cash flows from *investing activities*.

8.06 Cash equivalents are held for the purpose of meeting short-term cash commitments rather than for investing or other purposes. For an investment to qualify as a cash equivalent, it must be readily convertible to a known amount of cash and subject to an insignificant risk of changes in value. Therefore, an investment normally qualifies as a cash equivalent only when it has a short maturity of three months or less from the date of acquisition.

---

[1] Italicized terms are defined in the glossary.

8.07 In certain circumstances, investments that qualify to be treated as cash equivalents may be classified as investments. An entity should establish a policy concerning which short-term, highly liquid investments (that satisfy the definition in the glossary) will be treated as cash equivalents. For example, an investment entity, whose portfolio consists largely of short-term, highly liquid investments, may decide that all such items will be treated as investments rather than cash equivalents.

8.08 Bank borrowings are generally considered to be financing activities. An increase (decrease) in bank overdrafts represents an increase (decrease) in bank borrowing and should be classified as a financing inflow (outflow). The net change in overdrafts during the period should be classified as a financing activity. If an entity with multiple bank accounts (which do not have the right of offset) has one account in an overdraft position at year-end, then the entity should present as cash and cash equivalents on the statement of cash flows only the accounts with the positive balances.

8.09 The total amounts of cash and cash equivalents at the beginning and end of the period should be the same amounts as similarly titled line items or subtotals shown in the statements of financial position.

8.10 Cash flows exclude movements between items that constitute cash or cash equivalents because these components are part of the cash management of an entity rather than part of its operating, investing, and financing activities.

Classification of Cash Flows

8.11 The statement of cash flows should report cash flows during the period classified by operating, investing, and financing activities.

8.12 An entity presents its cash flows from operating, investing, and financing activities in a manner that is most appropriate to its business. Classification by activity provides information that allows users to assess the impact of those activities on the financial position of the entity and the amount of its cash and cash equivalents. This information may also be used to evaluate the relationships among those activities.

8.13 A single transaction may include cash flows that are classified differently. For example, when the cash repayment of a liability includes both interest and principal, the interest component is classified as an operating activity and the principal component as a financing activity.

Operating Activities

8.14 The amount of cash flows arising from *operating activities* is a key indicator of the extent to which the operations of the entity have generated sufficient cash flows to repay loans, maintain the operating capability of the entity, make new investments, and provide distributions to owners without recourse to external sources of financing. Information about the specific components of historical operating cash flows is useful in conjunction with other information in forecasting future operating cash flows.

8.15 Cash flows from operating activities are primarily derived from the principal revenue-producing activities of the entity. Therefore, they generally result from the transactions and other events that enter into the determination of net income or loss. Examples of cash flows from operating activities are

Statement of Cash Flows

    a. cash receipts from the sale of goods and the rendering of services;

    b. cash receipts from royalties, fees, commissions, and other revenue;

    c. cash payments to suppliers for goods and services;

    d. cash payments to, and on behalf of, employees;

    e. cash receipts and payments of interest and dividends received included in the determination of net income;

    f. cash payments and refunds of income and other taxes; and

    g. cash receipts and payments from contracts held for trading purposes or related to normal inventory purchase or sales.

Some transactions, such as the sale of a capital asset, may give rise to a gain or loss that is included in the determination of net income or loss. However, the cash flows relating to such transactions are cash flows from investing activities.

8.16 An entity may acquire securities and loans for trading purposes (that is, specifically for resale in the near term), in which case, they are similar to inventory acquired specifically for resale. Therefore, cash flows arising from the purchase and sale of such trading assets are classified as operating activities.

Investing Activities

8.17 The separate presentation of cash flows arising from investing activities is important because the cash flows represent the extent to which expenditures have been made for resources intended to generate future income and cash flows. Examples of cash flows arising from investing activities are

    a. cash payments to acquire capital assets and other long-term assets (these payments include those relating to capitalized development costs and self-constructed capital assets, including interest paid and capitalized before the assets are substantially complete and ready for productive use);

    b. cash receipts from sales of capital assets and other long-term assets;

    c. cash payments to acquire equity or debt instruments of other entities (other than payments for those instruments considered to be cash equivalents or those held for trading purposes) and interests in joint ventures;

    d. cash receipts from sales of equity or debt instruments of other entities (other than receipts for those instruments considered to be cash equivalents and those held for trading purposes) and interests in joint ventures;

    e. cash advances and loans made to other parties;

    f. cash receipts from the repayment of advances and loans made to other parties;

    g. cash payments for futures contracts, forward contracts, option contracts, and swap contracts, except when the contracts are held for trading purposes, related to normal inventory purchases or sales, or the payments are classified as financing activities; and

h. cash receipts from futures contracts, forward contracts, option contracts, and swap contracts, except when the contracts are held for trading purposes, related to normal inventory purchases or sales, or the receipts are classified as financing activities.

Financing Activities

8.18 The separate presentation of cash flows arising from financing activities is important because it is useful when predicting claims on future cash flows by providers of capital and debt financing to the entity. Examples of cash flows arising from financing activities are

　　a. cash proceeds from issuing equity instruments;

　　b. cash payments to owners to acquire or redeem the entity's shares;

　　c. cash proceeds from issuing debentures, loans, notes, bonds, mortgages, and other short- or long-term borrowings;

　　d. cash repayments of amounts borrowed;

　　e. cash payments by a lessee for the reduction of the outstanding liability relating to a capital lease; and

　　f. cash payments of dividends and interest charged to retained earnings.

Cash Flows From Operating Activities

8.19 An entity should report cash flows from operating activities using either the direct method or the indirect method. Examples of the major classes of cash flows from operating activities are contained in paragraph 8.15.

8.20 Under the direct method, an entity should present separately major classes of gross cash receipts and gross cash payments arising from operating activities. This information may be obtained either

　　a. from the accounting records of the entity or

　　b. by adjusting sales, cost of sales, interest income and expense, and other items in the statement of operations for

　　　　i. noncash items;

　　　　ii. changes during the period in inventories and operating receivables and payables;

　　　　iii. other deferrals or accruals of past or future operating cash receipts or payments; and

　　　　iv. items for which the cash effects are investing or financing cash flows.

8.21 When the direct method is used, a separate schedule that reconciles net income to net cash flows from operating activities should also be presented.

Statement of Cash Flows

8.22 Under the indirect method, the net cash flow from operating activities is determined by adjusting net income or loss for the effects of

a. noncash items, such as depreciation, provisions for losses, deferred taxes, unrealized foreign currency gains and losses, undistributed profits of equity-accounted investees, and noncontrolling interests;

b. changes during the period in inventories and operating receivables and payables;

c. other deferrals or accruals of past or future operating cash receipts or payments; and

d. revenues, expenses, gains, or losses associated with investing or financing cash flows.

Cash Flows From Investing and Financing Activities

8.23 An entity should present separately major classes of gross cash receipts and gross cash payments arising from investing and financing activities.

8.24 Examples of the major classes of investing activities are contained in paragraph 8.17. Examples of the major classes of financing activities are contained in paragraph 8.18.

Cash Flows on a Net Basis

8.25 Cash receipts and payments for items in which the turnover is quick, the amounts are large, and the maturities are short may be reported on a net basis. An example of such items is cash receipts and payments related to short-term borrowings (for example, those that have a maturity period of three months or less) and revolving credit lines.

Foreign Currency Cash Flows

8.26 Cash flows arising from transactions in a foreign currency should be recorded in an entity's reporting currency by applying to the foreign currency amount the exchange rate between the reporting currency and the foreign currency at the date of the cash flow.

Interest and Dividends

8.27 Cash inflows from interest and dividends received should be classified as cash flows from operating activities. Cash outflows related to interest paid should be classified as an operating activity, unless capitalized. Cash outflows related to dividends paid should be classified as cash flows used in financing activities. Cash outflows from dividends paid by subsidiaries to noncontrolling interests should be presented separately as cash flows used in financing activities.

8.28 When an entity acquires a financial asset or issues a financial liability at a discount, the amortization of the discount over the term of the instrument does not reflect a cash flow.

8.29 When an entity acquires a financial asset or issues a financial liability at a premium, the excess of the periodic interest payments, based on the stated rate, over the effective yield recognized in income is, in substance, a repayment of principal. Cash flows from operating activities should reflect interest income or expense recognized in income. The excess of actual cash flows over amounts recognized in income should be classified as cash flows from investing or financing activities.

Income Taxes

8.30 Cash flows arising from income taxes should be classified as cash flows from operating activities unless they can be specifically identified with financing and investing activities.

Business Combinations and Disposals of Business Units

8.31 The aggregate cash flows arising from each of the business combinations accounted for using the acquisition method and disposals of business units should be presented separately and classified as cash flows from investing activities.

8.32 The separate presentation of the cash flow effects of business combinations accounted for as acquisitions and disposals of business units, together with the separate disclosure of the total amounts of assets and liabilities acquired or disposed of, helps to distinguish those cash flows from the cash flows arising from the other operating, investing, and financing activities. The cash flow effects of disposals are not deducted from those of acquisitions.

8.33 The aggregate amount of the cash paid or received as purchase or sale consideration is presented in the statement of cash flows net of cash and cash equivalents acquired or disposed of.

Noncash Transactions

8.34 Investing and financing transactions that do not require the use of cash or cash equivalents should be excluded from a statement of cash flows but should be disclosed in accordance with paragraph 8.40.

8.35 Many investing and financing activities do not have a direct impact on current cash flows, although they do affect the capital and asset structure of an entity. The exclusion of noncash transactions from the statement of cash flows is consistent with the objective of a statement of cash flows because these items do not involve cash flows in the current period. Examples of noncash transactions are

    a. the acquisition of assets by assuming directly related liabilities;

    b. the acquisition of assets by means of a capital lease;

    c. the acquisition of an entity in exchange for shares of the acquirer; and

    d. the conversion of debt to equity.

Disclosure

Cash and Cash Equivalents

8.36 An entity should disclose the policy it adopts when determining the composition of cash and cash equivalents.

8.37 Any amounts of cash for which use is restricted should not be included in the composition of cash and cash equivalents. Material restrictions on cash should be disclosed.

8.38 As discussed in paragraph 8.07, in certain circumstances, an entity may classify investments that qualify to be treated as cash equivalents as investments. In such circumstances, the policy for determining components of cash and cash equivalents should be disclosed. Any change in the policy for determining the components of cash and cash equivalents should be disclosed in accordance with chapter 9, "Accounting Changes, Changes in Accounting Estimates, and Correction of Errors."

Business Combinations and Disposals of Business Units

8.39 An entity should disclose, in aggregate, in respect of both business combinations and disposals of business units during the period

    a. the total purchase or disposal consideration;

    b. the portion of the purchase or disposal consideration composed of cash and cash equivalents;

    c. the amount of cash and cash equivalents acquired or disposed of; and

    d. the total assets, other than cash or cash equivalents, and total liabilities acquired or disposed of.

Noncash Transactions

8.40 Investing and financing transactions that do not require the use of cash or cash equivalents should either be presented on the face of the statement of cash flows as "noncash investing or financing activities" or disclosed in the notes to the financial statements in a way that provides all the relevant information about these investing and financing activities.

Chapter 9

Accounting Changes, Changes in Accounting Estimates, and Correction of Errors

Purpose and Scope

9.01 The purpose of this chapter is to prescribe the criteria for changing accounting policies, together with the accounting treatment and disclosure of changes in accounting policies, changes in accounting estimates, and corrections of errors.

9.02 Disclosure requirements for accounting policies, except those for changes in accounting policies, are set out in chapter 2, "General Principles of Financial Statement Presentation and Accounting Policies."

9.03 The tax effects of corrections of *prior period errors*[1] and retrospective adjustments made to apply changes in accounting policies are accounted for and disclosed in accordance with chapter 21, "Income Taxes."

Changes in Accounting Policies

9.04 Management should change an accounting policy only if the change

    a. is required by the FRF for SMEs accounting framework or

    b. results in the financial statements providing reliable and more relevant information about the effects of transactions, other events, or conditions on the entity's financial position, financial performance, or cash flows.

9.05 Users of financial statements need to be able to compare the financial statements of an entity over time to identify trends in its financial position, financial performance, and cash flows. Therefore, the same accounting policies are applied within each period, and from one period to the next, unless a change in accounting policy meets one of the criteria in paragraph 9.04.

9.06 The following are not changes in accounting policies:

    a. The application of an accounting policy for transactions, other events, or conditions that differ in substance from those previously occurring

    b. The application of a new accounting policy for transactions, other events, or conditions that did not occur previously or were immaterial

---

[1] Italicized terms are defined in the glossary.

Applying Changes in Accounting Policies

9.07 Subject to paragraph 9.09

  a. an entity should account for a change in accounting policy resulting from the initial application of the FRF for SMEs accounting framework in accordance with the specific transitional provisions, if any, described in chapter 3, "Transition."

  b. an entity should account for a change in accounting policy retrospectively when

   i. management changes an accounting policy upon initial application of the FRF for SMEs accounting framework that does not include specific transitional provisions applying to that change (see chapter 3);

   ii. management changes an accounting policy voluntarily; or

   iii. management is required to change an accounting policy by the FRF for SMEs accounting framework.

Retrospective Application

9.08 Subject to paragraph 9.09, when a change in accounting policy is applied retrospectively in accordance with paragraph 9.07(a) or (b), management should adjust the opening balance of each affected component of equity for the earliest prior period presented and the other comparative amounts disclosed for each prior period presented, as if the new accounting policy had always been applied.

Limitations on Retrospective Application

9.09 When *retrospective application* is required by paragraph 9.07(a) or (b), a change in accounting policy should be applied retrospectively, except to the extent that it is *impracticable* to determine either the period-specific effects or the cumulative effect of the change.

9.10 When it is impracticable to determine the period-specific effects of changing an accounting policy on comparative information for one or more prior periods presented, management should apply the new accounting policy to the carrying amounts of assets and liabilities at the beginning of the earliest period for which retrospective application is practicable, which may be the current period, and should make a corresponding adjustment to the opening balance of each affected component of equity for that period.

9.11 At the beginning of the current period, when it is impracticable to determine the cumulative effect of applying a new accounting policy to all prior periods, management should apply the new accounting policy prospectively from the earliest date practicable.

9.12 When an entity applies a new accounting policy retrospectively, it applies the new accounting policy to comparative information for prior periods as far back as is practicable. Retrospective application to a prior period is not practicable unless the entity can determine the cumulative effect on the amounts in both the opening and closing statement of financial position for that period. The amount of the resulting adjustment relating to periods before those presented in the financial statements is made

FRF-SME 9.12

to the opening balance of each affected component of equity of the earliest prior period presented. Any other information presented about prior periods, such as historical summaries of financial data, is also adjusted as far back as is practicable.

9.13 When it is impracticable for an entity to apply a new accounting policy retrospectively because it cannot determine the cumulative effect of applying the policy to all prior periods, the entity, in accordance with paragraph 9.11, applies the new policy prospectively from the start of the earliest period practicable. Therefore, it disregards the portion of the cumulative adjustment to assets, liabilities, and equity arising before that date. Changing an accounting policy is permitted, even if it is impracticable to apply the policy retrospectively for any prior period. Paragraphs 9.25–9.28 provide guidance on when it is impracticable to apply a new accounting policy to one or more prior periods.

Changes in Accounting Estimates

9.14 As a result of the uncertainties inherent in business activities, many items in financial statements cannot be measured with precision but can only be estimated. Estimation involves judgments based on the latest available, reliable information. For example, estimates may be required of

 a. bad debts;
 b. inventory obsolescence;
 c. the useful lives of, or expected pattern of consumption of the future economic benefits embodied in, depreciable assets (see the example in paragraph 9.20);
 d. progress on uncompleted contracts under the percentage-of-completion method; and
 e. warranty obligations.

9.15 The use of reasonable estimates is an essential part of the preparation of financial statements and does not undermine their reliability.

9.16 An estimate may need revision if changes occur in the circumstances on which the estimate was based or as a result of new information or more experience. By its nature, the revision of an estimate does not relate to prior periods and is not the correction of an error.

9.17 Distinguishing between a change in an accounting principle and an accounting estimate is sometimes difficult. In some cases, a *change in accounting estimate* is effected by a change in accounting principle. The effect of the change in accounting principle, or the method of applying it, may be inseparable from the effect of the change in accounting estimate. Changes of that type often are related to the continuing process of obtaining additional information and revising estimates and, therefore, should be considered changes in estimates for purposes of applying this guidance.

9.18 The effect of a change in an accounting estimate should be recognized prospectively by including it in net income in

 a. the period of the change, if the change affects that period only or
 b. the period of the change, and future periods, if the change affects both.

Changes in Accounting Estimates and Correction of Errors

9.19 To the extent that a change in an accounting estimate gives rise to changes in assets and liabilities or relates to an item of equity, it should be recognized by adjusting the carrying amount of the related asset, liability, or equity item in the period of the change.

9.20 Prospective recognition of the effect of a change in an accounting estimate means that the change is applied to transactions, other events, and conditions from the date of the change in estimate. A change in an accounting estimate may affect only the current period's net income or the net income of both the current period and future periods. For example, a change in the estimate of the amount of bad debts affects only the current period's net income and, therefore, is recognized in the current period. However, a change in the estimated useful life of, or the expected pattern of consumption of the future economic benefits embodied in, a depreciable asset affects depreciation expense for the current period and each future period during the asset's remaining useful life. In both cases, the effect of the change relating to the current period is recognized as income or expense in the current period. The effect, if any, on future periods is recognized as income or expense in those future periods.

Errors

9.21 Errors can arise regarding the recognition, measurement, presentation, or disclosure of elements of financial statements. Financial statements do not comply with the FRF for SMEs accounting framework if they contain either material errors or immaterial errors made intentionally to achieve a particular presentation of an entity's financial position, financial performance, or cash flows. Potential current period errors discovered in that period are corrected before the financial statements are available to be issued. However, material errors are sometimes not discovered until a subsequent period, and these prior period errors are corrected in the comparative information presented in the financial statements for that subsequent period (see paragraphs 9.22–.23).

9.22 Management should correct material prior period errors retrospectively in the first set of financial statements available to be issued after their discovery by

   a. restating the comparative amounts for the prior period(s) presented when the error occurred or

   b. if the error occurred before the earliest prior period presented, restating the opening balances of assets, liabilities, and equity for the earliest prior period presented.

9.23 The correction of a prior period error is excluded from net income for the period when the error is discovered. Any information presented about prior periods, including any historical summaries of financial data, is restated.

9.24 Corrections of errors are distinguished from changes in accounting estimates. Accounting estimates, by their nature, are approximations that may need revision as additional information becomes known. For example, the gain or loss recognized on the outcome of a contingency is not the correction of an error.

Impracticability Regarding Retrospective Application

9.25 In some circumstances, it is impracticable to adjust comparative information for one or more prior periods to achieve comparability with the current period. For example, data may not have been collected in the prior period(s) in a way that allows retrospective application of a new accounting policy (including, for the purpose of paragraphs 9.26–9.28, its *prospective application* to prior periods), and it may be impracticable to recreate the information. See paragraph 9.13 for additional guidance.

9.26 It is frequently necessary to make estimates when applying an accounting policy to elements of financial statements recognized or disclosed regarding transactions, other events, or conditions. Estimation is inherently subjective, and estimates may be developed after the statement of financial position date. Developing estimates is potentially more difficult when retrospectively applying an accounting policy or making a *retrospective restatement* to correct a prior period error because of the longer period of time that might have passed since the affected transaction, other event, or condition occurred. However, the objective of estimates related to prior periods remains the same as for estimates made in the current period, namely, for the estimate to reflect the circumstances that existed when the transaction, other event, or condition occurred.

9.27 Therefore, retrospectively applying a new accounting policy requires distinguishing information that

    a. provides evidence of circumstances that existed on the date(s) the transaction, other event, or condition occurred and

    b. would have been available when the financial statements for that prior period were available to be issued

from other information. For some types of estimates, it is impracticable to distinguish these types of information. When retrospective application would require making a significant estimate for which it is impossible to distinguish these two types of information, it is impracticable to apply the new accounting policy retrospectively.

9.28 Hindsight is not used when applying a new accounting policy to, or correcting amounts for, a prior period, either in making assumptions about what management's intentions would have been in a prior period or estimating the amounts recognized, measured, or disclosed in a prior period. The fact that significant estimates are frequently required when amending comparative information presented for prior periods does not prevent reliable adjustment or correction of the comparative information.

Disclosure

Changes in Accounting Policies

9.29 When initial application of the FRF for SMEs accounting framework, or a required change in accounting policy, has an effect on the current period or any prior period, or would have such an effect, except that it is impracticable to determine the amount of the adjustment, an entity should disclose

a. when applicable, that the change in accounting policy is made in accordance with its transitional provisions;

b. the nature of the change in accounting policy;

c. when applicable, a description of the transitional provisions;

d. for the current period, to the extent practicable, the amount of the adjustment for each financial statement line item affected;

e. the amount of the adjustment relating to periods before those presented to the extent practicable; and

f. if retrospective application required by paragraph 9.07(a) or (b) is impracticable for a particular prior period or for periods before those presented, the circumstances that led to the existence of that condition and a description of how, and from when, the change in accounting policy has been applied.

Financial statements of subsequent periods need not repeat these disclosures, unless comparative financial statements are presented.

9.30 When a voluntary change in accounting policy has an effect on the current period or any prior period, or would have an effect on that period, except that it is impracticable to determine the amount of the adjustment, an entity should disclose

a. the nature of the change in accounting policy;

b. the reasons why applying the new accounting policy provides reliable and more relevant information (see paragraph 9.04);

c. for the current period, to the extent practicable, the amount of the adjustment for each financial statement line item affected;

d. the amount of the adjustment relating to periods before those presented to the extent practicable; and

e. if retrospective application is impracticable for a particular prior period or for periods before those presented, the circumstances that led to the existence of that condition and a description of how, and from when, the change in accounting policy has been applied.

Financial statements of subsequent periods need not repeat these disclosures.

Changes in Accounting Estimates

9.31 Management should disclose the nature and amount of a change in an accounting estimate that has an effect in the current period. Disclosure of those effects is not necessary for estimates made each period in the ordinary course of accounting for items such as uncollectible accounts, progress on uncompleted contracts, or inventory obsolescence; however, disclosure is required if the effect of a change in the estimate is material.

Errors

9.32 When applying paragraph 9.22, management should disclose the following:

    a. The nature of the prior period error

    b. For each prior period presented, the amount of the correction for each financial statement line item affected

    c. The amount of the correction at the beginning of the earliest prior period presented

Financial statements of subsequent periods need not repeat these disclosures.

Chapter 10
Risks and Uncertainties

Purpose and Scope

10.01 Volatility and uncertainty in the business and economic environment result in the need to disclose information about the risks and uncertainties that reporting entities face. This chapter establishes disclosure principles for certain risks and uncertainties in the financial statements. The risks and uncertainties addressed can stem from any of the following:

- Nature of operations
- Use of estimates in the preparation of financial statements
- Certain significant estimates
- Current vulnerability due to certain concentrations

Nature of Operations

10.02 A reporting entity should include in the financial statements a description of the major products or services the reporting entity sells or provides and its principal markets, including the locations of those markets. Disclosures concerning the nature of operations do not have to be quantified, and relative importance may be described by terms such as *predominantly, about equally,* and *major.*

Use of Estimates

10.03 A reporting entity should include in the financial statements an explanation that the preparation of financial statements in conformity with the FRF for SMEs accounting framework requires the use of management's estimates.

Significant Estimates

10.04 A reporting entity should include a discussion of significant estimates when, based on known information available before the financial statements are *available to be issued,*[1] it is reasonably possible that (*a*) the estimate will change in the *near term* (a period of time not to exceed one year from the date of the financial statements), and (*b*) the effect of the change will be material. The estimate of the effect of a change in a condition, situation, or set of circumstances that existed at the date of the financial statements should be disclosed, and the evaluation should be based on known information available before the financial statements are available to be issued.

10.05 The following are examples of assets and liabilities and gain and loss contingencies that may be based on estimates that are particularly sensitive to change in the near term and, therefore, require disclosure if they meet the criteria in paragraph 10.04:

---

[1] Italicized terms are defined in the glossary.

a. Inventory subject to rapid technological obsolescence
b. Specialized equipment subject to technological obsolescence
c. Valuation allowances for deferred tax assets based on future taxable income
d. Capitalized computer software costs
e. Valuation allowances for commercial and real estate loans
f. Environmental remediation-related obligations
g. Litigation-related obligations
h. Contingent liabilities for obligations of other entities
i. Amounts reported for long-term obligations, such as amounts reported for pensions and postemployment benefits
j. Estimated net proceeds recoverable, the provisions for expected loss to be incurred, or both, on disposition of a business or assets
k. Amounts reported for long-term contracts

Concentrations

10.06 Vulnerability from concentrations arises because an entity is exposed to risk of loss greater than it would have had it mitigated its risk through diversification. An entity should disclose in the financial statements certain concentrations if, based on information known to management before the financial statements are available to be issued, all the following criteria are met:

a. The concentration exists at the date of the financial statements.
b. The concentration makes the entity vulnerable to the risk of a near-term severe impact.
c. It is at least reasonably possible that the events that could cause the severe impact will occur in the near term.

10.07 The following are examples of concentrations that require disclosure if they meet the preceding criteria:

a. Concentrations in the volume of business transacted with a particular customer, supplier, or lender
b. Concentrations in revenue from particular products or services
c. Concentrations in the available sources of supply of materials, labor, or services or of licenses or other rights used in the entity's operations
d. Concentrations in the market or geographic area where an entity conducts its operations
e. Concentrations in credit risk (for example, funds deposited in financial institutions in excess of Federal Deposit Insurance Corporation insurance limits)
f. Concentrations in the workforce covered by collective bargaining agreements

Chapter 11

Equity, Debt, and Other Investments

Purpose and Scope

11.01 This chapter establishes principles for accounting for and measuring and disclosing equity and debt investments and certain other investments (such as works of art and other tangible assets held for investment purposes).

11.02 This chapter applies to investments, except subsidiaries of entities that are consolidated (see chapter 22, "Subsidiaries").

Accounting for Investments—Recognition and Measurement

11.03 An investor may be able to exercise significant influence over the strategic operating, investing, and financing policies of an investee, even when the investor does not control, or jointly control, the investee. For example, the ability to exercise significant influence may be indicated by representation on the board of directors, participation in policy-making processes, material intercompany transactions, interchange of managerial personnel, or technological dependency. If the investor holds 20 percent or more of the voting interest in the investee, a rebuttable presumption is that the investor has the ability to exercise significant influence. If the investor holds less than 20 percent of the voting interest in the investee, it is presumed that the investor does not have the ability to exercise significant influence, unless such influence is clearly demonstrated.

11.04 An investor that is able to exercise significant influence over an investee that is not a subsidiary as defined in chapter 22 should account for the investment using the equity method. An investor that is not able to exercise significant influence over an investee should account for the investment using the *cost method*,[1] except for investments in securities held for sale.

11.05 Equity method investees normally should follow the same basis of accounting (that is, the FRF for SMEs accounting framework) as the investor. Accordingly, financial statements of equity-method investees should be adjusted, if necessary, to conform with principles in the framework, unless it is impracticable to do so. As stated in chapter 22, a material difference in the basis of accounting between a parent and a subsidiary precludes the use of the equity method.

11.06 Equity and debt investments held for sale should be recognized and measured at market value. Changes in market value should be recognized in net income in the period incurred. Investments held for sale are securities that management is currently attempting to sell.

11.07 When an investor ceases to be able to exercise significant influence over an investee, the investment should be accounted for in accordance with the cost method, unless the investor has obtained *control*

---

[1] Italicized terms are defined in the glossary.

(as that term is used in chapter 22), in which case the investor applies chapter 22.

Equity Method

11.08 Investment income, as calculated by the *equity method*, should be the investor's share of the income or losses of the investee.

11.09 When accounting for an investment by the equity method, the investor's proportionate share of the investee's discontinued operations, changes in accounting policy, corrections of errors relating to prior period financial statements, and capital transactions should be presented in the investor's financial statements according to their nature.

11.10 In those situations in which the investor has the ability to exercise significant influence, shareholders would be informed of the results of operations of the investee, and it is appropriate to include in the results of operations of the investor its share of the income or losses of the investee. The equity method of accounting for the investment provides this information.

11.11 Depreciation and amortization of investee assets are based on the assigned costs of such assets at the date(s) of acquisition. The portion of the difference between the investor's cost and the amount of its underlying equity in the net assets of the investee that is similar to goodwill (equity method goodwill) is amortized. Unrealized intercompany gain or loss, and any gain or loss that would arise in accounting for intercompany bond holdings, are eliminated.

11.12 The investment account of the investor reflects

 a. the cost of the investment in the investee;

 b. the investment income or loss (including the investor's proportionate share of discontinued operations) relating to the investee subsequent to the date when the use of the equity method first became appropriate;

 c. the investor's proportionate share of a change in an accounting policy, a correction of an error relating to prior period financial statements, and capital transactions of the investee subsequent to the date when the use of the equity method first became appropriate; and

 d. the investor's proportion of *dividends* paid by the investee subsequent to the date when the use of the equity method first became appropriate.

11.13 Presentation of the individual steps involved in the calculation of investment income on the equity method includes a duplication of much of chapter 23, "Consolidated Financial Statements and Noncontrolling Interests," which deals with consolidations. However, the investor's proportionate share of any discontinued operations, changes in accounting policy, corrections of errors relating to prior period financial statements, or capital transactions of the investee is presented and disclosed separately, according to its nature, in the investor's financial statements.

11.14 The elimination of an unrealized intercompany gain or loss has the same effect on net income regardless of whether the consolidation or equity method is used. However, in consolidated financial statements, the elimination of a gain or loss may affect sales and cost of sales otherwise to be reported. In the application of the equity method, the gain or loss is eliminated by adjustment of investment income from the investee or by separate provision in the investor's financial statements, as is appropriate in the circumstances.

11.15 When an investor ceases to be able to exercise significant influence, cost is deemed to be the carrying amount of the investment at that time.

11.16 An investor generally should discontinue applying the equity method if the investment, and net advances, is reduced to zero. An investor's share of losses in excess of the carrying amount and net advances of the investment should be recorded if

    a. the investor has guaranteed the obligations of the investee;

    b. the investor is otherwise committed to provide further financial support to the investee; or

    c. the investee seems assured of imminently returning to profitability.

If the investee subsequently reports net income, the investor should resume applying the equity method only after its share of net income equals the share of net losses not recognized during the period where the equity method of accounting was suspended.

Cost Method

11.17 The cost method should be used when accounting for investments within the scope of this chapter other than for those for which the investor is able to exercise significant influence over an investee and equity and debt investments held for sale.

11.18 These types of investments include certain other investments, such as works of art and other tangible assets held for investment purposes.

Gains and Losses on Sales of Investments

11.19 For the purposes of calculating a gain or loss on the sale of an investment, the cost of the investment sold should be calculated on the basis of the average carrying amount.

Presentation

11.20 The following should be presented separately on the statement of financial position or in the notes to the financial statements:

    a. Investments in companies subject to significant influence accounted for using the equity method

    b. Other investments accounted for at cost

    c. Equity and debt investments held for sale

11.21 Income from investments in

    a. investments in companies subject to significant influence accounted for using the equity method;

b. other investments accounted for at cost; and

c. equity and debt investments held for sale

should be presented separately in the statement of operations or in the notes to the financial statements.

11.22 A significant factor when evaluating the investment income is the relationship of the income reported to the investments from which such income is derived. For this reason, investments reported on the statement of financial position and investment income reported in the statement of operations are grouped in the same way.

Disclosure

11.23 The basis used to account for investments should be disclosed.

11.24 When the fiscal periods of an investor and an investee are not the same and the equity method is used to account for the investee, events relating to, or transactions of, the investee that have occurred during the intervening period and significantly affect the financial position or results of operations of the investor should be disclosed. This disclosure is not necessary if these events or transactions are recorded in the financial statements.

11.25 Other than investments held for sale, an entity should disclose the name and description of each significant investment, including the carrying amounts, and proportion of ownership interests held in each investment.

Chapter 12

Inventories

Purpose and Scope

12.01 This chapter prescribes the accounting treatment for *inventories*.[1] A primary issue when accounting for inventories is the amount of cost to be recognized as an asset and carried forward until the related revenues are recognized. This chapter provides guidance on the determination of cost and its subsequent recognition as an expense, including any write-down to *net realizable value*. It also provides guidance on the cost formulas that are used to assign costs to inventories.

12.02 Certain specialized industries typically have their own unique inventory accounting policies (for example, agricultural activities), and this chapter does not preclude the use of those policies, as long as they are generally used and accepted in the industry and the disclosure requirements of paragraphs 12.28–12.29 are complied with.

12.03 *Inventories* encompass goods purchased and held for resale (for example, merchandise purchased by a retailer and held for resale or land and other property held for resale). Inventories also encompass finished goods produced or work in progress being produced by the entity and include materials and supplies awaiting use in the production process.

Measurement of Inventories

12.04 Inventories should be measured at the lower of cost or net realizable value.

Cost of Inventories

12.05 The cost of inventories should comprise all costs of purchase, costs of conversion, and other costs incurred when bringing the inventories to their present location and condition.

Costs of Purchase

12.06 The costs of purchase of inventories comprise the purchase price, import duties, and other taxes (other than those subsequently recoverable by the entity from the taxing authorities) and transport, handling, and other costs directly attributable to the acquisition of finished goods, materials, and services. Trade discounts, rebates, and other similar items are deducted when determining the costs of purchase.

Costs of Conversion

12.07 The costs of conversion of inventories include costs directly related to the units of production, such as direct labor. They also include a systematic allocation of fixed and variable production overheads that are incurred when converting materials into finished goods. Fixed production overheads are those indirect costs of production that remain relatively

---

[1] Italicized terms are defined in the glossary.

constant, regardless of the volume of production, such as depreciation and maintenance of factory buildings and equipment and the cost of factory management and administration. Variable production overheads are those indirect costs of production that vary directly, or nearly directly, with the volume of production, such as indirect materials and indirect labor.

12.08 The allocation of fixed production overheads to the costs of conversion is based on the normal capacity of the production facilities. *Normal capacity* is the production expected to be achieved on average over a number of periods or seasons under normal circumstances, taking into account the loss of capacity resulting from planned maintenance. The actual level of production may be used if it approximates normal capacity. The amount of fixed overhead allocated to each unit of production is not increased as a consequence of low production or idle plant. Unallocated overheads are recognized as an expense in the period in which they are incurred. In periods of abnormally high production, the amount of fixed overhead allocated to each unit of production is decreased so that inventories are not measured above cost. Variable production overheads are allocated to each unit of production on the basis of the actual use of the production facilities.

12.09 A production process may result in more than one product being produced simultaneously. For example, this is the case when joint products are produced or when there is a main product and a by-product. When the costs of conversion of each product are not separately identifiable, they are allocated between the products on a rational and consistent basis. For example, the allocation may be based on the relative sales value of each product either at the stage in the production process when the products become separately identifiable or at the completion of production. Most by-products are immaterial. When this is the case, they are often measured at net realizable value, and this value is deducted from the cost of the main product. As a result, the carrying amount of the main product is not materially different from its cost.

Other Costs

12.10 Other costs are included in the cost of inventories only to the extent that they are incurred when bringing the inventories to their present location and condition. For example, it may be appropriate to include nonproduction overheads or the costs of designing products for specific customers in the cost of inventories.

12.11 Examples of costs excluded from the cost of inventories and recognized as expenses in the period in which they are incurred are

   a. abnormal amounts of wasted materials, labor, or other production costs;

   b. storage costs, unless those costs are necessary in the production process before a further production stage;

   c. administrative overheads that do not contribute to bringing inventories to their present location and condition; and

   d. selling costs.

12.12 The cost of inventories that require a substantial period of time to get them ready for their intended use or sale includes interest costs, when the entity's accounting policy is to capitalize interest costs. The cost of inventories that are ready for their intended use or sale when acquired does not include interest costs.

12.13 An entity may purchase inventories on deferred settlement terms. When the arrangement effectively contains a financing element, that element (for example, a difference between the purchase price for normal credit terms and the amount paid) is recognized as interest expense over the period of the financing.

Techniques for the Measurement of Cost

12.14 Techniques for the measurement of the cost of inventories, such as the standard cost method or the retail method, may be used for convenience if the results approximate cost. Standard costs take into account normal levels of materials and supplies, labor, efficiency, and capacity utilization. They are regularly reviewed and, if necessary, revised in the light of current conditions.

12.15 The retail method is often used in the retail industry for measuring inventories of large numbers of rapidly changing items with similar margins for which it is impracticable to use other costing methods. The cost of the inventory is determined by reducing the sales value of the inventory by the appropriate percentage gross margin. The percentage used takes into consideration inventory that has been marked down to below its original selling price. An average percentage for each retail department is often used.

Cost Formulas

12.16 The cost of inventories of items that are not ordinarily interchangeable, and goods or services produced and segregated for specific projects, should be assigned by using specific identification of their individual costs.

12.17 *Specific identification of cost* means that specific costs are attributed to identified items of inventory. This is the appropriate treatment for items that are segregated for a specific project, regardless of whether they have been bought or produced. However, specific identification of costs is inappropriate when large numbers of items of inventory are ordinarily interchangeable. In such circumstances, the method of selecting those items that remain in inventories could be used to obtain predetermined effects on net income.

12.18 The cost of inventories, other than those dealt with in paragraph 12.16, should be assigned by using the first in, first out (FIFO), last in, first out (LIFO), or weighted average cost formulas.

12.19 Inventories used in one business segment may have a use to the entity different from the same type of inventories used in another business segment. However, a difference in geographical location of inventories (or in the respective tax rules), by itself, is not sufficient to justify the use of different cost formulas.

12.20 The FIFO formula assumes that the items of inventory that were purchased or produced first are sold first and, consequently, the items remaining in inventory at the end of the period are those most recently purchased or produced. The LIFO formula assumes that the items of

FRF-SME 12.20

inventory that were most recently purchased or produced are sold first and, consequently, the items remaining in inventory at the end of the period are those purchased or produced first. Under the weighted average cost formula, the cost of each item is determined from the weighted average of the cost of similar items at the beginning of a period and the cost of similar items purchased or produced during the period. The average may be calculated on a periodic basis or as each additional shipment is received, depending upon the circumstances of the entity.

Net Realizable Value

12.21 The cost of inventories may not be recoverable if those inventories are damaged, if they have become wholly or partially obsolete, or if their selling prices have declined. The cost of inventories also may not be recoverable if the estimated costs of completion or the estimated costs to be incurred to make the sale have increased. The practice of writing inventories down below cost to net realizable value is consistent with the view that assets are not carried in excess of amounts expected to be realized from their sale or use.

12.22 Inventories are usually written down to net realizable value item by item or in the aggregate. In some circumstances, it may be appropriate to group similar or related items. This may be the case with items of inventory relating to the same product line that have similar purposes or end uses, are produced and marketed in the same geographical area, and cannot be practicably evaluated separately from other items in that product line. It is not appropriate to write inventories down on the basis of a classification of inventory (for example, finished goods or all the inventories in a particular industry or geographical segment).

12.23 Estimates of net realizable value are based on the most reliable evidence available, at the time the estimates are made, of the amount the inventories are expected to realize. These estimates take into consideration fluctuations of price or cost directly relating to events occurring after the end of the period, to the extent that such events confirm conditions existing at the end of the period.

12.24 Estimates of net realizable value also take into consideration the purpose for which the inventory is held. For example, the net realizable value of the quantity of inventory held to satisfy firm sales contracts is based on the contract price. If the sales contracts are for less than the inventory quantities held, the net realizable value of the excess is based on general selling prices. Liabilities may arise from firm sales contracts in excess of inventory quantities held or from firm purchase contracts.

12.25 Materials and other supplies held for use in the production of inventories are not written down below cost if the finished products in which they will be incorporated are expected to be sold at or above cost. However, when a decline in the price of materials indicates that the cost of the finished products exceeds net realizable value, the materials are written down to net realizable value. In such circumstances, the replacement cost of the materials may be the best available measure of their net realizable value.

Recognition as an Expense

12.26 When inventories are sold, the carrying amount of those inventories should be recognized as an expense in the period in which the related revenue is recognized. The amount of any write-down of inventories to net realizable value and all losses of inventories should be recognized as an expense in the period the write-down or loss occurs. The use of a valuation allowance account is permitted.

12.27 Some inventories may be allocated to other asset accounts (for example, inventory used as a component of self-constructed property, plant, or equipment). Inventories allocated to another asset in this way are recognized as an expense during the useful life of that asset.

Disclosure

12.28 The financial statements should disclose

  a. the accounting policies adopted in measuring inventories, including the cost formula used;
  b. the total carrying amount of inventories and the carrying amount in classifications appropriate to the entity; and
  c. the amount of cost of goods sold during the period.

12.29 Information about the carrying amounts held in different classifications of inventories, and the extent of the changes in these assets, is useful to financial statement users. Common classifications of inventories are merchandise, production supplies, materials, works in progress, and finished goods.

12.30 When material and unusual losses result from measuring inventories at the lower of cost or net realizable value, the amount of the loss should be disclosed in the statement of operations separately identified from the consumed inventory costs described as cost of goods sold.

12.31 *Firm purchase commitments* should be disclosed. If the contract price of firm purchase commitments exceeds the market value, the estimated loss should be disclosed.

12.32 If the entity's accounting policy is to capitalize interest costs related to certain items of inventory, the amounts capitalized should be disclosed.

Chapter 13

Intangible Assets

Purpose and Scope

13.01 This chapter establishes principles for the recognition, measurement, presentation, and disclosure of *intangible assets*,[1] including *goodwill*.

13.02 This chapter applies to goodwill subsequent to initial recognition. Principles for the initial recognition, measurement, and disclosure of goodwill acquired in a business combination are provided in chapter 28, "Business Combinations."

13.03 This chapter does not apply to

  a. the initial recognition, measurement, and disclosure of intangible assets acquired in a business combination (see chapter 28);
  b. the establishment of a new cost basis for intangible assets as part of a comprehensive revaluation (see chapter 29, "New Basis (Push-Down) Accounting");
  c. intangible assets held by an entity for sale in the ordinary course of business (see chapter 12, "Inventories");
  d. leases that are within the scope of chapter 25, "Leases";
  e. assets arising from employee benefits (see chapter 20, "Retirement and Other Postemployment Benefits");
  f. deferred income tax assets (see chapter 21, "Income Taxes");
  g. noncurrent intangible assets classified as held for sale (or included in a disposal group that is classified as held for sale) in accordance with chapter 15, "Disposal of Long-Lived Assets and Discontinued Operations"; and
  h. *financial assets* as defined in the glossary.

13.04 Principles for the recognition, measurement, presentation, and disclosure of tangible capital assets are provided in chapter 14, "Property, Plant, and Equipment." Some intangible assets may be contained in or on a physical substance, such as a compact disc (in the case of computer software), legal documentation (in the case of a license or patent), or film. When determining whether an asset that incorporates both intangible and tangible elements is to be accounted for under chapter 14 or as an intangible asset under this chapter, management uses judgment to assess which element is more significant. For example, computer software for a computer-controlled machine tool that cannot operate without that specific software is an integral part of the related hardware, and it is treated as property, plant, and equipment. The same applies to the operating system of a computer.

13.05 Rights under licensing agreements for items such as motion picture films, video recordings, plays, manuscripts, patents, and copyrights are excluded from the scope of chapter 25 and are within the scope of this chapter.

---

[1] Italicized terms are defined in the glossary.

13.06 This chapter applies to, among other things, expenditure on advertising, training, start-up, and research and development activities. *Research* and *development* activities are directed to the development of knowledge. Therefore, although these activities may result in an asset with physical substance (for example, a prototype), the physical element of the asset is secondary to its intangible component (that is, the knowledge embodied in it).

Intangible Assets

13.07 Entities frequently expend resources or incur liabilities on the acquisition, development, maintenance, or enhancement of intangible resources, such as scientific or technical knowledge, design, and implementation of new processes or systems; licenses; intellectual property; market knowledge; and trademarks (including brand names and publishing titles). Common examples of items encompassed by these broad headings are computer software, patents, copyrights, motion picture films, customer lists, mortgage servicing rights, fishing licenses, import quotas, franchises, customer or supplier relationships, customer loyalty, market share, and marketing rights.

13.08 Not all the items described in paragraph 13.07 meet the definition of an intangible asset (that is, identifiability, control over a resource, and existence of future economic benefits). If an item within the scope of this chapter does not meet the definition of an intangible asset or goodwill, expenditure to acquire it or generate it internally is recognized as an expense when it is incurred.

Identifiability

13.09 The definition of an intangible asset requires an intangible asset to be identifiable to distinguish it from goodwill. Goodwill acquired in a business combination represents a payment made by the acquirer in anticipation of future economic benefits from assets that are not capable of being individually identified and separately recognized. The future economic benefits may result from synergy between the identifiable assets acquired or from assets that, individually, do not qualify for recognition in the financial statements but for which the acquirer is prepared to make a payment in the business combination.

13.10 An asset meets the identifiability criterion in the definition of an intangible asset when it

   a. is separable (that is, is capable of being separated or divided from the entity and sold, transferred, licensed, rented, or exchanged, either individually or together with a related contract, identifiable asset, or liability, regardless of whether the entity intends to do so) or

   b. arises from contractual or other legal rights, regardless of whether those rights are transferable or separable from the entity or from other rights and obligations.

Control

13.11 An entity controls an asset if the entity has the power to obtain the future economic benefits flowing from the underlying resource and to restrict the access of others to those benefits. The capacity of an entity to control the future economic benefits from an intangible asset would normally stem from legal rights that are enforceable in a court of law. In the absence of legal rights, it is more difficult to demonstrate control. However, legal enforceability of a right is not a necessary condition for control because an entity may be able to control the future economic benefits in some other way.

13.12 Market and technical knowledge may give rise to future economic benefits. An entity controls those benefits if, for example, the knowledge is protected by legal rights through copyrights, through a restraint of trade agreement (when permitted), or by a legal duty on employees to maintain confidentiality.

13.13 An entity may have a portfolio of customers or a market share and expect that, because of its efforts in building customer relationships and loyalty, the customers will continue to conduct business with the entity. However, in the absence of legal rights to protect or other ways to control the relationships with customers or the loyalty of the customers to the entity, the entity usually has insufficient control over the expected economic benefits from customer relationships and loyalty for such items (for example, portfolio of customers, market shares, customer relationships, and customer loyalty) to meet the definition of intangible assets. In the absence of legal rights to protect customer relationships, exchange transactions for the same or similar noncontractual customer relationships (other than as part of a business combination) provide evidence that the entity is, nonetheless, able to control the expected future economic benefits flowing from the customer relationships. Because such exchange transactions also provide evidence that the customer relationships are separable, those customer relationships meet the definition of an intangible asset.

Future Economic Benefits

13.14 The future economic benefits flowing from an intangible asset may include revenue from the sale of products or services, cost savings, or other benefits resulting from the use of the asset by the entity. For example, the use of intellectual property in a production process may reduce future production costs, rather than increase future revenues.

Recognition and Measurement

13.15 The recognition of an item as an intangible asset requires an entity to demonstrate that the item meets

> *a.* the definition of an intangible asset (see paragraphs 13.07–.14) and
>
> *b.* the recognition criteria (see paragraphs 13.18–.20).

This requirement applies to costs incurred initially to acquire or internally generate an intangible asset.

13.16 Paragraphs 13.22–.27 deal with the application of the recognition criteria to separately acquired intangible assets, and paragraphs

13.28–.30 deal with the treatment of internally-generated goodwill. Paragraphs 13.31–.46 deal with the initial recognition and measurement of internally-generated intangible assets.

13.17 The nature of intangible assets is such that, in many cases, there are no additions or replacements to such an asset or any part of it. Accordingly, most subsequent expenditures are likely to maintain the expected future economic benefits embodied in an existing intangible asset, rather than meet the definition of an intangible asset and the recognition criteria in this chapter. In addition, it is often difficult to attribute subsequent expenditure directly to a particular intangible asset rather than to the business as a whole. Therefore, only rarely will subsequent expenditure—expenditure incurred after the initial recognition of an acquired intangible asset or after completion of an internally-generated intangible asset—be recognized in the *carrying amount* of an asset. Consistent with paragraph 13.43, subsequent expenditure on brands, mastheads, publishing titles, customer lists, and items similar in substance (whether externally acquired or internally generated) is always recognized in net income as incurred because such expenditure cannot be distinguished from expenditure to develop the business as a whole.

13.18 An intangible asset should be recognized if, and only if

    a. it is probable that the expected future economic benefits that are attributable to the asset will flow to the entity;

    b. the *cost* of the asset can be measured reliably; and

    c. the *useful life* of the asset can be estimated.

13.19 Management should assess the probability of expected future economic benefits using reasonable and supportable assumptions that represent management's best estimate of the set of economic conditions that will exist over the useful life of the asset.

13.20 Management uses judgment to assess the degree of certainty attached to the flow of future economic benefits that are attributable to the use of the asset on the basis of the evidence available at the time of initial recognition, giving greater weight to external evidence.

13.21 An intangible asset should be measured initially at cost. If an intangible asset is acquired in a business combination and separately recognized, the cost of that intangible asset is its market value at the acquisition date.

Separate Acquisition

13.22 Normally, the price an entity pays to acquire separately an intangible asset reflects expectations about the probability that the expected future economic benefits embodied in the asset will flow to the entity. In other words, the effect of probability is reflected in the cost of the asset. Therefore, the probability recognition criterion in paragraph 13.18(a) is always considered to be satisfied for separately acquired intangible assets.

13.23 The cost of a separately acquired intangible asset can usually be measured reliably, particularly when the purchase consideration is in the form of cash or other *monetary assets*.

13.24 The cost of a separately acquired intangible asset comprises

  a. its purchase price, including import duties and nonrefundable purchase taxes, after deducting trade discounts and rebates, and

  b. any directly attributable cost of preparing the asset for its intended use.

13.25 Examples of directly attributable costs are

  a. costs of salaries, wages, and employee benefits arising directly from bringing the asset to its working condition;

  b. professional fees arising directly from bringing the asset to its working condition; and

  c. costs of testing whether the asset is functioning properly.

13.26 Examples of expenditures that are not part of the cost of an intangible asset are

  a. costs of introducing a new product or service (including costs of advertising and promotional activities);

  b. costs of conducting business in a new location or with a new class of customer (including costs of staff training); and

  c. administration and other general overhead costs.

13.27 Recognition of costs in the carrying amount of an intangible asset ceases when the asset is in the condition necessary for it to be capable of operating in the manner intended by management. Therefore, costs incurred when using or redeploying an intangible asset are not included in the carrying amount of that asset. For example, the following costs are not included in the carrying amount of an intangible asset:

  a. Costs incurred while an asset capable of operating in the manner intended by management has yet to be brought into use

  b. Initial operating losses, such as those incurred while demand for the asset's output builds up

Internally-Generated Goodwill

13.28 Internally-generated goodwill should not be recognized as an asset.

13.29 In some cases, expenditure is incurred to generate future economic benefits, but it does not result in the creation of an intangible asset that meets the recognition criteria in this chapter. Such expenditure is often described as contributing to internally-generated goodwill. Internally-generated goodwill is not recognized as an asset because it is not an identifiable resource (that is, it is not separable, nor does it arise from contractual or other legal rights) controlled by the entity that can be measured reliably at cost.

13.30 Differences between the market value of an entity and the carrying amount of its identifiable net assets at any time may capture a range of factors that affect the value of the entity. However, such differences do not represent the cost of intangible assets controlled by the entity.

Intangible Assets

Internally-Generated Intangible Assets

13.31 It is sometimes difficult to assess whether an internally-generated intangible asset qualifies for recognition because of problems when

   a. identifying whether and when there is an identifiable asset that will generate expected future economic benefits and

   b. determining the cost of the asset reliably. In some cases, the cost of generating an intangible asset internally cannot be distinguished from the cost of maintaining or enhancing the entity's internally-generated goodwill or of running day-to-day operations.

Therefore, in addition to complying with the general requirements for the recognition and initial measurement of an intangible asset, an entity should apply the requirements and guidance in paragraphs 13.32–.46 to all internally-generated intangible assets.

13.32 To assess whether an internally-generated intangible asset meets the criteria for recognition, an entity classifies the generation of the asset into

   a. a research phase and

   b. a development phase.

Although the terms *research* and *development* are defined, the terms *research phase* and *development phase* have a broader meaning for the purpose of this chapter.

13.33 If management cannot distinguish the research phase from the development phase of an internal project to create an intangible asset, the entity treats the expenditure on that project as if it were incurred in the research phase only.

Research Phase

13.34 No intangible asset arising from research (or from the research phase of an internal project) should be recognized. Expenditure on research (or on the research phase of an internal project) should be recognized as an expense when it is incurred.

13.35 In the research phase of an internal project, an entity cannot demonstrate that an intangible asset exists that will generate probable future economic benefits. Therefore, this expenditure is recognized as an expense when it is incurred.

13.36 Examples of research phase activities are

   a. activities aimed at obtaining new knowledge;

   b. the search for, evaluation, and final selection of applications of research findings or other knowledge;

   c. the search for alternatives for materials, devices, products, processes, systems, or services; and

   d. the formulation, design, evaluation, and final selection of possible alternatives for new or improved materials, devices, products, processes, systems, or services.

FRF-SME 13.36

Development Phase

13.37 When accounting for expenditures on internally-generated intangible assets during the development phase, management should make an accounting policy choice to either

    a. expense such expenditures as incurred or

    b. capitalize such expenditures as an intangible asset (provided the criteria in paragraph 13.38 are met).

This accounting policy choice should be applied consistently to expenditures on all internal projects in the development phase.

13.38 An intangible asset arising from development (or from the development phase of an internal project) is recognized if, and only if, an entity can demonstrate all of the following:

    a. The technical feasibility of completing the intangible asset so that it will be available for use or sale.

    b. Its intention to complete the intangible asset and use or sell it.

    c. Its ability to use or sell the intangible asset.

    d. The availability of adequate technical, financial, and other resources to complete the development and to use or sell the intangible asset.

    e. Its ability to measure reliably the expenditure attributable to the intangible asset during its development.

    f. How the intangible asset will generate probable future economic benefits. Among other things, the entity can demonstrate the existence of a market for the output of the intangible asset or the intangible asset itself or, if it is to be used internally, the usefulness of the intangible asset.

13.39 In the development phase of an internal project, in some instances, an entity can identify an intangible asset and demonstrate that the asset will generate probable future economic benefits because the development phase of a project is further advanced than the research phase.

13.40 Examples of development phase activities are

    a. the design, construction, and testing of preproduction or preuse prototypes and models;

    b. the design of tools, jigs, molds, and dies involving new technology;

    c. the design, construction, and operation of a pilot plant that is not of a scale economically feasible for commercial production; and

    d. the design, construction, and testing of a chosen alternative for new or improved materials, devices, products, processes, systems, or services.

13.41 Availability of resources to complete, use, and obtain the benefits from an intangible asset can be demonstrated by, for example, a business plan showing the technical, financial, and other resources needed and the entity's ability to secure those resources. In some cases, an entity demonstrates the availability of external finance by obtaining a lender's indication of its willingness to fund the plan.

Intangible Assets

13.42 An entity's costing systems can often measure reliably the cost of generating an intangible asset internally, such as salary and other expenditure incurred in securing copyrights or licenses or developing computer software.

13.43 Internally-generated brands, mastheads, publishing titles, customer lists, and items similar in substance should not be recognized as intangible assets.

Cost of an Internally-Generated Intangible Asset

13.44 The cost of an internally-generated intangible asset for the purpose of paragraph 13.21 is the sum of expenditures incurred from the date when the intangible asset first meets the recognition criteria in paragraphs 13.18–.19 and 13.38. Paragraph 13.52 prohibits reinstatement of expenditures previously recognized as an expense.

13.45 The cost of an internally-generated intangible asset comprises all directly attributable costs necessary to create, produce, and prepare the asset to be capable of operating in the manner intended by management. Examples of directly attributable costs are

 a. costs of materials and services used or consumed when generating the intangible asset;
 b. costs of employee salaries, wages, and benefits arising from the generation of the intangible asset;
 c. fees to register a legal right;
 d. *amortization* of patents and licenses that are used to generate the intangible asset; and
 e. interest costs when the entity's accounting policy is to capitalize interest costs.

13.46 The following are not components of the cost of an internally-generated intangible asset:

 a. Selling, administrative, and other general overhead expenditure, unless this expenditure can be directly attributed to preparing the asset for use
 b. Identified inefficiencies and initial operating losses incurred before the asset achieves planned performance
 c. Expenditure on training staff to operate the asset

Recognition of an Expense

13.47 Expenditure on an intangible item should be recognized as an expense when it is incurred unless

 a. for an internally-generated intangible asset in the development phase, management has made an accounting policy choice to capitalize such expenditures (see paragraph 13.37), and
 b. it forms part of the cost of an intangible asset that meets the recognition criteria (see paragraphs 13.15–.46).

13.48 In some cases, expenditure is incurred to provide future economic benefits to an entity, but no intangible asset or other asset is acquired or created that can be recognized. In the case of the supply of goods, the entity recognizes such expenditure as an expense when it has a right to access those goods. In the case of the supply of services, the entity recognizes the expenditure as an expense when it receives the services. Examples of expenditures that are recognized as an expense when it is incurred include expenditure on

   a. training activities;

   b. advertising and promotional activities (including mail-order catalogs and other similar documents intended to advertise goods, services, or events to customers); and

   c. relocating or reorganizing part or all of an entity.

13.49 An entity has a right to access goods when it owns them. Similarly, it has a right to access goods when they have been constructed by a supplier in accordance with the terms of a supply contract, and the entity can demand delivery of them in return for payment. Services are received when they are performed by a supplier in accordance with a contract to deliver them to the entity and not when the entity uses them to deliver another service (for example, to deliver an advertisement to customers).

13.50 Paragraph 13.48 does not preclude recognizing a prepayment as an asset when payment for the delivery of goods has been made in advance of the entity obtaining a right to access those goods. Similarly, paragraph 13.48 does not preclude an entity from recognizing a prepayment as an asset when payment for services has been made in advance of the entity receiving those services.

Start-Up Costs

13.51 Start-up costs may consist of establishment costs, such as legal and other administrative costs incurred when establishing a legal entity, expenditure to open a new facility or business (that is, preopening costs), or expenditures for starting new operations or launching new products or processes (that is, preoperating costs). Management should make an accounting policy election to either expense start-up costs as incurred or capitalize start-up costs and amortize the amount over 15 years.

Past Expenses Not to Be Recognized as Assets

13.52 Expenditure on an intangible item that was initially recognized as an expense should not be recognized as part of the cost of an intangible asset at a later date.

Subsequent Measurement

13.53 A recognized intangible asset should be amortized over its useful life. For the purpose of the FRF for SMEs accounting framework, all intangible assets should be considered to have a finite useful life. The useful life of an intangible asset that arises from contractual or other legal rights should not exceed the period of the contractual or other legal rights but may be shorter depending on the period over which the entity expects to use the asset. If the contractual or other legal rights are conveyed for a limited term that can be renewed, the useful life of the intangible asset should include the renewal period(s) only if there is evidence to support renewal by the entity without significant cost.

13.54 The amortization method and estimate of the useful life of an intangible asset should be reviewed on a regular basis.

13.55 When the precise length of an intangible asset's useful life is not known, the intangible asset is amortized over the best estimate of its useful life. Guidance for determining the useful life of an intangible asset is provided in paragraph 13.58.

13.56 The amount of an intangible asset to be amortized is the amount initially assigned to that asset less any *residual value*. The residual value of an intangible asset is assumed to be zero unless, at the end of its useful life to the reporting entity, the asset is expected to continue to have a useful life to another entity, and

> *a.* the reporting entity has a commitment from a third party to purchase the asset at the end of its useful life, or
>
> *b.* the residual value can be determined by reference to an exchange transaction in an existing market for that asset, and that market is expected to exist at the end of the asset's useful life.

13.57 The method of amortization will reflect the pattern in which the economic benefits of the intangible asset are consumed or otherwise used up. The guidance in chapter 14 related to identifying an appropriate depreciation method for a tangible asset is also conceptually relevant when identifying an appropriate amortization method for an intangible asset. When the pattern of economic benefits cannot be reliably determined, a straight-line amortization method is used.

Determining the Useful Life of an Intangible Asset

13.58 The estimate of the useful life of an intangible asset is based on an analysis of all pertinent factors, in particular

> *a.* the expected use of the asset by the entity;
>
> *b.* the expected useful life of another asset or a group of assets to which the useful life of the asset may relate;
>
> *c.* any legal, regulatory, or contractual provisions that may limit the useful life;
>
> *d.* any legal, regulatory, or contractual provisions that enable renewal or extension of the asset's legal or contractual life without substantial cost (provided there is evidence to support renewal or extension, and renewal or extension can be accomplished without material modifications to the existing terms and conditions);
>
> *e.* the effects of obsolescence, demand, competition, and other economic factors (such as the stability of the industry, known technological advances, legislative action that results in an uncertain or changing regulatory environment, and expected changes in distribution channels); and
>
> *f.* the level of maintenance expenditures required to obtain the expected future cash flows from the asset.

Goodwill

13.59 Goodwill should be recognized on an entity's statement of financial position at the amount initially recognized, less amortization.

13.60 Goodwill should be amortized generally over the same period as that used for federal income tax purposes or, if not amortized for federal income tax purposes, then a period of 15 years.

13.61 For equity method investments, the portion of the difference between the investor's cost and the amount of its underlying equity in the net assets of the investee that is similar to goodwill (equity method goodwill) is amortized.

Presentation

13.62 The aggregate amount of goodwill should be presented as a separate line item in an entity's statement of financial position.

13.63 Intangible assets should be aggregated and presented as a separate line item in an entity's statement of financial position.

Disclosure

13.64 The financial statements should disclose the following information:

   a. The carrying amount in total and by major intangible asset class
   b. The aggregate amortization expense for the period
   c. The amortization method used, including the amortization period or rate by major intangible asset class
   d. The accounting policy for internally-generated intangible assets, including the treatment of development costs, whether expensed or capitalized

13.65 An *intangible asset class* is a group of intangible assets that are similar, either by their nature or use in the operations of an entity.

13.66 If the entity has incurred expenditure on start-up costs, the policy for accounting for those costs should be disclosed.

Chapter 14

Property, Plant, and Equipment

Purpose and Scope

14.01 This chapter establishes principles for the recognition, measurement, presentation, and disclosure of *property, plant, and equipment*[1] (tangible capital assets). This chapter applies to property, plant, and equipment recognized under chapter 25, "Leases."

14.02 This chapter does not deal with goodwill or intangible assets (see chapter 13, "Intangible Assets") or with the disposal of property, plant, and equipment (see chapter 15, "Disposal of Long-Lived Assets and Discontinued Operations"). This chapter also does not deal with special circumstances in which it may be appropriate to undertake a comprehensive revaluation of all the assets and liabilities of an entity (see chapter 29, "New Basis (Push-Down) Accounting").

Measurement

Cost

14.03 Property, plant, and equipment should be recorded at cost.

14.04 The *cost* of an item of property, plant, and equipment includes the purchase price and other acquisition costs, such as option costs, when an option is exercised; brokers' commissions; installation costs, including architectural, design, and engineering fees; legal fees; survey costs; site preparation costs; freight charges; transportation insurance costs; duties; testing; and preparation charges. It may be appropriate to group together individually insignificant items of property, plant, and equipment.

14.05 The cost of each item of property, plant, and equipment acquired as part of a group purchase (that is, when a group of assets is acquired for a single amount), is determined by allocating the price paid for the group to each item on the basis of its relative market value at the time of acquisition.

14.06 When, at the time of acquisition, a portion of the acquired item of property, plant, and equipment meets the criteria in chapter 15 to be classified as held for sale at the acquisition date, that portion of the item is measured at market value less cost to sell. The remainder of the acquired item is measured at the cost of acquisition of the entire item less the amount assigned to the portion to be sold. For example, if a portion of land acquired is to be resold, the cost of the land to be retained would be the total cost of the purchase, minus the market value, less cost to sell of the portion of land held for sale. When, at the time of acquisition, a portion of the acquired item of property, plant, and equipment is not intended for use because it will be abandoned, its cost and any costs of disposal, net of any estimated proceeds, are attributed to that portion of the acquired asset that is intended for use. For example, the cost of acquired land that

---

[1] Italicized terms are defined in the glossary.

includes a building that will be demolished comprises the cost of the acquired property and the cost of demolishing the building.

Acquisition, Construction, or Development Over Time

14.07 The cost of an item of property, plant, and equipment includes direct construction or development costs (such as materials and labor) and overhead costs directly attributable to the construction or development activity.

14.08 The cost of an item of property, plant, and equipment that is acquired, constructed, or developed over time includes carrying costs directly attributable to the acquisition, construction, or development activity (such as interest costs when the entity's accounting policy is to capitalize interest costs.)

14.09 Capitalization of carrying costs ceases when an item of property, plant, and equipment is substantially complete and ready for productive use. Determining when an asset, or a portion thereof, is substantially complete and ready for productive use requires consideration of the circumstances and the industry in which it is to be operated. Normally, it would be predetermined by management with reference to such factors as productive capacity, occupancy level, or the passage of time.

14.10 Net revenue or expense derived from an item of property, plant, and equipment prior to substantial completion and readiness for use is included in the cost.

Improvement

14.11 The cost incurred to enhance the *service potential* of an item of property, plant, and equipment is an improvement. Service potential may be enhanced when there is an increase in the previously assessed physical output or service capacity; associated operating costs are lowered; the life or *useful life* is extended; or the quality of output is improved. The cost incurred in the maintenance of the service potential of an item of property, plant, and equipment is a repair, not an improvement. If a cost has the attributes of both a repair and an improvement, the portion considered to be an improvement is included in the cost of the asset.

14.12 A redevelopment project that adds significant economic value to rental real estate is treated as an improvement. When a building is removed for the purpose of redevelopment of rental real estate, the carrying amount of the building is included in the cost of the redeveloped property, as long as the net amount considered recoverable from the redevelopment project exceeds its cost.

Depreciation

14.13 *Depreciation* should be recognized over the useful life of the asset in a rational and systematic manner appropriate to the nature of an item of property, plant, and equipment with a limited life and its use by the entity. Depreciation expense is calculated on the cost less any expected *residual value*.

14.14 Property, plant, and equipment are acquired to earn income or supply a service over its useful life. An item of property, plant, and equipment, other than land that normally has an unlimited life, has a limited life. Its useful life is normally the shortest of its physical, technological, commercial, and legal life. Depreciation is the charge to income that recognizes that life is finite and that the cost, less any expected residual value of an item of property, plant, and equipment, is allocated to the periods of service provided by the asset. Depreciation may also be termed *amortization*.

14.15 The cost of an item of property, plant, and equipment made up of significant separable component parts is allocated to the component parts when practicable and when estimates can be made of the lives of the separate components.

14.16 Different methods of depreciating an item of property, plant, and equipment result in different patterns of charges to income. The objective is to provide a rational and systematic basis for allocating the depreciable amount of an item of property, plant, and equipment over its useful life. A straight-line method reflects a constant charge for the service as a function of time. A variable charge method reflects service as a function of usage. Other methods may be appropriate in certain situations. For example, an increasing charge method may be used when an entity can price its goods or services to obtain a constant rate of return on the investment in the asset; a decreasing charge method may be appropriate when the operating efficiency of the asset declines over time. When the pattern of allocating the depreciable amount of an item of property, plant, or equipment cannot be reliably determined, a straight-line depreciation method may be used.

14.17 Factors to be considered when estimating the life and useful life of an item of property, plant, and equipment include expected future usage, effects of technological or commercial obsolescence, expected wear and tear from use or the passage of time, the maintenance program, results of studies made regarding the industry, studies of similar items retired, and the condition of existing comparable items. As the estimate of the life of an item of property, plant, and equipment is extended into the future, it becomes increasingly difficult to identify a reasonable basis for estimating the life.

Review of Depreciation

14.18 The depreciation method and estimates of the life and useful life of an item of property, plant, and equipment should be reviewed on a regular basis. See chapter 9, "Accounting Changes, Changes in Accounting Estimates, and Correction of Errors," for guidance applicable to changes in estimates.

14.19 Significant events that may indicate a need to revise the depreciation method or estimates of the life and useful life of an item of property, plant, and equipment include

    a. a change in the extent to which the asset is used;

    b. a change in the manner in which the asset is used;

    c. removal of the asset from service for an extended period of time;

    d. physical damage;

    e. significant technological developments; and

    f. a change in the law, environment, or consumer styles and tastes affecting the period of time over which the asset can be used.

Asset Retirement Obligations

14.20 Obligations associated with the retirement of property, plant, and equipment are accounted for in accordance with the section, "Asset Retirement Obligations," in chapter 17, "Contingencies."

Disclosure

14.21 For each major category of property, plant, and equipment, the cost and the depreciation method used, including the depreciation period or rate, should be disclosed.

14.22 The carrying amount of an item of property, plant, and equipment not being depreciated because it is under construction or development or has been removed from service for an extended period of time should be disclosed.

14.23 The amount of depreciation of property, plant, and equipment charged to income for the period should be disclosed (see chapter 7, "Statement of Operations"). In addition, total accumulated depreciation should be disclosed.

14.24 Major categories of property, plant, and equipment are determined by reference to type (for example, land, buildings, machinery, leasehold improvements) or nature of operations (for example, manufacturing, processing, distribution).

14.25 The financial statements should disclose the following information in the period in which the carrying value of a *long-lived asset* is reduced (other than for depreciation) due to the cessation of the asset's use or write down in the carrying value of the asset:

    a. A description of the long-lived asset

    b. A description of the facts and circumstances leading to the reduction in carrying value

    c. If not separately presented on the face of the statement of operations, the amount of the reduction in carrying value and the caption in the statement of operations that includes that amount

14.26 Disclosure should be made of interest costs capitalized when the entity's accounting policy is to capitalize interest costs.

Chapter 15

Disposal of Long-Lived Assets and Discontinued Operations

Purpose and Scope

15.01 This chapter establishes principles for the recognition, measurement, presentation, and disclosure of the disposal of *long-lived assets*.[1] It also establishes principles for the presentation and disclosure of discontinued operations, regardless of whether they include long-lived assets.

15.02 This chapter applies to the disposal of nonmonetary long-lived assets, including property, plant, and equipment; intangible assets; and long-term prepaid assets. It does not apply to

   a. the disposal of goodwill (except in the case of a disposal group that constitutes a business);

   b. investments, including equity method accounted investments (see chapter 11, "Equity, Debt, and Other Investments"); and

   c. financial assets, financial liabilities, and contracts to buy or sell nonfinancial items accounted for in accordance with chapter 6, "Special Accounting Considerations for Certain Financial Assets and Liabilities."

Long-Lived Assets to Be Disposed of by Sale

Recognition

15.03 A long-lived asset to be sold should be classified as held for sale in the period when all the following criteria are met:

   a. Management, having the authority to approve the action, commits to a plan to sell.

   b. It is available for immediate sale in its present condition, subject only to terms that are usual and customary for sales of such assets.

   c. An active program to locate a buyer and other actions required to complete the sale plan have been initiated.

   d. The sale is probable and is expected to qualify for recognition as a completed sale within one year, except as permitted by paragraph 15.04.

   e. It is being actively marketed for sale at a price that is reasonable.

   f. Actions required to complete the plan indicate that it is not probable that significant changes to the plan will be made or that the plan will be withdrawn.

---

[1] Italicized terms are defined in the glossary.

15.04 Events or circumstances beyond an entity's control may extend the period required to complete the sale beyond one year. An exception to the one-year requirement in paragraph 15.03(d) applies in the following situations in which such events or circumstances arise:

    a. At the date an entity commits to a plan to sell a long-lived asset, it reasonably expects that others (not a buyer) will impose conditions on the transfer that will extend the period required to complete the sale, and

        i. actions necessary to respond to the conditions cannot be initiated until after a firm purchase commitment is obtained, and

        ii. a firm purchase commitment is probable within one year.

    b. An entity obtains a firm purchase commitment and, as a result, a buyer or others unexpectedly impose(s) conditions on the transfer of a long-lived asset previously classified as held for sale that will extend the period required to complete the sale, and

        i. actions necessary to respond to the conditions have been initiated or will be initiated in a timely manner, and

        ii. a favorable resolution of the delaying factors is expected.

    c. During the initial one-year period, circumstances arise that previously were considered not probable and, as a result, a long-lived asset previously classified as held for sale is not sold by the end of that period, and

        i. during the initial one-year period, the entity initiated actions necessary to respond to the change in circumstances;

        ii. the asset is being actively marketed at a price that is reasonable, given the change in circumstances; and

        iii. the criteria in paragraph 15.03 are met.

15.05 A *firm purchase commitment* is an agreement with an unrelated party, binding on both parties and usually legally enforceable, that

    a. specifies all the significant terms, including the price and timing of the transaction and

    b. includes a disincentive for nonperformance that is sufficiently large to make performance probable.

15.06 A long-lived asset that is newly acquired and will be sold, rather than held and used, is classified as held for sale at the acquisition date only if the one-year requirement in paragraph 15.03(d) is met (except as permitted by paragraph 15.04), and any other criteria in paragraph 15.03 that are not met at that date are probable of being met within a short period following the acquisition (usually within 3 months).

15.07 If the criteria in paragraph 15.03 are met after the statement of financial position date but before the financial statements are available to be issued, a long-lived asset continues to be classified as held and used in those financial statements, and the information required by paragraph 15.24(a) is disclosed in the notes to the financial statements (see chapter 27, "Subsequent Events").

15.08 A gain or loss recognized that results from the sale of a long-lived asset is recognized at the date of sale.

Measurement

15.09 A long-lived asset classified as held for sale should be measured at its *carrying amount*. Any costs to sell the asset are recorded as a period expense when the asset is sold. A long-lived asset should not be amortized while it is classified as held for sale. Interest and other expenses attributable to the liabilities of a *disposal group* classified as held for sale should continue to be accrued.

15.10 When a disposal group constitutes a business, goodwill is allocated to the disposal group and included in its carrying amount.

Changes to a Plan of Sale

15.11 If a long-lived asset no longer meets the criteria to be classified as held for sale, it should be reclassified as held and used. A long-lived asset that is reclassified should be measured individually at the carrying amount before it was classified as held for sale, adjusted for any depreciation (amortization) expense that would have been recognized had it been continuously classified as held and used.

15.12 Any required adjustment to the carrying amount of a long-lived asset that is reclassified as held and used is included in income before discontinued operations in the period of the subsequent decision not to sell. If a component of an entity (see paragraph 15.21) is reclassified as held and used, the results of operations of the component previously reported in discontinued operations in accordance with paragraph 15.22 are reclassified and included in income before discontinued operations for all periods presented.

15.13 If an entity removes an individual asset or liability from a disposal group previously classified as held for sale, the remaining assets and liabilities of the disposal group to be sold continue to be measured as a group only if the criteria in paragraph 15.03 are met.

Statement of Financial Position Presentation

15.14 A long-lived asset classified as held for sale should be presented separately in the entity's statement of financial position. The assets and liabilities of a disposal group classified as held for sale should be presented separately in the asset and liability sections, respectively, of the statement of financial position.

15.15 Assets and liabilities of a disposal group classified as held for sale are not offset, other than financial assets and liabilities that meet the conditions for offsetting (see chapter 6). Current and long-term assets (and liabilities) are presented separately unless the entity's statement of financial position is unclassified.

15.16 Long-lived assets classified as held for sale are not reclassified as current assets unless the entity has sold the assets prior to the date the financial statements are available to be issued, and the proceeds of the sale will be realized within a year of the date of the statement of financial position or within the normal operating cycle if that is longer than a year.

If the assets have been classified as current assets due to the subsequent sale, any liabilities to be assumed by the purchaser or required to be discharged on disposal of the assets are classified as current liabilities.

Long-Lived Assets to Be Disposed of Other Than by Sale

15.17 A long-lived asset to be disposed of other than by sale should continue to be classified as held and used until it is disposed of. Disposal other than by sale includes, for example, abandonment and a distribution to owners in a spin-off.

15.18 A long-lived asset to be abandoned is disposed of when it ceases to be used. If an entity commits to a plan to abandon a long-lived asset before the end of its previously estimated useful life, depreciation estimates are revised to reflect the use of the asset over its shortened useful life. The continued use of a long-lived asset demonstrates the presence of service potential.

15.19 A gain or loss recognized that results from the disposal of a long-lived asset other than by sale is recognized at the date of disposal. A long-lived asset to be distributed to owners in a spin-off is disposed of when it is distributed.

Discontinued Operations

15.20 The results of operations of a component of an entity that either has been disposed of (by sale, abandonment, or spin-off) or is classified as held for sale should be reported in discontinued operations if both of the following conditions are met:

 a. The operations and cash flows of the component have been (or will be) eliminated from the ongoing operations of the entity as a result of the disposal transaction.

 b. The entity will not have any significant continuing involvement in the operations of the component after the disposal transaction.

Only items meeting the preceding criteria should be reported in discontinued operations.

15.21 A component of an entity comprises operations and cash flows that can be clearly distinguished, operationally and for financial reporting purposes, from the rest of the entity.

15.22 The results of discontinued operations, less applicable income taxes, should be reported as a separate element of income for both current and prior periods (see chapter 7, "Statement of Operations").

15.23 Adjustments to amounts previously reported in discontinued operations that are directly related to the disposal of a component of an entity in a prior period are classified separately in the current period in discontinued operations. Examples of circumstances in which those types of adjustments may arise include the following:

 a. The resolution of contingencies that arise pursuant to the terms of the disposal transaction, such as the resolution of purchase price adjustments and indemnification issues with the purchaser

Disposal of Long-Lived Assets and Discontinued Operations

    b. The resolution of contingencies that arise from, and are directly related to, the operations of the component prior to its disposal, such as environmental and product warranty obligations retained by the seller

    c. The settlement of employee benefit plan obligations (pension, postemployment benefits other than pensions, and other postemployment benefits), provided that the settlement is directly related to the disposal transaction (that is, there is a demonstrated direct cause-and-effect relationship, and the settlement occurs no later than one year following the disposal transaction, unless it is delayed by events or circumstances beyond an entity's control, as permitted by paragraph 15.04.)

Disclosure

15.24 The financial statements should disclose the following information in the period in which a long-lived asset (or disposal group) either has been disposed of by sale or other than by sale or is classified as held for sale:

    a. A description of the facts and circumstances leading to the disposal or expected disposal

    b. If not separately presented on the face of the statement of operations, the amount of the gain or loss on disposal and the caption in the statement of operations that includes that gain or loss

    c. If applicable, amounts of revenue and pretax profit or loss reported in discontinued operations

15.25 In a period when a decision is made not to sell an asset previously classified as held for sale, the change in accounting treatment should be disclosed.

Chapter 16

Commitments

Purpose and Scope

16.01 This chapter establishes disclosure requirements with respect to commitments.

Disclosure

16.02 Commitments that are material in relation to the current financial position or future operations should be disclosed. Examples include

> *a.* commitments to purchase or construct new facilities;
>
> *b.* a commitment to reduce debts;
>
> *c.* an obligation to maintain working capital;
>
> *d.* commitments to acquire assets; and
>
> *e.* unconditional purchase obligations and firm purchase commitments.

16.03 For commitments involving related parties, see also chapter 26, "Related Party Transactions." (With reference to disclosures about guarantees, see also chapter 17, "Contingencies.")

Chapter 17

Contingencies

Purpose and Scope

17.01 This chapter establishes principles for the treatment of contingencies in financial statements. The issues discussed concern both the accrual for, and the disclosure of, contingencies when presenting the financial position and results of operations of an entity. (With reference to contingencies involving related parties, see also chapter 26, "Related Party Transactions.")

17.02 Contingencies would include, but are not limited to, pending or threatened litigation, threat of expropriation of assets, guarantees of the indebtedness or performance of others, and possible liabilities arising from discounted bills of exchange or promissory notes.

17.03 In the preparation of the financial statements of an entity, estimates are required for many ongoing and recurring activities. However, the mere fact that an estimate is involved does not, of itself, constitute the type of uncertainty that characterizes a *contingency*.[1] For example, amounts owed for goods or services received but not billed are not contingencies, even though the amounts may be estimated. No uncertainties exist about the fact that these obligations have been incurred; any uncertainty is related solely to the amounts thereof.

17.04 Although allowances for doubtful accounts, as well as nondiscretionary vendor rebates and provisions for warranties, have many of the characteristics of contingencies, such estimates are not regarded as contingencies, and for the purposes of this chapter, are excluded.

Measurement of Uncertainty

17.05 The uncertainty relating to the occurrence or nonoccurrence of the future event(s), which determines the outcome of a contingency, can be expressed by a range of probabilities that provide a basis for establishing the appropriate accounting treatment. This chapter identifies three areas of this range by a general description as follows:

- *Probable.* The chance of the occurrence (or nonoccurrence) of the future event(s) is likely to occur. Probable is a higher level of likelihood than "more likely than not." Probable does not mean virtually certain.

- *Remote.* The chance of the occurrence (or nonoccurrence) of the future event(s) is slight.

- *Reasonably possible.* The chance of the occurrence (or nonoccurrence) of the future event(s) is more than remote but less than likely.

17.06 Prediction of the outcome of contingencies, including estimation of the financial effects, is a matter for judgment by those responsible for preparing financial statements, taking into account the particular circumstances. When identifying contingencies and determining their amount,

---

[1] Italicized terms are defined in the glossary.

consideration should be given to all information available prior to the date the financial statements are available to be issued (see chapter 27, "Subsequent Events"), supplemented by experience in similar transactions and, in some cases, reports from independent experts.

Accounting Treatment

Contingent Losses

17.07 The treatment of contingent losses in financial statements depends upon the likelihood that a future event will confirm that the value of an asset has diminished or a liability incurred at the financial statement date.

17.08 The amount of a contingent loss should be accrued in the financial statements by a charge to income when both of the following conditions are met:

    a. It is probable that a future event will confirm that the value of an asset has diminished or a liability incurred at the date of the financial statements.

    b. The amount of the loss can be reasonably estimated.

17.09 If it is probable that a contingency existing at the financial statement date will result in a loss and the loss can be reasonably estimated, accrual of its financial effects is required. This accounting treatment recognizes that the probable diminishment of the value of an asset or incurrence of a liability is related to a condition or situation existing at the end of the reporting period and not to the confirming future event.

17.10 A probable loss to an entity may be reduced or avoided by a counterclaim or a claim against a third party (for example, an insurance claim). In such a case, the amount of the probable recovery is an element of the contingent loss and, therefore, should be taken into account in determining the amount to be recognized in the statement of operations. However, if the probability of success in the related action is not virtually certain, a potential recovery should not be taken into account. The amount of the probable recovery should be presented as a gross amount.

17.11 The estimation of the amount of a contingent loss to be accrued in the financial statements may be based on information that provides a range of the amount of loss. When a particular amount within such a range appears to be a better estimate than any other, that amount should be accrued. However, when no amount within the range is indicated as a better estimate than any other, the minimum amount in the range should be accrued.

Contingent Gains

17.12 Contingent gains usually should not be accrued in financial statements because this accounting treatment could result in the recognition of gains that might never be realized.

Disclosure

Contingent Losses

17.13 The existence of a contingent loss at the date of the financial statements should be disclosed in notes to the financial statements when

    a. the occurrence of the confirming future event is probable, but the amount of the loss cannot be reasonably estimated;

    b. the occurrence of the confirming future event is probable, and an accrual has been made, but an exposure to loss in excess of the amount accrued exists; or

    c. the occurrence of the confirming future event is reasonably possible.

17.14 At a minimum, the note disclosure should include

    a. the nature of the contingency;

    b. an estimate of the amount of the contingent loss or a statement that such an estimate cannot be made; and

    c. any exposure to loss in excess of the amount accrued.

17.15 Users of financial statements should be advised of conditions or situations existing at the end of a reporting period when management considers that the probability of realization of a loss or incurrence of a liability is probable or reasonably possible. Such information is important when evaluating the future prospects of an entity.

Contingent Gains

17.16 When it is probable that a future event will confirm that an asset has been acquired or a liability reduced at the date of the financial statements, the existence of a contingent gain should be disclosed in notes to the financial statements.

17.17 At a minimum, the note disclosure should include

    a. the nature of the contingency and

    b. an estimate of the amount of the contingent gain or a statement that such an estimate cannot be made.

17.18 Disclosure of the existence of a contingent gain that is considered probable to be realized provides useful information and, therefore, should be included in a note to the financial statements. However, it is necessary to exercise particular care in the disclosure of contingent gains to avoid a misleading implication about the likelihood of realization. It is not appropriate to disclose the existence of a contingent gain that is not probable to be realized.

Asset Retirement Obligations

17.19 This section establishes principles for the recognition, measurement, and disclosure of liabilities for *asset retirement obligations* and the associated *asset retirement costs*.

17.20 This section applies to legal obligations associated with the *retirement* of a tangible long-lived asset that result from its acquisition, construction, development, or normal operation. This section covers the obligations of both lessors and lessees in connection with leased assets, whether imposed by a lease agreement or by a party other than the lessor, except for those obligations of a lessee that meet the definition of either minimum lease payments or contingent rentals and are accounted for in accordance with chapter 25, "Leases." This section also covers obligations arising in connection with leasing and other agreements concerning the rights to explore for or exploit natural resources, to which chapter 25 does not apply. This section does not apply to

   a. obligations that arise solely from a plan to sell, or otherwise dispose of, a long-lived asset subject to chapter 15, "Disposal of Long-Lived Assets and Discontinued Operations," and

   b. obligations that result from the improper operation of an asset.

Recognition

17.21 An entity should recognize a liability for an asset retirement obligation in the period in which it is incurred when a reasonable estimate of the amount of the obligation can be made. If a reasonable estimate of the amount of the obligation cannot be made in the period the asset retirement obligation is incurred, the liability should be recognized when a reasonable estimate of the amount of the obligation can be made. Only a legal obligation associated with the retirement of a tangible long-lived asset, including an obligation created by promissory estoppel, establishes a clear duty or responsibility to another party that justifies recognition of a liability.

17.22 Various accounting principles deal with uncertainty in different ways. This section provides a measurement technique to deal with uncertainties about the amount and timing of the future cash flows necessary to settle a liability. This section requires that all asset retirement obligations within its scope be recognized when a reasonable estimate of the amount of the obligation can be made.

17.23 When a tangible long-lived asset with an existing asset retirement obligation is acquired, a liability for that obligation is recognized at the asset's acquisition date as if that obligation were incurred on that date.

Measurement

17.24 The amount recognized as an asset retirement obligation should be the best estimate of the expenditure required to settle the present obligation at the statement of financial position date.

17.25 The best estimate of the expenditure required to settle the present obligation is the amount that an entity would rationally pay to settle the obligation at the statement of financial position date or to transfer it to a third party at that time. It will often be impossible or prohibitively expensive to settle or transfer an obligation at the statement of financial position date. Therefore, the estimate of the amount that an entity would rationally pay to settle or transfer the obligation is reported.

17.26 The estimate of the expenditure required to settle the present obligation is determined by the judgment of the management of the entity, supplemented by experience of similar transactions and, in some cases, reports from independent experts.

17.27 Future events that may affect the amount required to settle an obligation are reflected in its measurement when there is sufficient, objective evidence that they will occur. Expected future events may be particularly important when measuring an asset retirement obligation. For example, an entity may believe that the cost of cleaning up a site at the end of its life will be reduced by future changes in technology. The amount recognized reflects a reasonable expectation of technically qualified, objective observers, taking account of all available evidence about the technology that will be available at the time of the clean-up. Thus, it is appropriate to include expected cost reductions associated with increased experience when applying existing technology, or the expected cost of applying existing technology, to a larger or more complex clean-up operation than has previously been carried out. However, an entity does not anticipate the development of a completely new technology for cleaning up unless it is supported by sufficient, objective evidence.

17.28 The effect of possible new legislation is taken into consideration when measuring an existing obligation when the new legislation is enacted. Any new legislation that is enacted after the statement of financial position date but before the financial statements are available to be issued would be subject to subsequent event disclosure as required by chapter 27.

17.29 A present value technique is often the best available technique with which to estimate the expenditure required to settle the present obligation at the statement of financial position date. When a present value technique is used, an entity estimates future cash flows used in that technique on a basis consistent with the objective of measuring the asset retirement obligation. Uncertainties surrounding the amount to be recognized as an asset retirement obligation are incorporated in the best estimate of the expenditure required to settle the obligation.

17.30 Asset retirement obligations are reviewed at each statement of financial position date and adjusted to reflect the current best estimate. Changes in an asset retirement obligation may be due to the passage of time, revisions to the timing or amount of cash flows, or the interest rate used when determining the best estimate of the expenditures required to settle the present obligation at the statement of financial position date.

Recognition and Allocation of an Asset Retirement Cost

17.31 Upon initial recognition of a liability for an asset retirement obligation, an entity should recognize an asset retirement cost by increasing the carrying amount of the related long-lived asset by the same amount as the liability. An entity should subsequently allocate that asset retirement cost to expense using a systematic and rational method over its useful life.

17.32 Application of a systematic and rational allocation method does not preclude an entity from capitalizing an amount of asset retirement cost and allocating an equal amount to expense in the same accounting period. For example, assume an entity acquires a long-lived asset with an estimated life of 10 years. As that asset is operated, the entity incurs additional asset retirement obligations of equal amount each year. Application of a systematic and rational allocation method would not preclude that entity from capitalizing, and then expensing, the asset retirement costs incurred each year.

17.33 In periods subsequent to initial measurement, an entity should recognize period-to-period changes in the liability for an asset retirement obligation resulting from

  a. the passage of time and

  b. revisions to either the timing, the amount of the original estimate of undiscounted cash flows, or the discount rate.

An entity should measure and incorporate changes due to the passage of time into the carrying amount of the liability before measuring changes resulting from a revision to either the timing or the amount of estimated cash flows.

17.34 An entity measures changes in the liability for an asset retirement obligation due to passage of time by applying an interest method of allocation to the amount of the liability at the beginning of the period. The interest rate used to measure that change is the discount rate applied to measure the liability at the beginning of the period. That amount is recognized as an increase in the carrying amount of the liability and an expense. The expense is classified as an operating item in the statement of operations, not as interest expense. It is referred to in this section as *accretion expense*, but an entity may use any descriptor, as long as it conveys the underlying nature of the expense.

17.35 Changes resulting from revisions to the timing or the amount of the original estimate of undiscounted cash flows or revisions to the discount rate are recognized as an increase or a decrease in the carrying amount of the liability for an asset retirement obligation and the related asset retirement cost capitalized as part of the carrying amount of the related long-lived asset. When asset retirement costs change as a result of a revision to estimated cash flows, an entity adjusts the amount of asset retirement cost allocated to expense in the period of change if the change affects that period only or in the period of change, and future periods, if the change affects more than one period (in accordance with chapter 9, "Accounting Changes, Changes in Accounting Estimates, and Correction of Errors" for a change in estimate). Changes in asset retirement costs that affect future periods will result in adjustments of capitalized asset retirement costs and will affect subsequent depreciation of the related asset. Such adjustments are depreciated on a prospective basis.

Effects of Funding and Assurance Provisions

17.36 Providing assurance that an entity will be able to satisfy its asset retirement obligation does not satisfy or extinguish the related liability. Methods of providing assurance include surety bonds, insurance policies, letters of credit, guarantees by other entities, and establishment of trust funds or identification of other assets dedicated to satisfy the asset retirement obligation. Setting assets aside to satisfy an asset retirement obligation does not satisfy the criteria for offsetting the assets and the liability on the statement of financial position. For a previously recognized asset retirement obligation, changes in funding and assurance provisions have no effect on the measurement of that liability. Costs associated with complying with funding or assurance provisions are accounted for separately from the asset retirement obligation.

Disclosure

17.37 An entity should disclose the following information about its asset retirement obligations:

    a. A general description of the asset retirement obligations and the associated long-lived assets

    b. The amount of the asset retirement obligation at the end of the year

    c. The total amount paid towards the liability during the year

    d. The carrying amount of assets legally restricted for purposes of settling asset retirement obligations

When a reasonable estimate of the amount of an asset retirement obligation cannot be made, that fact, and the reasons therefor, should be disclosed.

Guarantees

17.38 Guarantees are recognized and measured in accordance with paragraphs 17.07–.11.

17.39 A guarantor should disclose the following information about each guarantee, or each group of similar guarantees, even when the likelihood of the guarantor having to make any payments under the guarantee is remote:

    a. The nature of the guarantee, including the approximate term of the guarantee, how the guarantee arose, and the events or circumstances that require the guarantor to perform under the guarantee.

    b. The maximum potential amount of future payments (undiscounted) the guarantor could be required to make under the guarantee before any amounts that may possibly be recovered under recourse or collateralization provisions in the guarantee (see [d] and [e] that follow). When the terms of the guarantee provide for no limitation to the maximum potential future payments under the guarantee, that fact should be disclosed. When the guarantor is unable to develop an estimate of the maximum potential amount of future payments under its guarantee, the guarantor should disclose that it cannot make such an estimate.

    c. The current carrying amount of the liability, if any, for the guarantor's obligations under the guarantee, regardless of whether the guarantee is freestanding or embedded in another contract.

    d. The nature of any recourse provisions that enable the guarantor to recover from third parties any of the amounts paid under the guarantee.

    e. The nature of any assets held as collateral or by third parties that, upon the occurrence of any triggering event or condition under the guarantee, the guarantor can obtain and liquidate to recover all, or a portion of, the amounts paid under the guarantee.

17.40 Some guarantees are issued to benefit entities that meet the definition of a related party in chapter 26, such as joint ventures and equity method investees. In those cases, the disclosures required by this chapter may be in addition to the disclosures required by chapter 26.

Chapter 18

Equity

Purpose and Scope

18.01 This chapter establishes principles for the presentation of *equity*,[1] changes in equity during the reporting period, and capital transactions. It also establishes principles for the acquisition and redemption of shares and disclosure of capital stock. This chapter establishes principles for the presentation and disclosure of the equity and capital accounts of unincorporated businesses, partnerships, and limited liability entities.

18.02 Capital transactions include items such as

a. changes in capital, including premiums, discounts, and expenses relating to the issue, redemption, or cancellation of capital stock;

b. excess or deficiency of proceeds

  i. on purchase and resale by a company of its own issued common shares or

  ii. on purchase and cancellation by a company of its own issued common shares;

c. contributions by owners or others;

d. dividends (including stock dividends);

e. distributions—cash and property; and

f. taxes arising at the time of changes in shareholder status or capital stock transactions.

Acquisition or Redemption of Shares

18.03 When a company redeems or acquires its own shares, the cost will usually be different from their par, stated, or assigned values. Because such transactions are usually capital transactions, this difference should be excluded from the determination of net income.

Acquisition of Shares

18.04 This chapter allows two methods of accounting for the acquisition by an entity of its own shares: the cost method and the constructive retirement method. Note that the treatment of treasury stock can vary depending on state laws and regulations.

18.05 Under the cost method, the acquired shares should be carried at cost and shown as a deduction from shareholders' equity (contra-equity or treasury stock account) until cancelled, retired, or resold. Shares held are considered to be issued capital for purposes of paragraph 18.29. No adjustment is made to capital stock and related accounts that were credited upon original issuance.

---

[1] Italicized terms are defined in the glossary.

18.06 Under the constructive retirement method, the aggregate par or stated value of the reacquired shares are charged to the capital stock account rather than a treasury stock account. An excess of repurchase price over par or stated value is allocated between *additional paid-in capital* and *retained earnings*.

18.07 When a subsidiary acquires its own shares from interests outside the consolidated group, the accounting treatment to be followed in the parent company's consolidated financial statements is outlined in chapter 23, "Consolidated Financial Statements and Noncontrolling Interests."

Resale of Acquired Shares

18.08 When a company acquires its own shares and subsequently resells them, no part of the proceeds is taken into income.

18.09 Under the cost method, when an entity resells shares that it has acquired, the treasury stock account is credited, and any excess of the proceeds over cost should be credited to additional paid-in capital; any deficiency should be charged to additional paid-in capital to the extent that a previous net excess from resale or cancellation of shares of the same class is included therein, otherwise, to retained earnings.

18.10 Under the constructive retirement method, when an entity resells shares that it has acquired, they are treated as if they were an original issue. Capital stock and additional paid-in capital are credited with the appropriate amounts (see paragraph 18.21).

Retirement or Cancellation of Shares

18.11 When an entity retires or cancels shares that it has acquired, the accounting depends on the method that was used to reacquire the shares. If the cost method was used, the treasury stock account is credited, and the cost is allocated to the capital stock and related accounts (for example, additional paid-in capital). If the constructive retirement method was used, no further accounting would be necessary if those reacquired shares are retired or cancelled.

Dividends

18.12 Dividends should be recognized when declared.

18.13 Because a company cannot own a part of itself, it cannot receive dividend income on its own shares.

18.14 When a company has acquired its own shares and such shares have not been cancelled, any dividends otherwise payable with respect to these shares should be treated as a reduction of dividends and should not be reflected as income by the company.

Accounting for Stock and Other Equity Compensation

18.15 No compensation expense is recognized when stock or other equity compensation are issued in lieu of cash compensation. Such arrangements and related activities are disclosed in accordance with paragraphs 18.27–.28. Additionally, exercised stock options are accounted for as a normal stock issuance transaction.

Equity Transactions With Nonemployees

18.16 Transactions in which an entity acquires goods and services by granting equity should be recognized when the entity obtains the goods, or the counterparty renders the services. These transactions are measured based on the value of the consideration received, or the value of the equity instruments given, whichever can be measured more reliably.

Presentation

18.17 An entity should present separately changes in equity for the period arising from each of the following:

    a. Net income, showing separately the total amounts attributable to owners of the parent and *noncontrolling interests* (see chapter 23)

    b. Other changes in retained earnings

    c. Changes in additional paid-in capital

    d. Changes in capital stock

    e. Other changes in equity

18.18 As applicable, an entity should present separately the following components of equity either in the body of the financial statements or in the accompanying notes:

    a. Retained earnings

    b. Additional paid-in capital

    c. Capital stock

    d. Noncontrolling interests (see chapter 23)

    e. Other components of equity

18.19 The financial statements of unincorporated businesses and partnerships should include a statement detailing the changes in the owners' equity during the period, and this statement should detail separately contributions of capital, income or losses, and withdrawals.

18.20 It is important to understand the nature and amounts of the different types of excess or deficiency in proceeds that are included directly in equity. Therefore, this chapter requires an entity to present a separate component of equity for each category of equity.

18.21 Charges against additional paid-in capital should be limited to instances when that disposition is clearly warranted by the circumstances, such as a charge that is the direct opposite of a credit previously carried to additional paid-in capital.

18.22 An entity may receive a note, rather than cash, for the purchase of its equity. The transaction may be a sale of capital stock (or its equivalent in an unincorporated entity) or a contribution to paid-in capital. Reporting the note as an asset is generally not appropriate, except in very limited circumstances in which there is substantial evidence of ability and intent to pay within a reasonably short period of time. Consequently, the note should ordinarily be offset against stock in the equity section. However, such notes may be recorded as an asset if collected in cash before the financial statements are available to be issued.

18.23 Capital transactions should be excluded from the determination of net income and shown separately in the statement to which they relate (at least for the year in which the transactions occur). Stock issuance costs should be recorded as a deduction to equity.

18.24 The financial statements of an unincorporated business should indicate clearly the name under which the business is conducted.

18.25 Any salaries, interest, or similar items accruing to owners of an unincorporated business should be clearly indicated by showing such items separately, either in the body of the statement of operations or in a note to the financial statements. If no such charges are made in the accounts of an unincorporated business, this fact should be disclosed in the financial statements.

Disclosure

18.26 When a condition restricts or affects the distribution of retained earnings, the nature and extent thereof should be disclosed.

18.27 An entity with one or more stock-based compensation plans should provide a description of the plan(s), including the general terms of awards under the plan(s), such as vesting requirements, and the maximum term of options granted. An entity that uses equity instruments to acquire goods or services other than employee services should provide disclosures similar to those in accordance with this paragraph to the extent that those disclosures are important in understanding the effects of those transactions on the financial statements.

18.28 An entity that grants options under multiple, stock-based employee compensation plans should provide information separately for different types of awards to the extent that the differences in the characteristics of the awards make separate disclosure important to an understanding of the entity's use of stock-based compensation.

18.29 Disclosure should be made of authorized and issued capital stock, including

 a. the number of shares issued and outstanding for each class, giving a brief description and the par value, if any;
 b. dividend rates on preference shares and whether or not they are cumulative;
 c. the redemption price of redeemable shares;
 d. the existence and details of conversion provisions;
 e. the number of shares and the amount received or receivable that is attributable to capital for each class (when any shares have not been fully paid, disclosure should be made of the amounts that have not been called and the unpaid amounts that have been called or are otherwise due, as well as the number of shares in each of these categories); and
 f. arrears of dividends for cumulative preference shares.

18.30 Disclosure should be made of the number of shares of capital stock authorized.

18.31 Disclosure should be made of commitments to issue or resell shares.

18.32 Disclosure should be made of details of transactions during the period, including

    a. the number of shares of each class issued since the date of the last statement of financial position, indicating the value attributed thereto and distinguishing shares issued for cash (showing separately shares issued pursuant to options or warrants), shares issued directly or indirectly for services, and shares issued directly or indirectly for other considerations;

    b. the number of shares of each class redeemed or acquired since the date of the last statement of financial position and the consideration given and, when the consideration was other than cash, the nature of the consideration given and the value attributed thereto; and

    c. the number of shares of each class resold since the date of the last statement of financial position, indicating the value attributed thereto and distinguishing shares resold for cash (showing separately shares resold pursuant to options or warrants), shares resold directly or indirectly for services, and shares resold directly or indirectly for other considerations.

18.33 The fact that a business is unincorporated and that the statements do not include all the assets, liabilities, revenues, and expenses of the owners should be disclosed.

Limited Liability Entities

18.34 A limited liability entity should present information related to changes in owners' (members') equity for the period. This information may be presented as a separate statement, combined with the statement of operations, or in the notes to financial statements.

18.35 The equity section in the statement of financial position of a limited liability entity should be titled "Owners' (or Members') Equity." If more than one class of members exists, each having varying rights, preferences, and privileges, the limited liability entity is encouraged to report the equity of each class separately within the equity section.

18.36 If a limited liability entity records amounts due from owners for capital contributions, such amounts should be presented as deductions from owners' equity.

18.37 Even though an owner's liability may be limited, if the total balance of the owners' equity account or accounts is less than zero, a deficit should be reported in the statement of financial position.

Disclosure

18.38 If a limited liability entity does not report the amount of equity of each class of owners (members) separately within the equity section, it should disclose those amounts in the notes to financial statements.

18.39 If a limited liability entity maintains separate accounts for components of owners' equity (for example, undistributed earnings, earnings available for withdrawal, or unallocated capital), disclosure of those components, either on the face of the statement of financial position or in the notes to financial statements, is permitted.

18.40 Significant differences in the rights, preferences, and privileges of different classes of members should be disclosed.

Chapter 19
Revenue

Purpose and Scope

19.01 This chapter establishes principles for the timing of recognition of *revenue*[1] in the financial statements of entities. It addresses the recognition of revenue during the course of the ordinary activities of an entity, normally from the sale of goods, the rendering of services, a combination of both, and the use by others of entity resources yielding interest, royalties, and dividends. It does not comprehensively deal with the measurement of revenue. However, when uncertainties exist regarding the determination of the amount of revenue, these uncertainties may influence the timing of revenue recognition.

19.02 The timing of recognition of the following types of revenue is dealt with elsewhere in other chapters:

  a. Revenue arising from investments accounted for under the equity method (see chapter 11, "Equity, Debt, and Other Investments")

  b. Revenue arising from lease agreements (see chapter 25, "Leases")

Recognition

19.03 Revenue from sales and service transactions should be recognized when the requirements regarding performance set out in paragraphs 19.04–.05 are satisfied, provided that at the time of performance, ultimate collection is reasonably assured.

19.04 In a transaction involving the sale of goods, performance should be regarded as having been achieved when the following conditions have been fulfilled:

  a. The seller of the goods has transferred to the buyer the significant risks and rewards of ownership in that all significant acts have been completed, and the seller retains no continuing managerial involvement in, or effective control of, the goods transferred to a degree usually associated with ownership.

  b. Reasonable assurance exists regarding the measurement of the consideration that will be derived from the sale of goods and the extent to which goods may be returned.

19.05 In the case of rendering of services and long-term contracts and modifications to those contracts, performance should be determined using either the *percentage of completion method* or the *completed contract method*, whichever relates the revenue to the work accomplished. Such performance should be regarded as having been achieved when reasonable assurance exists regarding the measurement of the consideration that will be derived from rendering the service or performing the long-term contract.

---

[1] Italicized terms are defined in the glossary.

19.06 Performance should be regarded as being achieved under paragraphs 19.04–.05 when all the following criteria have been met:

    a. Persuasive evidence of an arrangement exists.

    b. Delivery has occurred, or services have been rendered.

    c. The seller's price to the buyer is fixed or determinable.

19.07 Some of the items management should consider when determining if persuasive evidence of an arrangement exists are as follows:

    a. Customary business practices and past dealings between parties

    b. Side arrangements

    c. Consignment arrangements

    d. Rights to return the product

    e. Requirements to repurchase the product

Other characteristics may exist. Accordingly, judgment is necessary when assessing whether the substance of a transaction is a consignment, a financing, or other arrangement for which revenue recognition is not appropriate.

19.08 Generally, delivery is not considered to have occurred unless the product has been delivered to the customer's place of business or another site specified by the customer. Some of the aspects of the revenue arrangement management should consider when determining if delivery has occurred or services have been rendered are as follows:

    a. Bill and hold arrangements.

    b. Customer acceptance of product.

    c. Layaway sales arrangements.

    d. Nonrefundable fee arrangements.

    e. Licensing and similar fee arrangements.

    f. Risk of loss has passed to the buyer.

19.09 When determining if the seller's price to the buyer is fixed or determinable, management should consider the impact of the following factors:

    a. Cancellable sales arrangements

    b. Right of return arrangements

    c. Price protections or inventory credit arrangements, or both

    d. Refundable fee for service arrangements

19.10 The recognition criteria in this chapter are usually applied separately to each transaction. However, in certain circumstances, it is necessary to apply the recognition criteria to the separately identifiable components of a single transaction to reflect the substance of the transaction. A single sales transaction may involve the delivery or performance of multiple products, services, or rights to use assets, and performance may occur at different points in time or over different periods of time. In some cases, the arrangements include initial installation, initiation, or activation services and involve consideration in the form of a fixed fee or a fixed fee coupled with a continuing payment stream. For example, when the selling price of a product includes an identifiable amount for subsequent servicing, that amount is deferred and recognized as revenue over the period during which the service is performed. Conversely, the recognition criteria are applied to two or more transactions together when they are linked in such a way that the commercial effect cannot be understood without reference to the series of transactions as a whole. For example, an entity may sell goods and, at the same time, enter into a separate agreement to repurchase the goods at a later date, thus, negating the substantive effect of the transaction. In such a case, the two transactions are dealt with together.

19.11 Revenue arising from others' use of entity resources yielding interest, royalties, and dividends should be recognized when reasonable assurance exists regarding measurement and collectability. These revenues should be recognized on the following bases:

    a. Interest, on a time proportion basis

    b. Royalties, as they accrue, in accordance with the terms of the relevant agreement

    c. Dividends, when the shareholder's right to receive payment is established

19.12 Revenue from a transaction involving the sale of goods should be recognized when the seller has transferred to the buyer the significant risks and rewards of ownership of the goods sold. When the seller retains significant risks of ownership, it is normally inappropriate to recognize the transaction as a sale. Examples of a significant risk of ownership being retained by a seller are when a liability for unsatisfactory performance is not covered by normal warranty provisions; when the purchaser has the right to rescind the transaction; and when the goods are shipped on consignment.

19.13 Assessing when the risks and rewards of ownership are transferred to the buyer with sufficient certainty requires an examination of the circumstances of the transaction. In most cases, revenue is recognized on the passing of possession of the goods. In retail sales, this is usually coincident with the passing of legal title. In other cases, the passing of legal title may occur at a different time from the passing of possession or of the risks and rewards of ownership.

19.14 The percentage of completion method is used when performance consists of the execution of more than one act, and revenue would be recognized proportionately by reference to the performance of each act. Revenue recognized under this method should be determined on a rational and consistent basis, such as on the basis of sales value, associated costs, extent of progress, or number of acts. For practical purposes, when services are provided by an indeterminate number of acts over a specific period of time, revenue should be recognized on a straight-line basis over the period, unless there is evidence that some other method better reflects the pattern of performance. The amount of work accomplished should be assessed by reference to measures of performance that are reasonably determinable and relate as directly as possible to the activities critical to the completion of the contract. (Measures of performance include output measures, such as units produced and project milestones, or input measures, such as cost, labor hours, or machine use.) Amounts billed are not an appropriate basis of measurement unless they reflect the work accomplished.

FRF-SME 19.14

19.15 The completed contract method is used when the entity cannot reasonably estimate the extent of progress toward completion. The completed contract method may also be used if both of the following conditions are met:

   a. The completed contract method is used for income tax reporting purposes.

   b. The financial position and results of operations of the entity would not vary materially from those resulting from the use of the percentage of completion method (for example, in circumstances in which an entity has primarily short-term contracts).

Accounting for Contract-Related Claims

19.16 Recognition of amounts of additional contract revenue relating to contract-related claims is appropriate only if it is probable that the claims will result in additional contract revenue and if amounts can be reliably estimated, as evidenced by satisfying the following conditions:

   a. There is a legal basis for the claims.

   b. Additional costs are caused by circumstances that were unforeseen at the contract date and are not the result of contractor performance deficiencies.

   c. Costs associated with the claims are identifiable or otherwise determinable and are reasonable in view of the work performed.

   d. Evidence supporting the claims is objective and verifiable.

19.17 If the foregoing requirements are met, revenue from contract-related claims should be recorded only to the extent that contract costs relating to the claims have been incurred. Costs attributable to claims should be treated as costs of contract performance as incurred.

19.18 A practice such as recording revenues from claims only when the amounts have been received or awarded may be used.

Effect of Uncertainties

19.19 Recognition of revenue requires that the revenue is measurable and that ultimate collection is reasonably assured. When there is reasonable assurance of ultimate collection, revenue is recognized, even though cash receipts are deferred. When there is uncertainty about ultimate collection, it may be appropriate to recognize revenue only as cash is received.

19.20 When the uncertainty relates to collectability and arises subsequent to the time revenue was recognized, a separate provision to reflect the uncertainty should be made. The amount of revenue originally recorded should not be adjusted.

19.21 Uncertainties relating to the measurement of revenue may result from one or both of the following issues:

   a. *Consideration.* When consideration is not determinable within reasonable limits, for example, when payment relating to goods sold depends on the resale of the goods by the buyer, revenue should not be recognized.

b. *Returns.* Revenue should not be recognized when an entity is subject to material and unpredictable amounts of returns, (for example, when the market for a returnable good is untested). If an entity is exposed to material and predictable amounts of returns, it may be sufficient to provide for an allowance for returns.

19.22 Consideration may include a note or other financial instrument issued by the purchaser to be settled in cash and, under the terms of the note, the seller effectively has recourse only against the assets sold. The transaction is considered to be a sale because the total amount of the consideration received is determinable within reasonable limits (see paragraph 19.21). However, income from the sale is only recognized when

a. a substantial commitment by the purchaser exists, demonstrating its intent to honor its obligations under the note, and

b. the seller has reasonable assurance of collecting the note.

A commitment would include, for example, nonrefundable cash consideration from resources other than those transferred from the seller or the assumption of an obligation of the seller to a third party when the third party thereby releases the seller from that obligation.

Reporting Revenue Gross or Net

19.23 Revenue includes only the gross inflows of economic benefits received and receivable by the entity on its own account. Amounts collected on behalf of third parties, such as sales taxes and goods and services taxes, are not economic benefits that flow to the entity and do not result in increases in equity. Therefore, they are excluded from revenue. Similarly, in an agency relationship, the gross inflows of economic benefits include amounts collected on behalf of the principal that do not result in increases in equity for the entity. The amounts collected on behalf of the principal are not revenue. Instead, revenue is the amount of commission.

19.24 An entity is acting as a principal (and not as an agent) when it is exposed to the significant risks and rewards associated with the sale of goods or the rendering of services. Features that indicate that an entity is acting as a principal include the following:

a. The entity has the primary responsibility for providing the goods or services to the customer or for fulfilling the order (for example, by being responsible for the acceptability of the products or services ordered, contracted, or purchased by the customer).

b. The entity has inventory risk before or after the customer order, during shipping, or on return.

c. The entity has latitude in establishing prices, either directly or indirectly (for example, by providing additional goods or services).

d. The entity bears the customer's credit risk for the amount receivable from the customer.

One feature indicating that an entity is acting as an agent is that the amount the entity earns is predetermined, whether it is either a fixed fee per transaction or a stated percentage of the amount billed to the customer.

Presentation

19.25 The amount of revenue recognized during the period should be presented separately in the statement of operations.

Disclosure

19.26 An entity should disclose its revenue recognition policy. If an entity has different policies for different types of revenue transactions, the policy for each material type of transaction should be disclosed. If sales transactions have multiple elements, such as a product and service, the entity should clearly state the accounting policy for each element, as well as how multiple elements are determined and measured.

19.27 If sales transactions have multiple elements, the policy may contain items such as a description and nature of such an arrangement, including performance, cancellation, termination, or refund-type provisions.

19.28 If the completed contract method is used, the entity should disclose the reasons why that method, and not the percentage of completion method, is used.

19.29 Additional revenue from a contract-related claim that is recorded by the entity should be disclosed. In addition, if the entity has claims related to additional contract revenue and the requirements of paragraph 19.16 are not met or if those requirements are met but the claim exceeds the recorded contract costs, a contingent asset should be disclosed in accordance with chapter 17, "Contingencies."

19.30 If the practice of recording revenues from claims only when the amounts have been received or awarded is followed, the amounts should be disclosed in the notes to the financial statements.

19.31 An entity should disclose separately, either on the face of the statement of operations or in the notes to the financial statements, the major categories of revenue recognized during the period.

19.32 The objective of this disclosure is to assist the reader with understanding the sources of revenue and their effect on the financial statements.

19.33 Judgment is necessary to determine the categories that an entity uses. An entity may separate out sources based on life expectancy (for example, initial and ongoing franchise fees) and significantly differing profit margins or sources that differ from the standard operation of the business (for example, a manufacturing business that has material investment income).

Chapter 20

Retirement and Other Postemployment Benefits

Purpose and Scope

20.01 This chapter establishes principles for the recognition, measurement, and disclosure of the cost of retirement and other postemployment benefits. It requires an entity to recognize the cost of retirement benefits and certain postemployment benefits over the periods in which employees render services to the entity in return for the benefits. Other postemployment benefits are recognized when the event that obligates the entity occurs.

20.02 This chapter applies to benefits earned by *active employees*[1] and expected to be provided to them when they are no longer providing active service, pursuant to the terms of an entity's undertaking to provide such benefits. These benefits include the following:

 a. Pension and other retirement benefits expected to be provided after retirement to employees and their beneficiaries, such as pension income, health care benefits, life insurance, and other miscellaneous benefits provided to employees after retirement

 b. Postemployment benefits expected to be provided after employment but before retirement to employees and their beneficiaries, such as long- and short-term disability income benefits (including workers' compensation), severance benefits, salary continuation, supplemental unemployment benefits, job training and counseling, and continuation of benefits, such as health care benefits and life insurance

 c. Termination benefits

20.03 An entity's arrangements to provide future benefits to employees may take a variety of forms and may be financed in different ways. Future benefits may be provided either directly by an entity or through an intermediary, such as a pension plan or an insurance entity. This chapter applies to any arrangement that is, in substance, a benefit plan, regardless of its form or the manner or timing of its funding. Absent evidence to the contrary, it is presumed that an entity that has provided benefits in the past and is currently promising those benefits to employees will continue to provide those benefits in the future. This chapter applies to the future benefits for which an entity pays all or part of the cost.

20.04 This chapter does not apply to benefits provided by an entity to employees during their active employment. Examples of these benefits are

 a. salaries, wages, bonuses, fringe benefits, and similar items that are provided by an entity in the current reporting period or within 12 months thereafter, in exchange for services rendered by employees in the current reporting period;

---

[1] Italicized terms are defined in the glossary.

b. occasional sick days and vacation days that do not vest or accumulate beyond 12 months after the current reporting period; and

  c. benefits provided under stock-based compensation arrangements.

Basic Principles

20.05 An *obligation for retirement and other postemployment benefits* possesses all the characteristics of liabilities. First, an entity has a responsibility to its employees to provide the benefits at a specified time in the future (that is, when an employee retires or leaves the entity). Second, although the responsibility is not always contractual, the obligation is constructive or equitable in almost all cases, thereby leaving an entity little or no discretion to avoid it. Finally, an entity is obligated either by the rendering of service by the employee or, in the case of certain postemployment benefits, by an event such as an application for long-term disability benefits.

20.06 The two basic types of pension plans are defined contribution and defined benefit.

20.07 If deferred compensation contracts, as a group, are equivalent to a pension plan, they are accounted for the same as a pension plan. Other deferred compensation contracts should be accounted for on an individual basis for each employee.

Recognition, Measurement, and Disclosure—Defined Contribution Plans

Recognition and Measurement

20.08 An entity should recognize pension cost for its *defined contribution plans* as an expense for the period. The pension cost to be recorded as expense for an accounting period should normally be the contribution that applies to that period accounted for on the accrual basis.

Disclosure

20.09 An entity should disclose the following information about defined contribution plans:

  a. A general description of each plan

  b. The amount of cost recognized in the period

Recognition, Measurement, and Disclosure—Multiemployer Plans

Recognition and Measurement

20.10 An entity should recognize pension cost for *multiemployer plans* it participates in as an expense for the period. Pension cost consists solely of the contribution required for the year, unless termination of participation in the plan is probable; then, any amounts due should be accrued.

Disclosure

20.11 An entity should disclose the following information about significant multiemployer plans:

   a. The name of the plan and a description of the type of plan

   b. If withdrawal from the plan is probable or reasonably possible, whether withdrawal from the plan would give rise to an obligation

   c. The amount of cost recognized in the period

Recognition, Measurement, and Disclosure—Individual Deferred Compensation Contracts

Recognition and Measurement

20.12 If the contract is based on current and future employment, only the cost of benefits attributable to current employment should be accrued.

20.13 If benefits expected in the future are attributable to more than one year of service, the cost of those benefits should be accrued over the period of the employee's service. At the end of that service period, the total amount accrued should equal the present value of the benefits expected to be provided.

Disclosure

20.14 An entity should disclose the following information in aggregate about individual deferred compensation contracts:

   a. A general description of the contracts, including expected timing of benefit payments and the discount rate used to determine present value

   b. The liability at the statement of financial position date and the amount charged to expense in the current period

Recognition, Measurement, and Disclosure—Defined Benefit Plans

20.15 An entity should make an accounting policy choice to account for *defined benefit plans* (except multiemployer plans; see paragraph 20.10) using either

   a. the current contribution payable method or

   b. one of the *accrued benefit obligation* methods.

Current Contribution Payable Method

20.16 Under this method, only the contribution attributable to the current year is expensed.

20.17 Under this method, the following disclosures are required:

   a. A description of the plan, including plan participants, and the nature of determining benefits

    b. Information about the funded status of the plan, including benefit obligation, market value of *plan assets*, and the excess of the benefit obligation over market value of plan assets at the end of the reporting period
    c. The current year's contribution and expected contribution for the subsequent year
    d. The plan's expected rate of return on plan assets and the discount rate used to determine the accrued benefit obligation.

Accrued Benefit Obligation Methods

20.18 The accrued benefit obligation methods require the recording of the accrued benefit obligation. This alternative permits an entity to account for its defined benefit plans using the immediate recognition approach or the deferral and amortization approach discussed in the following paragraphs. The entity should apply the same approach to all of its defined benefit plans:

    a. Under the *immediate recognition approach*, an entity determines the accrued benefit obligation based on an actuarial valuation report prepared for funding purposes. When an appropriate valuation report is not available, the entity determines the accrued benefit obligation using the same assumptions that are required under the deferral and amortization approach. The entity recognizes the net amount of the accrued benefit obligation and the market value of plan assets, if any, in the statement of financial position. Actuarial gains and losses and prior service costs are included in the cost of the plan for the year.
    b. Under the *deferral and amortization approach*, an entity determines the accrued benefit obligation based on an actuarial valuation report prepared specifically for accounting purposes. The entity recognizes in the statement of financial position an accrued benefit liability or accrued benefit asset, which represents the sum of the current and prior years' benefit costs, less the entity's accumulated cash contributions to the plan. Prior service costs are deferred and amortized over future periods. Actuarial gains and losses may also be deferred and amortized over future periods. The market value of plan assets, if any, and the accrued benefit obligation are disclosed in the notes to the financial statements.

Immediate Recognition Approach

Recognition

20.19 For a defined benefit plan accounted for under the immediate recognition approach, an entity should recognize

    a. the accrued benefit obligation net of the market value of any plan assets in the statement of financial position at the end of the year and
    b. the cost of the plan for the year.

Measurement

Accrued Benefit Obligation

20.20 The accrued benefit obligation at the end of the year should be determined based on the most recent actuarial valuation report prepared for funding purposes.

20.21 When a defined benefit plan does not have an appropriate funding valuation as described in paragraph 20.20, an entity should determine the accrued benefit obligation for that plan based on an actuarial valuation using the discount rate in accordance with paragraph 20.36 and management's best estimates for each actuarial assumption other than the discount rate.

20.22 The actuarial valuation of the accrued benefit obligation should be determined in accordance with paragraph 20.20 or 20.21 at least every 3 years but may occur more frequently (for example, when a significant event takes place). In the years between valuations, the entity uses a roll-forward technique to estimate the accrued benefit obligation. In doing so, management exercises judgment and takes into account

  a. the amount from the last actuarial determination of the accrued benefit obligation;
  b. the increase in the obligation due to the passage of time;
  c. the increase in the obligation due to the rendering of service in the current year;
  d. the effects of changes in employee composition and salaries;
  e. any benefit payments; and
  f. any other significant changes.

A similar process occurs when an actuarial valuation is performed during the year and rolled forward to the end of the year.

20.23 An actuarial valuation of the accrued benefit obligation should be performed in the year in which a significant event takes place. This valuation may be as of the date of the significant event, the end of the year in which the significant event occurs, or any date in between. Examples of a significant event include a settlement, a curtailment, or a plan amendment.

Plan Assets

20.24 Plan assets should be measured at market value at the statement of financial position date. When market values are not readily available for certain assets, such as real estate investments, a method that provides an approximation of market value should be used. For example, an entity may obtain independent appraisals or review market values of similar assets.

Limit on the Carrying Amount of an Accrued Benefit Asset

20.25 When the market value of plan assets exceeds the accrued benefit obligation, that plan excess should be recognized on the statement of financial position only to the extent it is expected to be recoverable by the entity, either through reduced contributions in the future or through refunds from the plan.

Determination of Cost for the Year

20.26 The cost of a plan for a year should comprise

   a. changes in the accrued benefit obligation other than those resulting from benefit payments to plan members and net of any employee contributions and

   b. the actual return on plan assets, determined in accordance with paragraph 20.27.

20.27 The actual return on plan assets for a year should be determined by calculating the difference between

   a. the market value of plan assets at the beginning of the year, reduced for any benefit payments and increased by any contributions and

   b. the market value of plan assets at the end of the year.

Entities With Two or More Plans

20.28 An entity that has two or more defined benefit plans accounted for using the immediate recognition approach should determine a cost, an accrued benefit obligation, and plan assets by applying paragraphs 20.19–.27 separately to each plan.

20.29 An entity that has two or more defined benefit plans accounted for using the immediate recognition approach should present separately the information in accordance with paragraph 20.19(a) in the statement of financial position for plans in an excess position and plans in a deficit position, except when an entity

   a. has a right to use the assets of one plan to pay for the benefits to be provided by the other plan and

   b. intends to exercise that right.

Deferral and Amortization Approach

20.30 Accounting by an entity for a defined benefit plan using the deferral and amortization approach includes the following steps:

   a. Making estimates (actuarial assumptions) about demographic variables (such as employee turnover and mortality) and financial variables (such as future increases in salaries and medical costs) that will affect the cost of retirement and other postemployment benefits

   b. Determining the obligation for retirement and other postemployment benefits using actuarial techniques to make a reliable estimate of the present value of employees' future benefits

   c. Attributing the cost of benefits to employee service periods in order to determine the accrued benefit obligation and the current service cost

   d. Determining the interest cost on the accrued benefit obligation

e. Determining the market value of any plan assets

f. Determining the expected return on plan assets

g. When a plan has been initiated or amended, determining the resulting prior service costs and the amount of those prior service costs to be recognized

h. Determining the total amount of actuarial gains and losses and the amount of those actuarial gains and losses to be recognized

i. When a plan has been curtailed or settled, determining the resulting gain or loss

In some circumstances, estimates, averages, and computational shortcuts may provide a reliable approximation of the detailed computations.

Recognition

20.31 For a defined benefit plan, an entity should recognize a liability and a cost for retirement and other postemployment benefits, other than postemployment benefits and compensated absences that do not vest or accumulate, in the period in which employees render services to the entity in return for the benefits. An entity should recognize a liability and a cost for postemployment benefits and compensated absences that do not vest or accumulate when the event that obligates the entity occurs.

Measurement

Actuarial Valuation Method

20.32 An entity should determine its accrued benefit obligation using

a. the *projected benefit method* prorated on services, when future salary levels or cost escalation affect the amount of the retirement and other postemployment benefits or

b. the *accumulated benefit method*, when future salary levels and cost escalation do not affect the amount of the retirement and other postemployment benefits.

20.33 An accrued benefit method attributes a distinct unit of future benefit to each year of credited service, and the actuarial present value of that unit is computed separately for the period in which it is deemed to have been earned.

20.34 The amount of an obligation for retirement and other postemployment benefits is determined from actuarial valuations performed periodically. In the years between valuations, an extrapolation of the actuarial valuation of the obligation is used. Each year, management reviews matters such as changes to the plan, the actuarial assumptions, occurrence of settlements and curtailments, changes to the employee group, and the rate of return on plan assets and determines whether such matters necessitate any adjustments to the extrapolations. When the effect of any change is significant, a new valuation may be necessary.

Measurement Date of Plan Assets and Accrued Benefit Obligation

20.35 The plan assets and the accrued benefit obligation should be measured as of the date of the annual financial statements, except that they may be measured as of a date not more than three months prior to that date, provided the entity adopts this practice consistently from year to year.

Discount Rate

20.36 The discount rate used to determine the accrued benefit obligation should be an interest rate determined by reference to

   a. market interest rates at the measurement date on high-quality debt instruments, with cash flows that match the timing and amount of expected benefit payments or

   b. the interest rate inherent in the amount at which the accrued benefit obligation could be settled.

20.37 The discount rate is reevaluated at each measurement date. When long-term interest rates rise or decline, the discount rate changes in a similar manner.

Plan Assets

20.38 Plan assets should be measured at market value. When market values are not readily available for certain assets, such as real estate investments, a method that provides an approximation of market value is used. For example, an entity may obtain independent appraisals or review market values of similar assets.

Determination of Cost for the Period

20.39 Cost for a period should comprise

   a. the current service cost;

   b. the interest cost on the accrued benefit obligation;

   c. the expected return on plan assets;

   d. the amortization of prior service costs arising from a plan initiation or amendment;

   e. the amortization of a net actuarial gain (loss);

   f. the amount recognized as a result of a temporary deviation from the plan;

   g. the increase or decrease in a valuation allowance against the carrying amount of an accrued benefit asset;

   h. the gain or loss on a settlement or curtailment; and

   i. the expense recognized for a termination benefit.

Entities With Two or More Plans

20.40 An entity that has two or more defined benefit plans accounted for using the deferral and amortization approach should determine a cost, an accrued benefit obligation, and plan assets by applying paragraphs 20.30–.39 to each separately measured plan or aggregation of plans.

20.41 For purposes of paragraph 20.40, each funded benefit plan is a separately measured plan. Unfunded benefit plans may be aggregated for measurement purposes only when they provide

   a. different benefits to the same group of employees and their beneficiaries or

   b. the same benefits to different groups of employees and their beneficiaries.

20.42 When an entity has a benefit plan in which the accrued benefit obligation exceeds the market value of the plan assets and another benefit plan in which the market value of the plan assets exceeds the accrued benefit obligation, the amounts in the two plans are generally not netted. Netting in such circumstances is appropriate only when the entity has a clear right to use the assets of one plan to pay for the benefits to be provided by the other plan.

20.43 An entity that has two or more defined benefit plans accounted for using the deferral and amortization approach should present separately in the statement of financial position an accrued benefit asset of one defined benefit plan and an accrued benefit liability of another defined benefit plan, except when the entity

   a. has a right to use the assets of one plan to pay for the benefits to be provided by the other plan and

   b. intends to exercise that right.

Limit on the Carrying Amount of an Accrued Benefit Asset

20.44 When a defined benefit plan gives rise to an accrued benefit asset, the asset should be recognized in the statement of financial position only to the extent it is expected to be recoverable by the entity, whether through reduced contributions in the future or through refunds from the plan.

Settlements, Insurance Contracts and Arrangements, and Curtailments

Settlements and Curtailments

20.45 An entity should account for a settlement or curtailment in the current period by decreasing (increasing) the accrued benefit obligation and recognizing any gain or loss in income for the period.

Insurance Contracts and Arrangements

20.46 When an entity has settled an accrued benefit obligation through the purchase of an insurance contract, the benefits provided or funded by the insurance contract are excluded from the accrued benefit obligation, and the insurance contract is excluded from plan assets, except for any participation right (see paragraph 20.47).

20.47 The purchase price of a participating insurance policy ordinarily is higher than the price of an equivalent policy without a participating right. The difference represents the cost of the participating right, which is recognized separately at the date of purchase as an investment.

Disclosure

20.48 An entity should disclose the following information about defined benefit plans:

    a. A description of the plan, including plan participants and the nature of determining benefits

    b. Information about the funded status of the plan, including benefit obligation, market value of plan assets, and the plan deficit or excess, at the end of the reporting period

    c. The expected rate of return on plan assets and the discount rate used to determine the accrued benefit obligation

Termination Benefits

20.49 Termination benefits should be recognized as a liability and expense when it is probable that employees will be entitled to benefits, and the amount can be reasonably estimated.

20.50 When determining whether the payment of termination benefits is probable, one of the following conditions should be met:

    a. The termination benefits are contractually required to be provided to employees.

    b. Management has approved and committed to a detailed plan of termination, and withdrawal from the plan is not realistically possible.

Disclosure

20.51 An entity should disclose the nature and effect of any termination benefits provided in the period.

Chapter 21
Income Taxes

Purpose and Scope

21.01 This chapter establishes principles for the recognition, measurement, presentation, and disclosure of income and refundable taxes in an entity's financial statements.

Accounting Policy

21.02 An entity should make an accounting policy choice to account for *income taxes*[1] using either

    a. the *taxes payable method* or

    b. the *deferred income taxes* method.

Entities Not Subject to Income Taxes

21.03 Certain entities (for example, unincorporated businesses and subchapter S corporations) are not liable for income taxes on income earned. Although its income or losses do affect the tax liability of the owners, any calculation of the owners' tax liability relating specifically to the business would necessarily be arbitrary because it would be affected by factors completely unrelated to the operations of the business.

21.04 No provision for income taxes should be made in the financial statements of businesses for which income is taxed directly to the owners.

Taxes Payable Method

21.05 Under the taxes payable method, only current income tax assets and liabilities are recognized.

Recognition

21.06 Current income taxes, to the extent unpaid or refundable, should be recognized as a liability or asset.

21.07 The benefit relating to a tax loss arising in the current period that will be carried back to recover income taxes of a previous period should be recognized as a current asset. When a tax loss is used to recover income taxes previously paid, the benefit is recognized in the period in which the tax loss occurs because the benefit will be realized.

21.08 The liability for current income taxes included in the statement of financial position is the amount due for current and prior periods, less amounts already paid in respect of these income taxes. When the amount already paid for current income taxes for a period exceeds the liability for that period, any excess amount is shown as an asset.

---

[1] Italicized terms are defined in the glossary.

Measurement

21.09 Income tax liabilities and income tax assets should be measured in accordance with paragraphs 21.43–.47.

Intraperiod Allocation

21.10 The relevant intraperiod allocation provisions of paragraphs 21.48–.52 should be applied when using the taxes payable method.

Deferred Income Taxes Method

The Basic Principles of Deferred Income Taxes

21.11 The fundamental principle upon which the deferred income taxes method is based is that an entity recognizes a deferred income tax liability whenever recovery or settlement of the carrying amount of an asset or liability would result in deferred income tax outflows. Similarly, an entity recognizes a deferred income tax asset whenever recovery or settlement of the carrying amount of an asset or liability would generate deferred income tax reductions. An extension of this fundamental principle is that in the case of unused tax losses, income tax reductions, and certain items that have a tax basis but cannot be identified with an asset or liability on the statement of financial position, the recognition of deferred income tax benefits is determined by reference to the probable realization of a deferred income tax reduction.

Recovery or Settlement of the Carrying Amount of an Asset or Liability

21.12 The rules established by the taxation authorities to determine the *taxable income* that will arise from the recovery or settlement of an asset or liability are often different from the accounting policies followed by an entity in the preparation of its financial statements that govern the amounts included in income or expense from the recovery or settlement of an asset or liability. The determination of whether recovery or settlement of an asset or liability will result in deferred income tax outflows or benefits is determined by reference to the difference between the carrying amounts and tax bases of assets and liabilities. The tax basis of an asset or liability is the amount, determined with reference to the rules established by the taxation authorities, that could be deducted in the determination of taxable income if the asset was recovered or the liability was settled for its carrying amount. At any point in time, there may be a difference between the tax basis of an asset or liability and its carrying amount. Such differences are *temporary differences*. Temporary differences may be either taxable or deductible. *Taxable temporary differences* give rise to *deferred income tax liabilities*. *Deductible temporary differences* give rise to *deferred income tax assets*.

21.13 To determine the extent of any temporary differences, it is first necessary to establish the tax basis of the assets and liabilities. The following guidance assists in determining the tax basis of an asset for the purposes of this chapter:

    a. When an amount related to an asset is deductible when determining taxable income over one or more periods, the tax basis

Income Taxes

at the end of a period is that amount less all amounts already deducted when determining taxable income of the current and prior periods.

b. When an amount related to an asset is deductible when determining taxable income only when the asset is disposed of or permanently withdrawn from use, the tax basis of the asset is that amount.

c. When the cost of an asset is not deductible when determining taxable income, but any proceeds of a disposal of the asset would not be included in the determination of taxable income, the tax basis of the asset is equal to the carrying amount.

d. When the amount related to an asset that will be deductible when determining future taxable income depends on whether the asset is utilized or sold, the tax basis of the asset is the greater of those amounts.

21.14 The tax basis of a liability is its carrying amount less any amount that will be deductible for income tax purposes in respect of that liability in future periods. In the case of amounts received but not yet recognized as revenue, the tax basis of the resulting liability is its carrying amount less any amount that will not be taxable in future periods. When a liability can be settled for its carrying amount without tax consequences, the tax basis of the liability is considered to be the same as its carrying amount.

21.15 As discussed previously, the difference between the carrying amount of an asset or liability and its tax basis will determine the extent of any temporary differences, and these differences will, in turn, determine the extent of deferred income tax assets or liabilities. The following guidance assists in determining the nature of any temporary differences for the purposes of this chapter:

a. When the carrying amount of an asset and its tax basis are the same, the amount included in taxable income on the recovery of the asset is offset by the amount allowed as a deduction in the determination of taxable income. Therefore, there is no temporary difference because the recovery of the carrying amount has no effect on taxable income of the entity.

b. When the carrying amount of an asset is greater than its tax basis, the recovery of the carrying amount in a future period will result in a taxable amount in excess of the future amount allowed as a deduction in the determination of taxable income. Therefore, a taxable temporary difference exists that gives rise to a deferred income tax liability in respect of the income taxes that will be payable in future periods.

c. When the carrying amount of an asset is less than its tax basis, the amount allowed as a deduction in the determination of taxable income in respect of that asset will be greater than the taxable amount arising from the recovery of the carrying amount. Therefore, a deductible temporary difference exists that gives rise to a deferred income tax asset in respect of the income tax that will be recoverable in future periods.

FRF-SME 21.15

d. When the carrying amount of a liability is equal to its tax basis, there will be no tax consequences associated with settling the liability. Therefore, there is no temporary difference.

e. When an amount related to a liability is deductible for income tax purposes in future periods when the liability is settled, it has a tax basis of zero. The settlement of the liability will result in a deduction for tax purposes. Therefore, the difference between the carrying amount of the liability and its tax basis is a deductible temporary difference that gives rise to a deferred income tax asset.

Unused Tax Losses, Income Tax Reductions, and Certain Other Items

21.16 Unused tax losses and income tax reductions that are not related to particular assets or liabilities in the statement of financial position may generate benefits that meet the conceptual definition of assets and should be recognized if appropriate criteria are met. In addition, some items have a tax basis but cannot be identified with a particular asset or liability in the statement of financial position, such as the following:

a. Research costs are recognized as an expense in the financial statements in the period in which they are incurred but might not be deducted when determining taxable income until a later period. The difference between the tax basis of the research costs (that is, the amount the taxation authorities will permit as a deduction in the future) and the carrying amount of zero is a deductible temporary difference that gives rise to a deferred income tax asset.

b. For financial statement purposes, an entity might recognize profits on a long-term contract using the percentage of completion method but use the completed contract method when determining taxable income. Income is deferred for tax purposes, with no corresponding amount being deferred for accounting purposes. The income deferred for tax purposes represents a taxable temporary difference that gives rise to a deferred tax liability.

Business Combinations

21.17 In consolidated financial statements, *temporary differences* are the differences between the carrying amounts in the consolidated financial statements of assets and liabilities of each entity and the appropriate tax basis. The tax bases of the assets and liabilities are determined by reference to the individual entities in the group.

21.18 In a business combination, temporary differences might exist between the assigned market values and the tax bases of the related assets and liabilities. Such temporary differences can be either taxable temporary differences or deductible temporary differences and, therefore, result in either deferred income tax liabilities or assets. For example, when the carrying amount of an asset is increased to market value but the tax basis of the asset is not adjusted, a taxable temporary difference arises, resulting in a deferred income tax liability. When a liability is recognized on the acquisition but the related costs are not deductible when determining taxable income until a later period, a deductible temporary difference arises, resulting in a deferred income tax asset. These deferred income tax assets and liabilities are treated as identifiable assets and liabilities as of the acquisition date.

Recognition

Current Income Tax Liabilities and Current Income Tax Assets

21.19 Current income tax liabilities and current income tax assets are recognized in accordance with paragraphs 21.06–.08 and should not be included in deferred income tax assets and deferred income tax liabilities.

Deferred Income Tax Liabilities and Deferred Income Tax Assets

Taxable and Deductible Temporary Differences, Unused Tax Losses, and Income Tax Reductions

21.20 At each statement of financial position date, except as provided in paragraphs 21.28 and 21.30, a deferred income tax asset or liability should be recognized for all deductible and taxable temporary differences, unused tax losses, and income tax reductions. The amount recognized as a deferred income tax asset should be limited to the amount that is *more likely than not* to be realized.

21.21 Future realization of the tax benefit of an existing deductible temporary difference, unused tax loss, or unused income tax reduction ultimately depends on the existence of sufficient taxable income of an appropriate nature, relating to the same taxable entity and the same taxation authority, within the carryback and carryforward periods available under the tax law. The following sources of taxable income may be available under the tax law to realize a tax benefit for deductible temporary differences, unused tax losses, or income tax reductions:

  a. Future reversals of existing taxable temporary differences

  b. Future taxable income before the effects of reversing temporary differences, unused tax losses, and income tax reductions

  c. Taxable income in prior year(s) if carryback is permitted under the tax law

  d. Tax-planning strategies that, if necessary, would be implemented to realize a deferred income tax asset

21.22 An entity would consider tax-planning strategies when determining the extent to which it is more likely than not that a deferred income tax asset will be realized. Tax-planning strategies are actions that

  a. are prudent and feasible;

  b. an entity ordinarily might not take, but would take, to prevent a tax loss or income tax reduction from expiring unused; and

  c. would result in realization of deferred income tax assets.

The carrying amount of any deferred income tax asset recognized as a result of a tax-planning strategy would reflect the cost of implementing that strategy.

21.23 Forming a conclusion that it is appropriate to recognize a deferred income tax asset is difficult when unfavorable evidence exists, such as cumulative losses in recent years. Other examples of unfavorable evidence include

> a. a history of tax losses or income tax reductions expiring unused;
>
> b. losses expected in early future years (by a currently profitable entity);
>
> c. unsettled circumstances that, if unfavorably resolved, would adversely affect future operations and profit levels on a continuing basis in future years; and
>
> d. a carryback or carryforward period that is so brief that it would limit realization of tax benefits, particularly if the entity operates in a traditionally cyclical business.

21.24 Examples of favorable evidence that might support a conclusion that recognition of a deferred income tax asset is appropriate despite the existence of unfavorable evidence include

> a. existing sufficient taxable temporary differences relating to the same taxable entity and the same taxation authority that result in taxable amounts against which the unused tax losses or income tax reductions can be utilized;
>
> b. existing contracts or firm sales backlog that will produce more than enough taxable income to realize the deferred income tax asset based on existing sales prices and cost structures;
>
> c. an excess of market value over the tax basis of the entity's net assets in an amount sufficient to realize the deferred income tax asset; or
>
> d. a strong earnings history exclusive of the loss that created the future deductible amount (unused tax loss carryforward or deductible temporary difference), together with evidence indicating that the loss is an aberration, rather than a continuing condition.

21.25 An entity must use judgment when considering the relative impact of unfavorable and favorable evidence on the recognition of a deferred income tax asset. The weight given to the potential effect of unfavorable and favorable evidence is commensurate with the extent to which it can be verified objectively. The more unfavorable evidence that exists, the more favorable evidence is necessary, and the more difficult it is to support a conclusion that recognition of some portion of, or all of, the deferred income tax asset is appropriate.

21.26 An entity should recognize a deferred income tax asset for all deductible temporary differences, unused tax losses, and income tax reductions, reduced by a valuation allowance to the extent that it is more likely than not that some portion of, or all, the assets will not be realized. The valuation allowance reduces the deferred income tax asset to the amount that is more likely than not to be realized. This results in the same net asset as that determined in accordance with paragraph 21.20 and after applying the considerations described in paragraphs 21.21–.25 when determining the amount of the valuation allowance.

Reassessment of Deferred Income Tax Assets

21.27 At each statement of financial position date, an entity reassesses recognized and unrecognized deferred income tax assets. When it is more likely than not that sufficient future taxable income will be available to allow a previously unrecognized deferred income tax asset to be realized, the deferred income tax asset is recognized to the extent of that taxable income. For example, an improvement in existing contracts or firm sales backlog may increase the probability of the entity's ability to generate future taxable income such that the deferred income tax asset meets the recognition criteria in paragraphs 21.20–.25. Conversely, a significant weakening of an entity's financial position may indicate that the entity will not be able to generate sufficient taxable income to allow recognized deferred income tax assets to be realized, in which case, the deferred income tax asset is reduced by a valuation allowance to the amount that is considered more likely than not to be realized.

Intragroup Transfers

21.28 When an asset is transferred between entities within a consolidated group, a deferred income tax liability or asset should not be recognized in the consolidated financial statements for a temporary difference arising between the tax basis of the asset in the buyer's tax jurisdiction and its cost as reported in the consolidated financial statements. Any taxes paid or recovered by the transferor as a result of the transfer should be recorded as an asset or liability in the consolidated financial statements until the gain or loss is recognized by the consolidated entity.

21.29 A transfer of assets, such as the sale of inventory or depreciable assets between entities within a consolidated group, is a taxable event that might establish a new tax basis for those assets in the buyer's tax jurisdiction. The new tax basis of those assets is deductible on the buyer's income tax return when the cost of those assets, as reported in the consolidated financial statements, is recovered. However, from the point of view of the consolidated financial statements, no profit or loss has been realized, and there will be no change in net assets until such time as that asset is transferred, by sale or otherwise, outside the consolidated group. Although the difference between the buyer's tax basis and the cost of transferred assets as reported in the consolidated financial statements technically meets the definition of a temporary difference, the substance of accounting for it as such would be to recognize income taxes related to intercompany gains or losses that are not recognized in accordance with chapter 23, "Consolidated Financial Statements and Noncontrolling Interests." Similar principles apply to investments subject to significant influence and interests in joint ventures.

Investments in Subsidiaries, Interests in Joint Ventures, and Equity Method Investments

21.30 At each statement of financial position date, a deferred income tax liability or deferred income tax asset should be recognized for all temporary differences arising from investments in subsidiaries and interests in joint ventures, except with respect to the difference between the carrying amount of the investment and the tax basis of the investment, when it is apparent that this difference will not reverse in the foreseeable future. Any deferred income tax asset should be recognized only to the extent that it is more likely than not that the benefit will be realized.

21.31 Temporary differences may arise from investments in subsidiaries and interests in joint ventures in a number of different circumstances. Examples include

- a. differences between the carrying amounts (in the consolidated financial statements) of individual assets and liabilities of subsidiaries and joint ventures and their tax basis (inside basis differences) or
- b. differences between the carrying amount of an investment in a subsidiary or an interest in a joint venture and its tax basis (outside basis differences) because of items such as the existence of undistributed income of subsidiaries and joint ventures.

Such temporary differences are differences between the carrying amounts of assets and liabilities of each entity in the financial statements of the investor and the appropriate tax basis, even when they are eliminated on consolidation. The tax basis of the assets and liabilities is determined by reference to the individual entities in the group.

21.32 In consolidated financial statements, the taxable temporary difference arising from an investment in a subsidiary reflects the parent's share of the undistributed income of the subsidiary and differences arising from other transactions and events that affect the carrying amount of the parent's investment.

21.33 As a parent controls the dividend policy of its subsidiary, it is able to control the timing of the reversal of temporary differences associated with its investment. When the parent considers the reinvestment of a subsidiary's profits as part of its permanent investment in the subsidiary, and it has determined that those profits will not be distributed for the foreseeable future, a deferred income tax liability is not recognized. When it is apparent that all or part of the temporary difference will reverse in the foreseeable future, a deferred income tax liability is recognized.

21.34 A *venturer* is a party to a joint venture and has joint control over that joint venture. *Joint control* is the contractually agreed sharing of the continuing power to determine the strategic, operating, investing, and financing policies of the joint venture. Decisions relating to distributions from the joint venture usually require the venturers' consent in such a manner as defined in the terms of the contractual arrangement. Therefore, when the venturer can exercise joint control over distributions and it is apparent that distributions will not be made for the foreseeable future, a deferred income tax liability is not recognized.

21.35 The temporary differences described in paragraph 21.31 might also exist for investments subject to significant influence accounted for by the equity method. A deferred income tax liability or asset is recorded for such temporary differences because the investor is not normally able to control the timing of their reversal.

Assets Acquired Other Than in a Business Combination

21.36 In some circumstances, an asset acquired, other than an asset acquired in a business combination, has a tax basis that is less than its cost. This gives rise to a taxable temporary difference that results in the recognition of a deferred income tax liability. Adding the *cost of deferred income taxes* to the cost of the asset reflects the following:

    a. The carrying amount of the asset will include the cost to acquire the asset and the unavoidable income tax consequences of utilizing the asset.

    b. The carrying amount will represent the minimum future cash flows necessary to recover the investment in the asset, including any tax consequences associated with the asset.

21.37 There may be circumstances in which an asset acquired, other than an asset acquired in a business combination, has a tax basis in excess of its cost. This chapter requires the recognition of a deferred income tax asset in respect of the origination or reversal of the resulting temporary difference. The most appropriate manner of recognizing this deferred income tax asset is to reduce the cost of the asset by the deferred income tax benefit in order to reflect the consideration paid for the asset and take into account the effect of the tax treatment applied by the taxation authorities to the difference between the cost of the asset and its tax basis.

Business Combinations, New Basis (Push-Down) Accounting, Investments Subject to Significant Influence, and Interests in Joint Ventures

21.38 In certain circumstances, an acquirer may consider it more likely than not that, as a result of a business combination, it will be able to realize a deferred income tax asset of its own or its subsidiaries that was unrecognized immediately before the acquisition. For example, the acquirer may be able to utilize the benefits of its unused tax losses against the future taxable income of the acquiree or through the use of tax-planning strategies. Alternatively, as a result of the business combination, it might no longer be more likely than not that future taxable profit will allow the deferred income tax asset to be recovered. In such cases, the acquirer recognizes a change in the deferred income tax asset in the period of the business combination but does not include it as part of the accounting for the business combination. Therefore, the acquirer does not take the deferred income tax asset into account when measuring the goodwill or bargain purchase gain it recognizes in the business combination.

21.39 When a deferred income tax asset acquired in a business combination that was not recognized as an identifiable asset by the acquirer at the date of the acquisition is subsequently recognized by the acquirer within the measurement period, the benefit should be applied

    a. first to reduce to zero any unamortized goodwill related to the acquisition and

    b. then to reduce income tax expense.

21.40 The *measurement period* is the period after the acquisition date during which the acquirer may adjust the provisional amounts recognized for a business combination (see chapter 28, "Business Combinations").

21.41 When a deferred income tax asset acquired in a business combination that was not recognized as an identifiable asset by the acquirer at the date of the acquisition is recognized by the acquirer after the measurement period, the benefit should be recognized in income tax expense.

21.42 The principles in paragraphs 21.38–.39 and 21.41 should be applied

  a. when accounting for an investment subject to significant influence or an interest in a joint venture and

  b. when recognizing deferred income tax assets in periods subsequent to the application of push-down accounting (see chapter 29, "New Basis [Push-Down] Accounting").

Measurement

21.43 Income tax liabilities and income tax assets should be measured using the income tax rates and income tax laws that, at the statement of financial position date, are expected to apply when the liability is settled or the asset is realized, which are those enacted at the statement of financial position date.

21.44 Deferred income tax liabilities and deferred income tax assets should not be discounted.

21.45 For changes in income tax rates and tax laws enacted after the date of the financial statements but before the date they are available to be issued, disclosure as a subsequent event may be appropriate in accordance with chapter 27, "Subsequent Events."

21.46 When the effective tax rate that applies to capital gains and losses differs from the tax rate that applies to other taxable income, the rate used to measure deferred income tax assets and liabilities reflects the expected manner of recovery of the asset.

21.47 When different income tax rates apply to different levels of taxable income, deferred income tax assets and liabilities are measured using the rates that are expected to apply to the taxable income of the periods in which the temporary differences are expected to reverse. When income tax rate reductions must be allocated among companies in a related group, deferred income tax liabilities and deferred income tax assets are measured in the financial statements of the individual companies based on the allocations of these reductions expected to occur in the future, regardless of the actual allocations in the current year.

Intraperiod Allocation

21.48 The cost (benefit) of current and deferred income taxes should be recognized as income tax expense included in the determination of net income or loss for the period before discontinued operations, except that

  a. any portion of the cost (benefit) of current and deferred income taxes related to discontinued operations of the current period should be included in the statement of operations with the results of discontinued operations;

  b. any portion of the cost (benefit) of current and deferred income taxes relating to capital transactions in the current period, or relating to items that are credited or charged directly to equity in the current period, should be charged or credited directly to equity;

  c. any portion of the cost (benefit) of current and deferred income taxes arising at the time of changes in shareholder status should be treated as a capital transaction (see paragraph 21.52 and chapter 18, "Equity");

d. any portion of the cost of deferred income taxes arising at the time an entity renounces the deductibility of expenditures to an investor should be treated as a cost of issuing the security to the investor;

e. any portion of the cost (benefit) of deferred income taxes arising at the time of acquisition of an asset, other than an asset acquired in a business combination, should be recognized in accordance with paragraphs 21.36–.37;

f. any portion of the cost (benefit) of deferred income taxes recognized at the time of a business combination should be recognized in accordance with paragraph 21.18;

g. any other portion of the cost (benefit) of deferred income taxes related to a business combination, investment in a significantly influenced investee, interest in a joint venture, or comprehensive revaluation of assets and liabilities should be recognized in accordance with paragraphs 21.39 and 21.41–.42;

h. any portion of the cost (benefit) of current and deferred income taxes relating to the correction of an error or a change in accounting policy should be recognized in a manner consistent with the underlying item (see chapter 9, "Accounting Changes, Changes in Accounting Estimates, and Correction of Errors").

21.49 Changes in deferred income tax balances recognized in accordance with paragraph 21.43 as a result of changes in tax laws or rates should be included in deferred income tax expense reported in income before discontinued operations because such changes are considered to be a result of normal business activities.

21.50 The *cost (benefit) of current income taxes* represents the amount of income taxes payable or recoverable in respect of the period. The cost (benefit) of deferred income taxes represents the amount of deferred income tax liabilities and deferred income tax assets recognized in the period. The cost (benefit) of current and deferred income taxes is recognized in a manner consistent with the transaction or event that gave rise to the current or deferred income tax liability or asset. Therefore, the cost (benefit) of current and deferred income taxes is recognized as income tax expense, except for any portions allocated elsewhere in accordance with paragraph 21.48.

21.51 The tax benefit of an unused tax loss or income tax reduction, to the extent recognized in the year of the loss, is reported in the same manner as the related loss. When included in net income, the tax benefit of a loss carryforward recognized in a period, after the period of the loss, is reported in income before discontinued operations, regardless of the classification of the loss in the prior period.

21.52 Deferred income tax liabilities and assets may change because of changes in shareholder status or capital stock transactions that affect the entity's tax status (for example, changes in the residence of shareholders and changes in control). The changes in deferred income tax assets and liabilities related to the shareholders' action or the injection of new equity are recorded as capital transactions. The effects of changes in tax status related to the entity's actions or decisions, such as a change in the entity's residency, are included in income tax expense, which is included in the determination of net income before discontinued operations.

Alternative Minimum Tax

21.53 Any amounts of income tax payable currently that may reduce income taxes of a future period should be recorded as a deferred income tax asset if it is more likely than not that income taxes will be sufficient to recover the amounts payable currently. Any amounts not more likely than not to be recovered should be included in current income tax expense.

Presentation

Income Tax Expense

21.54 Income tax expense included in the determination of net income or loss before discontinued operations should be presented on the face of the statement of operations.

Income Tax Liabilities and Income Tax Assets

21.55 Income tax liabilities and income tax assets should be presented separately from other liabilities and assets. Current income tax liabilities and current income tax assets should be presented separately from deferred income tax liabilities and deferred income tax assets.

21.56 When an entity segregates assets and liabilities between current and noncurrent assets and liabilities, the current and noncurrent portions of deferred income tax liabilities and deferred income tax assets should also be segregated. The classification between current and noncurrent should be based on the classification of the liabilities and assets to which the deferred income tax liabilities and deferred income tax assets relate. A deferred income tax liability or deferred income tax asset that is not related to a liability or asset recognized for accounting purposes should be classified according to the expected reversal date of the temporary difference. Deferred income tax assets related to unused tax losses and income tax reductions should be classified according to the date that the benefit is expected to be realized.

21.57 Current income tax liabilities and current income tax assets should be offset if they relate to the same taxable entity and the same taxation authority. Deferred income tax liabilities and deferred income tax assets should be offset if they relate to the same taxable entity and the same taxation authority. However, when an entity classifies assets and liabilities as current and noncurrent, the current portion of deferred income tax balances should not offset any deferred income tax balances classified as noncurrent.

21.58 When entities in a group are taxed separately by the same taxation authority, a deferred income tax asset recognized by one entity in the group should not be offset against a deferred income tax liability of another entity in the group unless tax-planning strategies could be implemented to satisfy the requirements of paragraph 21.57 when the deferred income tax liability becomes payable.

21.59 Although current income tax assets and current income tax liabilities are separately recognized and measured, they may be offset in the statement of financial position to the extent that they relate to income taxes levied on the same taxable entity by the same taxation authority. Similarly, deferred income tax assets and deferred income tax liabilities are offset to the extent that they relate to income taxes levied on the same taxable entity by the same taxation authority. However, current and noncurrent income tax balances are not offset by an entity that makes a distinction between current and noncurrent assets and liabilities, irrespective of whether the balances relate to income taxes levied by the same taxation authorities. In addition, current income tax liabilities and current income tax assets are not offset with deferred income tax liabilities and deferred income tax assets, irrespective of whether the balances relate to income taxes levied by the same taxation authorities. However, it is appropriate to consider available tax planning strategies that can be implemented. A tax planning strategy is assumed only when it is practical and when management has both the ability and the intent to employ the strategy, if necessary, to offset tax balances. An example of a tax planning strategy that might result in an offset of deferred income tax assets and liabilities in a consolidated group is an amalgamation of companies in the group.

Disclosure

21.60 An entity that is not subject to income taxes because its income is taxed directly to its owners should disclose that fact.

21.61 An entity should disclose which of the following accounting methods were chosen to account for income taxes:

   a. The taxes payable method

   b. The deferred income taxes method

21.62 When an entity applies the taxes payable method of accounting for income taxes, the financial statements should disclose the following:

   a. Income tax expense (benefit) included in the determination of income or loss before discontinued operations.

   b. A discussion of the differences of income tax rate or expense related to income or loss for the period before discontinued operations to the statutory income tax rate or the dollar amount that would result from its application, including the nature of each significant reconciling item. The entity may include or omit a numerical reconciliation.

   c. The amount of unused income tax losses carried forward and unused income tax credits.

   d. The portion of income tax expense (benefit) related to transactions charged (or credited) to equity.

21.63 When an entity applies the deferred income taxes method of accounting for income taxes, the following should be disclosed separately:

   a. Current income tax expense (benefit) included in the determination of income or loss before discontinued operations.

   b. Deferred income tax expense (benefit) included in the determination of income or loss before discontinued operations.

c. The portion of the cost (benefit) of current and deferred income taxes related to capital transactions or other items that are charged or credited to equity.

d. The total amount of unused tax losses and income tax reductions and the amount of deductible temporary differences for which no deferred income tax asset has been recognized.

e. A discussion of the differences of income tax rate or expense related to income or loss for the period before discontinued operations to the statutory income tax rate or the dollar amount that would result from its application, including the nature of each significant reconciling item. The entity may include or omit a numerical reconciliation.

f. The amount of unused income tax losses carried forward and unused income tax credits.

Chapter 22

Subsidiaries

Purpose and Scope

22.01 This chapter establishes principles for accounting for subsidiaries in the general purpose financial statements. This chapter is closely related to chapter 28, "Business Combinations," which sets out the basis of accounting for transactions by which subsidiaries are acquired; chapter 23, "Consolidated Financial Statements and Noncontrolling Interests," which describes the preparation of consolidated financial statements and the accounting for a noncontrolling interest in a *subsidiary*[1] subsequent to a business combination; and chapter 26, "Related Party Transactions," which establishes principles for the disclosure of related party transactions in the financial statements.

22.02 This chapter does not deal with accounting for investments, which is covered in chapter 11, "Equity, Debt, and Other Investments."

Recognition and Presentation

22.03 An entity should make an accounting policy choice to either

a. consolidate its subsidiaries or

b. account for its subsidiaries using the equity method.

An entity choosing the equity method should provide the disclosures required by chapter 11. All subsidiaries should be accounted for using the same method. A material difference in the basis of accounting between a parent and a subsidiary precludes the preparation of consolidated financial statements and the use of the equity method.

Consolidated Financial Statements

22.04 Consolidated financial statements recognize that even though the parent and its subsidiaries may be separate legal entities, together, they constitute a single economic unit. Such financial statements provide an appropriate basis for informing users of the parent's financial statements about the resources and results of operations of the parent and its subsidiaries as a group. However, some users are more interested in financial statements on a nonconsolidated basis. For example, lenders may want information only about the entity to which they have made a loan. Consolidated financial statements may include cash flows, assets, and liabilities for entities that are separate from the entity to which the lender has made the loan and, thus, may be less informative than nonconsolidated financial statements.

22.05 When an entity prepares consolidated financial statements, it should describe these financial statements as being prepared on a consolidated basis, and each statement should be labeled accordingly.

---

[1] Italicized terms are defined in the glossary.

22.06 A holding of an interest in an entity that is not a subsidiary qualifies as an investment and is subject to the requirements of chapter 11.

22.07 Consolidation of a subsidiary commences at the date the parent acquires control and continues as long as control exists. Accordingly, a parent does not retroactively consolidate a subsidiary for periods prior to its acquisition of control.

22.08 When an entity ceases to meet the definition of a subsidiary, the former parent ceases to consolidate the entity from that time. Amounts reported on a consolidated basis for periods prior to the cessation of consolidation are not retroactively restated on a nonconsolidated basis.

22.09 Subsequent to a decision to dispose of a subsidiary, and prior to the disposal date, the provisions of chapter 15, "Disposal of Long-Lived Assets and Discontinued Operations," apply to a business of the subsidiary that meets the criteria in that chapter to be classified as held for sale. Application of the requirements of that chapter does not result in cessation of consolidation.

Nonconsolidated Financial Statements

22.10 When an entity applies the accounting policy choice as set out in paragraph 22.03(b), it should describe its financial statements as being prepared on a nonconsolidated basis, and each statement should be labeled accordingly.

22.11 Investments in nonconsolidated subsidiaries should be presented separately from other investments in the statement of financial position. Income or loss from those investments may be presented as a gross or net amount in the statement of operations.

Disclosure

Consolidated Financial Statements

22.12 Management should provide a listing and description of all subsidiaries, including their names, income from each subsidiary, and the proportion of ownership interests held in each subsidiary.

Nonconsolidated Financial Statements

22.13 An entity that prepares nonconsolidated financial statements should disclose the basis used to account for its subsidiaries.

22.14 An entity that prepares nonconsolidated financial statements should provide a listing and description of all subsidiaries, including their names, carrying amounts, income from each subsidiary, and the proportion of ownership interests held in each subsidiary.

Chapter 23

Consolidated Financial Statements and Noncontrolling Interests

Purpose and Scope

23.01 This chapter establishes principles for the preparation of consolidated financial statements and for accounting for a *noncontrolling interest*[1] in a subsidiary in *consolidated financial statements*. Five other chapters deal with closely related matters, as follows:

   a. Chapter 28, "Business Combinations," deals with the application of the acquisition method of accounting for business combinations. In particular, this chapter addresses the determination of the carrying amount of the assets and liabilities of a subsidiary entity, goodwill, and accounting for a noncontrolling interest at the time of the business combination.

   b. Chapter 22, "Subsidiaries," deals with the circumstances in which consolidation is used in the general purpose financial statements and provides an accounting policy choice for an entity to either consolidate its subsidiaries or account for them using the equity method.

   c. Chapter 11, "Equity, Debt, and Other Investments," deals with the circumstances in which the equity method of accounting is used.

   d. Chapter 13, "Intangible Assets," addresses accounting for goodwill subsequent to a business combination.

   e. Chapter 26, "Related Party Transactions," establishes principles for the disclosure of related party transactions in the financial statements.

23.02 Consolidated financial statements recognize that the separate legal entities are components of one economic unit and distinguishable from the separate parent and subsidiary company statements and combined statements of affiliated companies. The distinction is based both on the nature of such statements and the difference in circumstances justifying their use.

Combined Financial Statements

23.03 Combined financial statements (as distinguished from consolidated financial statements) may be useful in certain circumstances, although they are not a substitute for consolidated financial statements. Combined financial statements could be useful when one individual, or a group of individuals, owns a controlling interest in several entities. They could also be used to present the financial position and the results of operations of a group of subsidiaries or to combine the financial statements of entities under common management.

---

[1] Italicized terms are defined in the glossary.

23.04 When combined financial statements are prepared, similar principles to those used when preparing consolidated financial statements apply.

Preparation of Consolidated Financial Statements

23.05 The accounting principles that apply to the preparation of consolidated financial statements can be presented in three segments:

   a. Those that apply to the initial preparation of consolidated financial statements at the date of an acquisition
   b. Those that apply to transactions reported in subsequent consolidated financial statements
   c. Those that apply to miscellaneous transactions or relationships between the parent and subsidiary company

At the Date of Acquisition

23.06 When consolidated financial statements are prepared, the investment account of the parent should be replaced by the identifiable assets and liabilities of the subsidiary, any noncontrolling interest therein, and any goodwill arising as a result of the investment. Preparation of such financial statements requires that appropriate carrying amounts at the date of acquisition be determined for each asset and liability for the noncontrolling interest and goodwill (see chapter 28).

Intercompany Balances

23.07 Consolidated financial statements present two or more distinct legal entities as one single economic unit. To the extent that the two legal entities have receivables or payables from or to the other, intercompany balances should be eliminated upon consolidation.

Consolidated Retained Earnings

23.08 The retained earnings or deficit of a subsidiary company at the date(s) of acquisition by the parent should be excluded from consolidated retained earnings.

23.09 Sometimes the carrying amount of the assets of the parent company or the subsidiary company includes gains or losses arising from transactions between the two companies prior to the date of acquisition. Because transactions that took place prior to the date of acquisition are ordinarily assumed to have taken place at arm's length, the amounts involved in such transactions constitute objective evidence of value. Accordingly, such gains or losses should not be eliminated in the preparation of consolidated financial statements unless the transactions were made in contemplation of acquisition. However, gains and losses arising as a result of a business combination between related parties are eliminated on consolidation.

At Dates Subsequent to an Acquisition

23.10 Consolidated financial statements prepared on dates subsequent to the date of an acquisition are based on the amount assigned to assets, liabilities, and noncontrolling interest at the date of acquisition and, in addition, indicate the effects of transactions subsequent to that date.

Normal Operating Transactions Subsequent to an Acquisition

23.11 The existence of intercompany sales and purchases of goods and services, including inventory and fixed asset items and intercompany lending and borrowing transactions, will require the adjustment in the consolidated financial statements of the amounts included in the individual company financial statements.

23.12 A transaction between a parent and a subsidiary that results in a difference between the carrying amount in the subsidiary and the amount at which the item or service received is measured requires adjustment on consolidation.

Intercompany Balances, Gains and Losses, and Transactions

23.13 In consolidated financial statements prepared subsequent to the date of an acquisition, intercompany balances and postacquisition transactions should be eliminated. Unrealized intercompany gains or losses arising subsequent to the date of an acquisition on assets remaining within the consolidated group should be eliminated. The amount of elimination from assets should not be affected by the existence of a noncontrolling interest. Intercompany transactions may involve items reported as revenue or expense in the statements of operations of the individual companies. Such transactions often result in the creation of intercompany receivable and payable balances. These assets, liabilities, revenues, and expense amounts are eliminated in the preparation of consolidated financial statements.

Depreciation and Amortization

23.14 The assets and liabilities of the subsidiary company that were consolidated at the date of acquisition are deemed to have been purchased by the consolidated entity on that date. The amounts determined at that date are the basis for subsequent accounting for these assets and liabilities (such as calculation of depreciation charges). Therefore, the sum of the depreciation charges in the parent and subsidiary company records may not equal the appropriate depreciation charge to be presented in the consolidated financial statements, and adjustments may be necessary. Similarly, interest recognized on financial assets and liabilities measured at *amortized cost* may differ from the sum of interest amounts recorded by the parent and subsidiary.

23.15 The depreciation, depletion, and amortization of the assets of a subsidiary company should be computed for the purposes of consolidated financial statements on the basis of the amounts determined at the date of acquisition by the parent company.

Shareholders' Equity Transactions With Interests Outside the Consolidated Group

23.16 Transactions subsequent to the date of acquisition may affect the proportional equity positions of the parent and the noncontrolling

FRF-SME 23.16

interests. These include, for example, the sale by the parent company of some of its holdings in the subsidiary company, the issue by the subsidiary company of some of its own shares, and the repurchase by a subsidiary company of its own shares. Other equity transactions of the consolidated group with outside interests are similar in nature and may be accounted for accordingly.

23.17 When a parent company acquires additional shares in a subsidiary, that transaction will be accounted for in accordance with the guidelines provided in paragraphs 23.25–.26. Declaration of a stock dividend by a subsidiary company will also affect the number of shares held but not the relative positions of the parent and noncontrolling interests.

23.18 When the parent company sells part of its shareholdings in a subsidiary company to outside interests or the subsidiary company issues its own shares to outside interests, the shares sold or issued reduce the parent's interest and increase the noncontrolling interest. Guidance on accounting for changes in an ownership interest in a subsidiary is provided in paragraphs 23.25–.30.

Acquisition by a Subsidiary of Its Own Shares From Interests Outside the Group

23.19 When a subsidiary acquires its own shares for cancellation from outside interests, the proportionate interest of the parent company after the transaction is increased. Because the transaction is similar in effect to the situation when the parent company acquires an additional interest in a subsidiary, it is accounted for in accordance with paragraphs 23.25–.26.

Miscellaneous

Basis of Accounting

23.20 A material difference in the basis of accounting between a parent and a subsidiary precludes the preparation of consolidated financial statements.

23.21 Financial statements of foreign operations are adjusted, if necessary, to conform to standards in the FRF for SMEs accounting framework when incorporating them in the financial statements of the reporting entity.

Statements at Different Dates

23.22 A difference in fiscal periods of a parent and a subsidiary does not, of itself, justify the exclusion of the subsidiary from consolidation.

Noncontrolling Interests

Procedures

23.23 When preparing consolidated financial statements, an entity identifies noncontrolling interests in the net income of consolidated subsidiaries for the reporting period and noncontrolling interests in the net assets of consolidated subsidiaries separately from the parent's ownership interests in them. Noncontrolling interests in the net assets consist of the amount of those noncontrolling interests at the date of the original combination calculated in accordance with chapter 28 and the noncontrolling interests' share of changes in equity since the date of the combination.

23.24 When potential voting rights exist, the proportions of net income and changes in equity allocated to the parent and noncontrolling interests are determined on the basis of present ownership interests and do not reflect the possible exercise or conversion of potential voting rights.

Change in Ownership Interest in a Consolidated Subsidiary

23.25 Changes in a parent's ownership interest in a consolidated subsidiary that do not result in a loss of control should be accounted for as equity transactions (that is, transactions with owners in their capacity as owners).

23.26 In such circumstances, the carrying amounts of the controlling and noncontrolling interests should be adjusted to reflect the changes in their relative interests in the subsidiary. Any difference between the amount by which the noncontrolling interests are adjusted and the market value of the consideration paid or received should be recognized directly in equity and attributed to the owners of the parent.

Loss of Control of a Consolidated Subsidiary

23.27 A parent might lose control of a consolidated subsidiary in two or more arrangements (transactions). However, sometimes circumstances indicate that the multiple arrangements should be accounted for as a single transaction. When determining whether to account for the arrangements as a single transaction, a parent should consider all the terms and conditions of the arrangements and their economic effects. One or more of the following may indicate that the parent should account for the multiple arrangements as a single transaction:

   a. They are entered into at the same time or in contemplation of each other.

   b. They form a single transaction designed to achieve an overall commercial effect.

   c. The occurrence of one arrangement is dependent on the occurrence of at least one other arrangement.

   d. One arrangement considered on its own is not economically justified, but it is economically justified when considered together with other arrangements. An example is when one disposal of shares is priced below market value and is compensated for by a subsequent disposal priced above market value.

23.28 If a parent loses control of a consolidated subsidiary, it should

   a. derecognize the assets (including any goodwill) and liabilities of the subsidiary at their carrying amounts at the date when control is lost;

   b. derecognize the carrying amount of any noncontrolling interests in the former subsidiary at the date when control is lost (including any components of equity attributable to them);

   c. recognize

FRF-SME 23.28

        i. the market value of the consideration received, if any, from the transaction, event, or circumstances that resulted in the loss of control and

        ii. if the transaction that resulted in the loss of control involves a distribution of shares of the subsidiary to owners in their capacity as owners, that distribution;

    d. recognize any investment retained in the former subsidiary at its carrying amount at the date when control is lost; and

    e. recognize any resulting difference as a gain or loss in net income attributable to the parent.

23.29 On the loss of control of a consolidated subsidiary, any investment retained in the former subsidiary and any amounts owed by or to the former subsidiary should be accounted for in accordance with other chapters from the date when control is lost.

23.30 The carrying amount of a consolidated subsidiary is the carrying amount in the nonconsolidated financial statements of the parent. This will be the cost of the subsidiary. The carrying amount of the retained investment is a proportionate share of the carrying amount of the subsidiary at the date of loss of control.

Presentation of Consolidated Financial Statements and Noncontrolling Interests

23.31 Consolidated financial statements adhere to the disclosure and presentation requirements for all financial statements. Also, certain disclosure requirements are specific to consolidated financial statements.

Statement of Operations Presentation in a Period of an Acquisition or Disposal

23.32 Only postacquisition and predisposal income of a subsidiary company is included in consolidated net income. The guidelines for determining the date of disposal may be inferred from the guidelines for determining the date of acquisition contained in chapter 28.

Noncontrolling Interests

23.33 If an entity consolidates its subsidiaries, noncontrolling interests should be presented in the consolidated statement of financial position within equity, separately from the equity of the owners of the parent.

23.34 Net income is attributed to the owners of the parent and the noncontrolling interests. Total income is attributed to the owners of the parent and the noncontrolling interests, even if this results in the noncontrolling interests having a deficit balance.

Disclosure

23.35 The entity's consolidation policy should be disclosed.

23.36 When, for purposes of consolidation, it is not possible to use financial statements for a period that substantially coincides with that of the investor's financial statements, this fact, and the period covered by the financial statements used, should be disclosed.

23.37 When the fiscal periods of a parent and a subsidiary, the investment in which is accounted for by the consolidation method, are not the same, events relating to, or transactions of, the subsidiary that have occurred during the intervening period that significantly affect the financial position or results of operations of the group should be recorded or disclosed, as appropriate.

Chapter 24

Interests in Joint Ventures

Purpose and Scope

24.01 This chapter establishes principles for accounting for interests in *joint ventures*[1] and the reporting of joint venture assets, liabilities, revenue, and expenses in the financial statements of *venturers*, regardless of the structures and forms under which the joint venture activities take place. However, this chapter does not deal with accounting by the joint venture itself.

24.02 This chapter applies when economic activities meet the definitions and criteria outlined in the glossary and paragraphs 24.03–.13, even though such activities may not be referred to as *joint ventures*. However, this chapter does not apply when economic activities do not meet the definitions and criteria set out in the glossary definitions and paragraphs 24.03–.13, even though they may sometimes be referred to as *joint ventures*. Accounting for investments in such activities is governed by the nature of the investments (see chapter 11, "Equity, Debt, and Other Investments").

Definitions

24.03 A distinctive characteristic common to all joint ventures is that two or more venturers are bound by a contractual arrangement that establishes that the venturers have *joint control* over the joint venture, regardless of the difference that may exist in their ownership interest. None of the individual venturers is in a position to exercise unilateral control over the joint venture. Decisions in all areas essential to the accomplishment of the joint venture require the consent of the venturers in such manner as defined in the terms of the contractual arrangement.

24.04 Interests in an economic activity, as described previously, may exist without entitling all the investors to share in joint control. In such cases, this would not be considered an interest in a joint venture for those investors who do not share in joint control, even though the economic activity may be viewed as a joint venture by those investors who do have joint control. The interest of an investor who does not have joint control over the joint venture qualifies as an investment and is subject to the requirements of chapter 11.

24.05 A venturer has joint control over a joint venture and has the right and ability to obtain future economic benefits from the resources of the joint venture and is exposed to related risks. Future economic benefits normally include cash flows or other forms of output generated by the joint venture, and related risks normally include exposure to losses of the joint venture or the direct exposure of the venturer to loss. An investor who has made a loan to a joint venture does not have similar exposure to the benefits and related risks of the joint venture. For example, an arrangement whereby an investor is not entitled to share in the net income of the joint venture and has recourse to assets of the other venturers would suggest

---

[1] Italicized terms are defined in the glossary.

that the risks and rewards of the investor are similar to those associated with a loan. Accordingly, the investor should account for the arrangement as a loan.

24.06 The contractual arrangement that binds the venturers may take different forms. For example, it may be evidenced by a contract between the venturers or, in some cases, the arrangement may be incorporated in the articles or other bylaws of the joint venture. In other cases, the arrangement may be evidenced by a contract between the venturers and an outside entity. Whatever its form, the contractual arrangement is usually in writing and covers matters such as the activities, duration, policies, and procedures of the joint venture; the allocation of ownership; the decision-making process; the capital contributions by the venturers; and the sharing by the venturers of the output, revenue, expenses, or results of the joint venture.

24.07 The contractual arrangement may designate a venturer as the manager or the operator of the joint venture. The operator does not control the joint venture but acts within the financing and operating policies that have been agreed to by the venturers in accordance with the contractual arrangement and delegated to the operator.

24.08 Often, the activities of a joint venture are an extension of, or complementary to, those of the venturers. For example, joint ventures are often formed to access new markets, gain economies of scale, perform a contract, or access new skills and resources. Joint ventures may take various forms and structures, such as partnerships, co-tenancies, corporate or unincorporated entities, or undivided interests. Whatever the form, joint ventures may fall into one of the following broad categories, which are commonly described as, and meet the definition of, joint ventures: jointly controlled operations, jointly controlled assets, and jointly controlled entities.

24.09 Joint venture agreements can and often designate different allocations among the venturers of (*a*) the profits and losses, (*b*) the specified costs and expenses or revenues, (*c*) the distributions of cash from operations, (*d*) the distributions of cash proceeds from liquidation, and (*e*) prices for determination of sales or rentals to the joint venture (such as prices for the use of each venturer's equipment used to perform the venture contractual obligations). Such agreements may also provide for changes in the allocations at specified future dates or on the occurrence of specified future events. For the purpose of determining the amount of income or loss to be recognized by the venturer, the percentage of ownership interest should be based on the percentage by which costs and profits will ultimately be shared by the venturers. An exception to this general rule may be appropriate if changes in the percentages are scheduled or expected to occur so far in the future that they become meaningless for current reporting purposes. In those circumstances, the percentage interest specified in the joint venture agreement should be used with appropriate disclosures.

Jointly-Controlled Operations

24.10 The operations of some joint ventures involve the use of the assets and other resources of the venturers, rather than the establishment of a corporation, partnership, or other entity, or a financial structure that is separate from the venturers themselves. Each venturer uses its own property, plant, and equipment for the purposes of the joint venture activities.

The assets remain under the ownership and control of each venturer. Each venturer also incurs its own expenses and liabilities and raises its own financing, which represents its own obligations. The joint venture activities may be carried out by the venturer's employees alongside the venturer's similar activities. The contractual arrangement usually provides a means by which the revenue from the sale of goods or performance of services by the joint venture, and any expenses incurred in common are shared among the venturers.

Jointly-Controlled Assets

24.11 Some joint ventures involve joint control, and often, joint ownership, by the venturers of one or more assets contributed to, or acquired for, the purpose of a joint venture and dedicated to the purposes of a joint venture. Jointly-controlled assets are used to obtain benefits for the venturers. Each venturer may take a share of the output from the assets, and each bears an agreed share of the expenses incurred. Such a joint venture does not involve the establishment of a corporation, partnership, or other entity or a financial structure that is separate from the venturers themselves.

Jointly-Controlled Entities

24.12 A *jointly-controlled entity* is a joint venture that involves the establishment of a corporation, partnership, or other entity in which each venturer has an interest. The entity operates in the same way as other entities, except that a contractual arrangement between the venturers establishes joint control over the economic activity of the entity.

24.13 In a jointly-controlled entity, each venturer usually contributes cash or other resources to the joint venture. The jointly-controlled entity owns the assets of the joint venture, incurs liabilities and expenses, and earns revenue. It may enter into contracts in its own name and raise financing for the purposes of the joint venture activity. Each venturer is entitled to a share of the income of the jointly-controlled entity, although some jointly-controlled entities also involve a sharing of the output of the joint venture. An example of a jointly-controlled entity is when two or more entities combine their activities in a particular line of business by transferring the relevant assets and liabilities into a jointly-controlled entity.

Recognition

24.14 A venturer should make an accounting policy choice to account for its interests in joint ventures using

    a. the equity method (see chapter 11); or

    b. the *proportionate consolidation* method, only applicable to unincorporated entities when it is an established industry practice.

All interests in joint ventures should be accounted for using the same method. Equity method investees normally should follow the same basis of accounting (that is, the FRF for SMEs accounting framework) as the investor. Accordingly, financial statements of equity method investees should be adjusted, if necessary, to conform with principles in the FRF for SMEs accounting framework, unless it is impracticable to do so.

Proportionate Consolidation

24.15 Accounting for an interest in jointly-controlled unincorporated operations, assets, or an interest in a jointly-controlled unincorporated entity using the proportionate consolidation method results in the venturer recognizing

   a. in its statement of financial position, the assets that it controls and the liabilities that it incurs; its share of the jointly-controlled assets and liabilities incurred jointly with the other venturers in relation to the joint venture; or its share of the assets and liabilities of the jointly-controlled joint venture; and

   b. in its statement of operations, its share of the revenue of the joint venture and its share of the expenses incurred by the joint venture, or any revenue from the sale or use of its share of the output of, and any expenses incurred by, the joint venture, or its share of the revenue and expenses of the joint venture.

24.16 To the extent that assets are transferred between a venturer and a joint venture, or services are performed by a venturer for the joint venture, the application of proportionate consolidation requires that the venturer's share of interentity transactions and interentity gains and losses be eliminated. The treatment of the portion of gains or losses on the contribution of assets to a joint venture or transactions between a venturer and a joint venture that relates to the interest of the other venturers is dealt with subsequently.

24.17 When an investor ceases to have joint control over a jointly-controlled entity, the investor ceases to proportionately consolidate its interest. Such interests are accounted for as investments (see chapter 11). Amounts reported on a proportionate consolidation basis for periods prior to the cessation of proportionate consolidation are not retroactively restated on a nonconsolidated basis.

24.18 An interest in a jointly-controlled entity that is intended for disposal should continue to be proportionately consolidated in the financial statements of the venturer until such time as the venturer ceases to have joint control over the jointly-controlled entity.

Presentation

24.19 The following should be presented separately in the statement of financial position:

   a. Interests in joint ventures accounted for using the equity method

   b. Assets and liabilities in joint ventures accounted for using the proportionate consolidation method as its share of each asset or liability, such as share of accounts receivable from joint venture activities

24.20 Income from participation in a joint venture in the following should be presented separately in the statement of operations:

   a. Interests in joint ventures accounted for using the equity method

FRF-SME 24.20

b. Interests in joint ventures accounted for using the proportionate consolidation method as a total of its share of the joint venture's revenue, gross profit, and other expenses categories

24.21 A significant factor when evaluating the investment income is the relationship of the income reported to the investments from which such income is derived. For this reason, investments reported in the statement of financial position and investment income reported in the statement of operations are grouped in the same way.

Disclosure

24.22 The basis used to account for an entity's interests in joint ventures should be disclosed.

24.23 A venturer should provide a listing and description of interests in significant joint ventures, including the names, business purposes, carrying amounts, and proportion of ownership interests held in each joint venture.

24.24 A venturer should disclose its share of any contingencies and commitments of joint ventures and those contingencies that exist when the venturer is contingently liable for the liabilities of the other venturers of the joint ventures.

24.25 If investments in common stock of *corporate joint ventures* are, in the aggregate, material in relation to the statement of financial position or statement of operations of an investor, it may be necessary for summarized information about assets, liabilities, and results of operations of the investees to be presented in the notes or in separate statements, either individually or in groups, as appropriate.

24.26 Separate disclosure of the venturer's share of any contingencies and commitments of joint ventures should include, as appropriate, the venturer's share of any contingencies and commitments of joint ventures and the venturer's responsibility for the other venturers' share of the contingencies of joint ventures. If a venturer guarantees more than its proportionate share of a joint venture's liabilities, such a guarantee should be disclosed.

24.27 When the fiscal periods of a venturer and a joint venture are not the same, events relating to, or transactions of, the joint venture that have occurred during the intervening period and significantly affect the financial position or results of operations of the entity should be disclosed. This disclosure is not necessary if these events or transactions are recorded in the financial statements.

Chapter 25

Leases

Purpose and Scope

25.01 This chapter establishes principles for methods of accounting for lease transactions and circumstances in which these methods are appropriate.

25.02 This chapter does not apply to licensing agreements for items such as motion pictures, videotapes, plays, manuscripts, patents, and copyrights (see chapter 13, "Intangible Assets").

Classification

25.03 This chapter classifies *leases*[1] as follows:

a. From the point of view of the lessee—capital and *operating leases*

b. From the point of view of the lessor—sales-type, direct financing, and operating leases

25.04 This chapter adopts the view that property has benefits and risks associated with its ownership. Benefits may be represented by the expectation of profitable operation over the property's economic life and gain from appreciation in value or realization of a residual value. Risks include possibilities of losses from idle capacity or technological obsolescence and variations in return due to changing economic conditions. This chapter adopts the view that a lease that transfers substantially all the benefits and risks of ownership to the lessee is, in substance, an acquisition of an asset and an incurrence of an obligation by the lessee and a sale or financing by the lessor.

25.05 From the point of view of a lessee, a lease normally transfers substantially all the benefits and risks of ownership to the lessee when, at the *inception of the lease*, one or more of the following conditions are present:

a. The terms of the lease result in ownership being transferred to the lessee by the end of the *lease term*, or the lease provides for a *bargain purchase option*.

b. The lease term is of such a duration that the lessee will receive substantially all the economic benefits expected to be derived from the use of the leased property over its remaining life span. Although the lease term may not be equal to the *economic life of the leased property* in terms of years, the lessee is normally expected to receive substantially all the economic benefits to be derived from the leased property when the lease term is equal to a substantial portion (usually 75 percent or more) of the remaining economic life of the leased property. This is due to the fact that new equipment, reflecting later technology and in prime

---

[1] Italicized terms are defined in the glossary.

condition, may be assumed to be more efficient than old equipment that has been subject to obsolescence and wear.

    c. The lessor is assured of recovering the investment in the leased property and earning a return on the investment as a result of the lease agreement. This condition exists if the present value at the beginning of the lease term of the *minimum lease payments*, excluding any portion thereof relating to *executory costs*, is equal to substantially all (usually 90 percent or more) of the market value of the leased property at the inception of the lease. When determining the present value, the discount rate used by the lessee is the lower of the *lessee's rate for incremental borrowing* and the *interest rate implicit in the lease*, if known.

In view of the fact that land normally has an indefinite useful life, it is not possible for the lessee to receive substantially all the benefits and risks associated with its ownership, unless there is reasonable assurance that ownership will pass to the lessee by the end of the lease term.

25.06 From the point of view of a lessor, a lease normally transfers substantially all the benefits and risks of ownership to the lessee when, at the inception of the lease, all the following conditions are present:

    a. Any one of the conditions in paragraph 25.05.

    b. The credit risk associated with the lease is normal when compared to the risk of collection of similar receivables.

    c. The amounts of any nonreimbursable costs that are probable to be incurred by the lessor under the lease can be reasonably estimated. If such costs are not reasonably estimable, the lessor may retain substantial risks in connection with the leased property. For example, this may occur when the lessor has a commitment to guarantee the performance of, or to effectively protect the lessee from obsolescence of, the leased property.

When assessing whether the condition set out in paragraph 25.05(c) exists, the discount rate used by the lessor is the interest rate implicit in the lease.

25.07 The existence of any of the following conditions, by themselves, is not sufficient evidence that substantially all the benefits and risks of ownership have been transferred to the lessee:

    a. Lessee pays cost incident to ownership. This condition is considered inappropriate because in virtually all leasing agreements, the lessee will either directly or indirectly pay such costs.

    b. Lessee has the option to purchase the asset for the lessor's unrecovered investment. This condition is considered inappropriate because there is no assurance that the lessee will exercise the option.

    c. Leased property is special purpose to the lessee. This condition is considered insufficient because the concept of special purpose is relative and difficult to define. In addition, the fact that the leased property is special purpose does not, in itself, evidence a transfer of substantially all the benefits and risks of asset ownership. Although it is expected that most lessors lease special purpose property only under terms that transfer substantially all of those benefits and risks to the lessee, nothing in the nature of special purpose property necessarily entails such terms.

    d. Lessee records the lease as a *capital lease* for federal income tax purposes.

25.08 A lease that transfers substantially all the benefits and risks of ownership related to the leased property from the lessor to the lessee should be accounted for as a capital lease by the lessee and as a sales-type or *direct financing lease* by the lessor.

25.09 A lease in which the benefits and risks of ownership related to the leased property are substantially retained by the lessor should be accounted for as an operating lease by the lessee and lessor.

25.10 A renewal, an extension, or a change in the provisions of an existing lease that was not contemplated in the original lease agreement should be treated as a new lease and classified in accordance with paragraphs 25.08–.09 (for a renewal or extension of an existing *sales-type lease*, see paragraph 25.42).

25.11 When the classification of a lease arising from a renewal, an extension, or a change in the provisions of an existing lease results in a capital lease being replaced by an operating lease, the asset and related obligation are removed from the accounts of the lessee. The net adjustment is included in income of the period. When the classification of the new lease is the same as the original lease, the asset and obligation related to the original lease are adjusted to conform to the recalculated balances.

25.12 When the classification of a lease arising from a renewal, an extension, or change in the provisions of an existing lease results in a sales-type or direct financing lease being replaced by an operating lease, the remaining net investment is removed from the accounts of the lessor and the leased asset recorded as an asset at the lower of its original cost, present market value, or present carrying amount. The net adjustment is included in income of the period.

Accounting Treatment by a Lessee

Method of Accounting for a Capital Lease

25.13 To report the total resources at the lessee's disposal and all aspects of the lessee's long-term obligations, a capital lease should be accounted for by the lessee as an acquisition of an asset and an assumption of an obligation.

25.14 The asset value and the amount of the obligation recorded at the beginning of the lease term are the present value of the minimum lease payments, excluding the portion thereof relating to executory costs. The amount relating to executory costs included in the minimum lease payments are estimated if not known to the lessee. The interest rate implicit in the lease is affected by the *residual value of the leased property* in which the lessee usually has no interest. As a result, to use the interest rate implicit in the lease as the discount rate when it is higher than the lessee's rate for incremental borrowing would produce an amount that is less representative of the value of the asset to the lessee than would be obtained by using the lessee's rate for incremental borrowing as the discount rate. Therefore, the discount rate used by the lessee when determining the present value of minimum lease payments should be the lower of the lessee's rate for incremental borrowing and the interest rate implicit in the lease, if practicable to determine. Notwithstanding the foregoing, the maximum value recorded for the asset and obligation may not exceed the leased asset's market value.

25.15 The capitalized value of a depreciable asset under a capital lease should be amortized over the period of expected use on a basis that is consistent with the lessee's depreciation policy for other similar fixed assets (see chapter 14, "Property, Plant, and Equipment"). If the lease contains terms that allow ownership to pass to the lessee or a bargain purchase option, the period of amortization should be the economic life of the asset. Otherwise, the property should be amortized over the lease term.

25.16 An obligation under a capital lease is similar to a loan. Lease payments should be allocated to a reduction of the obligation, interest expense, and any related executory costs. The interest expense is calculated using the discount rate used when computing the present value of the minimum lease payments applied to the remaining balance of the obligation.

25.17 A lessee that has a liability to a lessor under a capital lease should remove the liability from its statement of financial position when, and only when, it is extinguished (that is, when the obligation specified in the lease is discharged or cancelled).

25.18 *Contingent rentals* should be charged to expense as incurred.

Presentation of a Capital Lease

25.19 In order to distinguish between assets that the entity owns and those that it only has the right to use, assets leased under capital leases should be presented separately on the statement of financial position or in the notes to the financial statements.

25.20 Obligations related to leased assets should be presented separately from other long-term obligations on the statement of financial position or in the notes to the financial statements.

25.21 Any portion of lease obligations payable within a year out of current funds should be included in current liabilities.

Method of Accounting for an Operating Lease

25.22 Because of the nature of operating leases, charging lease rentals to expense on a straight-line basis over the lease term, even if not payable in such a manner, would normally result in recognition of the expense in a manner that is representative of the time pattern in which the user derives benefit from the leased property. However, circumstances may indicate that another basis is required to achieve this result.

25.23 The terms of a renegotiated lease are interdependent with those of the original lease. On renegotiation, a lessee should continue to account for the lease in accordance with the terms of the original lease contract until the original lease term expires. To the extent that the payments required under the renegotiated lease arrangement differ from those otherwise due under the original lease, the differences are considered to relate to the term of the lease extension.

25.24 Payments under a residual value guarantee are included in lease rentals when it becomes probable that the lessee will be required to honor the guarantee because the estimated value of the property at the end of the lease term is less than the residual value guaranteed by the lessee.

25.25 *Lease inducements* are an inseparable part of the lease agreement and, accordingly, are accounted for as reductions of the lease expense over the term of the lease.

25.26 Lease rentals under an operating lease should be included in the determination of net income over the lease term on a straight-line basis, unless another systematic and rational basis is more representative of the time pattern of the user's benefit. Increases in rentals under lease arrangements that include inflationary-type escalation clauses may be accounted for on an as-incurred basis, rather than a straight-line basis.

Accounting Treatment by a Lessor

Method of Accounting for a Direct Financing Lease

25.27 Direct financing leases normally arise when a lessor acts as a financing intermediary between a manufacturer or dealer and a lessee. Such leases give rise to income in the form of finance income.

25.28 Finance income arising on a direct financing lease is composed of the difference between

   a. the total minimum lease payments, net of any executory costs and related profit included therein, plus any *unguaranteed residual value* of the leased property accruing to the lessor and

   b. the carrying amount of the leased property.

25.29 A lessor enters into a direct financing lease with the intention of earning a return on funds invested in the lease transaction. When assessing whether proposed terms of a lease will produce an acceptable return on the required investment, a lessor considers the pattern of cash flows associated with the lease transaction. In some instances, the pattern of cash flows will be significantly affected by the fact that income taxes will be reduced as a result of an investment tax credit. When income tax elements that affect the cash flow are predictable with reasonable assurance, it may be appropriate to take these elements into consideration in accounting for income from the lease.

25.30 When income tax factors are taken into consideration in accounting for a direct financing lease, the lessor's initial and continuing investment in the lease, for purposes of income recognition, is the net of the balances of the following accounts:

   a. Minimum lease payments receivable, less any executory costs and related profit included therein

   b. The unguaranteed residual value of the lease property accruing to the lessor

   c. Unearned finance income, after deducting *initial direct costs*, remaining to be allocated to income over the lease term

FRF-SME 25.30

d. The investment tax credit remaining to be allocated to income over the lease term

25.31 When income tax factors are not taken into consideration in accounting for a direct financing lease, the lessor's initial and continuing investment in the lease, for purposes of income recognition, is the net balances of the accounts set out in paragraph 25.30(a)–(c).

25.32 When a lease is a direct financing lease, initial direct costs should be expensed as incurred, and a portion of unearned income equal to the initial direct costs should be recognized in income in the same period. The remaining unearned income should be deferred and taken into income over the lease term to produce a constant rate of return on the investment in the lease.

25.33 The estimated residual value is reviewed annually to determine whether a decline in its value has occurred. If the decline in value is other than temporary, the accounting for the lease transaction should be revised using the changed estimate. The resulting reduction in the net investment in the lease is charged to income. An upward adjustment of the residual value is not made.

Method of Accounting for a Sales-Type Lease

25.34 Sales-type leases normally arise when a manufacturer or dealer uses leasing to effect a sale of its products. Such lease transactions give rise to two types of income: the initial profit or loss on the sale of the product at the inception of the lease and finance income over the lease term.

25.35 The sales revenue recorded at the inception of a sales-type lease is the present value of the minimum lease payments net of any executory costs and related profit included therein, computed at the interest rate implicit in the lease. The cost of sale recognized at the inception of the lease is the carrying amount of the leased property reduced by the present value of the unguaranteed residual accruing to the lessor, computed at the interest rate implicit in the lease.

25.36 Finance income arising from a sales-type lease is composed of the difference between

   a. total minimum lease payments, net of any executory costs and related profit included therein, plus any unguaranteed residual value of the leased property accruing to the lessor and

   b. the aggregate of the present value of the minimum lease payments.

The discount rate for determining the present values is the interest rate implicit in the lease.

25.37 When it is appropriate to take income tax factors into consideration in accounting for a sales-type lease, the lessor's initial and continuing investment in a sales-type lease, for purposes of income recognition, is the net of the balances of the accounts set out in paragraph 25.30(a)–(d).

25.38 When income tax factors are not taken into consideration in accounting for a sales-type lease, the lessor's initial and continuing investment for purposes of recognizing unearned finance income in the lease is the net balances of the accounts set out in paragraph 25.30(a)–(c).

25.39 Initial direct costs are considered to be incurred in order to produce the sale; therefore, they are recognized as an expense at the inception of the lease.

25.40 When a lease is a sales-type lease, a sale should be recorded with the manufacturer's or dealer's profit or loss being recognized at the time of the transaction. Unearned finance income should be deferred and taken into income over the lease term to produce a constant rate of return on the investment in the lease.

25.41 The estimated residual value is reviewed annually to determine whether a decline in its value has occurred. If the decline in value is other than temporary, the accounting for the lease transaction should be revised using the changed estimate. The resulting reduction in the net investment in the lease is charged to income. An upward adjustment of the residual value is not made.

25.42 Providing it transfers substantially all the benefits and risks of ownership related to the leased property from the lessor to the lessee, a renewal or an extension of an existing sales-type lease should be classified as a direct financing lease because the manufacturer's or dealer's profit will have been recognized at the inception of the original lease.

Collectability and Recoverability Issues

25.43 At the end of each reporting period, management should assess whether there are any indications that each direct financing lease, sales-type lease, operating lease receivables (the lease asset), or group of similar lease assets are not collectible or recoverable. When there is an indication of collectability or recoverability issues, management should determine whether a significant adverse change has occurred during the period in the expected timing or amount of future cash flows from the lease asset or group of lease assets.

25.44 Indicators of collectability or recoverability issues include

    a. significant financial difficulty of the lessee;

    b. a breach of contract, such as a default or delinquency in payment;

    c. the entity granting a concession to the lessee;

    d. the probability that the lessee will enter bankruptcy or other financial reorganization; and

    e. a significant adverse change in the technological, market, economic, or legal environment in which the lessee operates. (For example, a sharp decline in the price of a commodity may cause economic instability in the lessee's industry or have an adverse effect on other entities in a region that is dependent on the lessee's industry.)

25.45 When management identifies a significant adverse change in the expected timing or amount of future cash flows from a lease asset, or group of similar lease assets, it should reduce the carrying amount of the asset, or group of assets, to the highest of the following:

    a. The present value of the cash flows expected to be generated by holding the lease asset, discounted using a current market rate of interest appropriate to the asset

b. The amount that could be realized by selling the lease at the statement of financial position date net of disposal costs

The carrying amount of the lease asset, or group of assets, should be reduced directly or through the use of an allowance account.

Presentation of a Direct Financing or Sales-Type Lease

25.46 The result of these types of lease transactions is to create a long-term receivable, although the lessor may also hold an interest in the residual value of an asset under lease. As a consequence, the net investment in the lease is considered to be distinct from other assets and presented separately.

25.47 For purposes of statement presentation, the lessor's net investment in the lease includes

  a. the minimum lease payments receivable, less any executory costs and related profit included therein; plus
  b. any unguaranteed residual value of the leased property accruing to the lessor; less
  c. unearned finance income remaining to be allocated to income over the lease term.

25.48 When income tax factors have been considered in accounting for a direct financing or sales-type lease, any unamortized investment tax credit should either be deducted in computing the net investment in the lease or shown as a deferred credit. Deferred income taxes, if any, relating to the net investment in the lease are presented separately from the net investment in accordance with paragraph 21.55.

25.49 The lessor's net investment in direct financing and sales-type leases should be segregated between current and long-term portions in a classified statement of financial position.

Method of Accounting for an Operating Lease

25.50 Rental revenue from an operating lease should be recognized as income over the term of the lease as it becomes due. However, if rentals vary from a straight-line basis, the income should be recognized on a straight-line basis unless another systematic and rational basis is more representative of the time pattern in which the benefit from the leased property is utilized.

25.51 When initial direct costs are associated with a specific lease agreement, the costs are applicable to all revenue earned during the lease term and should be deferred and amortized over the lease term in proportion to the recognition of rental income.

Participation by a Third Party

25.52 The terms of either an assignment of lease payments due under an operating lease or a sale of property that is already, or that is intended to be, subject to an operating lease may result in the assignee or purchaser being given an effective guarantee that the investment will be recovered. For example, the terms of the transaction provide that in the case of default by the lessee or termination of the lease, the seller must reacquire the property, substitute an existing lease, or give priority to securing a replacement lessee or buyer under a remarketing agreement. When the substance of a transaction is such that the purchaser looks to the seller, rather than to the property or lease in order to recover his investment, the transaction is regarded as a secured loan by both parties because the seller or assignor has retained substantial risks of ownership.

25.53 An assignment of lease payments due under an operating lease or a sale of property that is already, or that is intended to be, subject to an operating lease should be accounted for as a loan whenever the assignor or seller retains substantial risks of ownership in connection with the leased property.

25.54 When a sale of property that is already, or that is intended to be, subject to an operating lease is classified as a secured loan, the seller should record the proceeds of sale as a loan. The interest rate applicable to the loan is that which an unrelated lender would negotiate with the lessor for a loan under similar terms and conditions. Until the loan is paid, the seller records as revenue rental payments made by the lessee, even if such rentals are paid directly to the third party purchaser, and records as interest expense an appropriate portion of each rental payment with the remainder reducing the amount of the loan. The asset is depreciated over the amortization period of the loan. The assignment by the lessor of lease payments due under an operating lease should be accounted for as a loan.

25.55 A sale of property already subject to a sales-type or direct financing lease, or an assignment of lease payments due under a sales-type or direct financing lease, does not negate the original accounting treatment of the lease.

Subleases

25.56 When leased property is subleased by the original lessee to a third party, the sublease is evaluated by both parties in accordance with paragraphs 25.08–.09. There is no effect on the accounting treatment of the obligation under the original lease.

Sale-Leaseback Transaction

25.57 A *sale-leaseback transaction* involves the sale of property with the purchaser concurrently leasing the same property back to the seller.

25.58 In a sale-leaseback transaction, the lease should be accounted for as a capital, direct financing, or operating lease, as appropriate, by the seller-lessee and the purchaser-lessor.

25.59 In view of the interdependence of the terms and the inability to objectively and practically separate the sale and lease, any profit or loss arising on the sale is generally deferred and taken to income over the lease term. However, when the leaseback is of a portion of the remaining use of the property sold, it may be possible to separate the accounting aspects of the terms of the sale and the lease. The 'portion' may be a part of the property, such as one floor of an office tower, or may consist of a portion of the property's remaining economic life, such as 3 years of an estimated life of 10 years. In substance, such a leaseback is not a lease of the same property as that sold to the purchaser-lessor.

25.60 Except as noted in paragraph 25.64, when the leaseback is classified as a capital lease, any profit or loss arising on the sale should be deferred and amortized in proportion to the amortization of the leased asset, except for leases involving land only, in which case, it should be amortized over the lease term on a straight-line basis.

25.61 Except as noted in paragraph 25.64, when the leaseback is classified as an operating lease, any profit or loss arising on the sale should be deferred and amortized in proportion to rental payments over the lease term.

25.62 When the seller-lessee retains the right to only a minor portion of the property sold, the sale and leaseback is accounted for as separate transactions based on their respective terms. The entire gain or loss is included in the determination of net income at the date of the sale unless the amount of rentals called for by the lease is unreasonable under market conditions at the inception of the lease. In these circumstances, an appropriate amount is deferred or accrued by adjusting the profit or loss on the sale and amortized to adjust those rentals to a reasonable amount. If the present value of the minimum lease payments represents 10 percent or less of the market value of the asset sold, the seller-lessee could be presumed to have transferred to the purchaser-lessor the right to substantially all the remaining use of the property sold, and the seller-lessee could be presumed to have retained only a minor portion of such use.

25.63 When the seller-lessee retains the right to more than a minor portion of the property but less than substantially all the property, the amount of the gain or loss included in the determination of net income immediately is equal to the excess, if any, of the gain on sale over

    a. the present value of the minimum lease payments over the lease term, if the leaseback is classified as an operating lease or

    b. the recorded amount of the leased asset, if the leaseback is classified as a capital lease.

25.64 When, at the time of the sale-leaseback transaction, the market value of the property is less than its carrying amount, the difference should be recognized as a loss immediately.

Leases Involving Land and Buildings

25.65 Under a capital lease, the terms of which allow ownership to pass or provide for a bargain purchase option, a lessee should capitalize the land separately from building(s) in proportion to their market values at the inception of the lease.

25.66 When a lease involving land and building(s) does not contain terms that allow ownership to pass or provide for a bargain purchase option, and the market value of land at the inception of the lease is minor in relation to the total market value of the leased property, the land and the building(s) are considered a single unit for the purposes of classification of the lease. The economic life of the building(s) is considered the economic life of the unit.

25.67 When a lease involving land and building(s) does not contain terms that allow the ownership to pass or provide for a bargain purchase option, and the market value of land at the inception of the lease is significant in relation to the total market value of the leased property, the land and building(s) are considered separately for purposes of classification. The lessee and lessor allocate the minimum lease payments between the land and building(s) in proportion to their market values. Both parties classify the portion of the lease applicable to land as an operating lease.

Related Party Leases

25.68 Lease transactions between related parties should be accounted for and classified in accordance with the terms of the lease agreement and the provisions of this chapter, similar to other leases.

Disclosure

Capital Lease—Lessee

25.69 For each major category of leased property, plant, and equipment, there should be disclosure of

   a. cost;

   b. accumulated amortization, including the amount of any write-downs; and

   c. the amortization method used, including the amortization period or rate.

25.70 For an obligation under a capital lease, an entity should disclose

   a. the interest rate;

   b. the maturity date;

   c. the amount outstanding; and

   d. if the leases are secured, the fact that they are secured.

25.71 Interest expense related to lease obligations should be disclosed separately or as part of interest on long-term indebtedness.

25.72 The aggregate amount of payments estimated to be required in each of the next five years to meet repayment, sinking fund, or retirement provisions should be disclosed.

Operating Lease—Lessee

25.73 Disclosure should be made of the future minimum lease payments in the aggregate and for each of the five succeeding years under operating leases. In addition, rent expense for each period presented in the financial statements should be disclosed. The nature of other commitments under such leases should also be described. Leases with an initial term of one year or less may be excluded from this disclosure requirement.

Direct Financing or Sales-Type Lease—Lessor

25.74 The lessor's net investment in direct financing and sales-type leases should be disclosed, along with the interest rates implicit in the leases.

Operating Lease—Lessor

25.75 Disclosure should be made of the cost of property, plant, and equipment held for leasing purposes and the amount of accumulated depreciation.

Chapter 26

Related Party Transactions

Purpose and Scope

26.01 This chapter establishes principles for the measurement and disclosure of related party transactions in the financial statements.

26.02 This chapter does not apply to management compensation arrangements, including retirement and other postemployment benefits accounted for in accordance with chapter 20, "Retirement and Other Postemployment Benefits," expense allowances, and other similar payments, including loans and receivables, to individuals, in the normal course of operations.

Identification of Related Parties

26.03 The most commonly encountered *related parties*[1] of a reporting entity include the following:

a. An entity that directly or indirectly, through one or more intermediaries, controls, is controlled by, or is under common control with, the reporting entity.

b. An individual who directly, or indirectly through one or more intermediaries, controls the reporting entity.

c. The other party, when an investment is accounted for by the equity or the proportionate consolidation method and the reporting entity, is either the investor or the investee.

d. Management. Any person(s) having authority and responsibility for planning, directing, and controlling the activities of the reporting entity. (In the case of a company, management includes the directors, officers, and other persons fulfilling a senior management function. When an independent committee of the board of directors is established in accordance with regulatory requirements to represent the noncontrolling interests of an entity, the directors serving on that committee are deemed not to be related parties for the transaction under consideration.)

e. An individual having an ownership interest in the reporting entity that results in *significant influence* or joint *control*.

f. Members of the immediate family of individuals described in (b), (d), and (e). (Immediate family comprises an individual's spouse and those dependent on either the individual or the individual's spouse.)

g. The other party, when a management contract or other management authority exists, and the reporting entity is either the managing or managed party.

---

[1] Italicized terms are defined in the glossary.

h. Any party that is subject to significant influence, whether by reason of an ownership interest, management contract, or other management authority, by another party that also has significant influence over the reporting entity.

i. Any party that is subject to *joint control* by the reporting entity. (In this instance, a party subject to joint control is related to each of the venturers that share that joint control. However, the venturers themselves are not related to one another solely by virtue of sharing of joint control.)

26.04 A transaction between a venturer and a joint venture involving the exchange of an asset for an interest in the joint venture is considered to be a transaction between the venturers. When the venturers are unrelated, such a transaction is not a *related party transaction*.

26.05 The degree of influence that one party may exert on another is a major factor in determining whether they are related. In some cases, the degree of influence may be so remote that they need not be considered related. For example, two companies may be unrelated, even though one director serves on the board of each company; in such a case, the degree of influence exercised by the director over the strategic policies of each company determines whether the companies are related.

26.06 Management should make reasonable efforts to identify all related parties. Circumstances that might indicate the existence of related parties include abnormal terms of trade or transactions not normally entered into by the reporting entity. When identifying related parties, management takes into account any beneficial ownership of an entity that it knows is held through nominees. When management has identified circumstances indicating that the other party to a transaction may be related, management has a responsibility to ascertain whether that party is, indeed, related.

Measurement

26.07 A related party transaction that occurs in the ordinary course of business should be measured in the same manner as the transaction would have been measured if it took place between unrelated parties. A related party transaction that does not occur in the ordinary course of business should be measured at the carrying amount, unless there is objective third-party evidence supporting the market value of what was exchanged in the transaction (for example, market value of the asset received or transferred).

Disclosure

26.08 An entity should disclose the following information about its transactions with related parties:

a. A description of the relationship between the transacting parties

b. A description of the transaction(s), including those for which no amount has been recognized

c. The recognized amount of the transactions classified by financial statement category

d. The measurement basis used

Related Party Transactions

    e. Amounts due to, or from, related parties and the terms and conditions relating thereto

    f. Commitments with related parties, separate from other commitments

    g. Contingencies involving related parties, separate from other contingencies

26.09 Information about related party transactions is often of more significance to a financial statement user than information about unrelated party transactions, regardless of the size of such transactions.

Description of Relationship

26.10 Terms such as *affiliate*, *associate*, and *related company* are insufficiently precise to describe relationships. With additional explanation, the effect of the related party relationship on the entity is more understandable. Terms such as *controlled investee, significantly influenced investee, jointly-controlled entity, common control entity, management, shareholder, member of the immediate family of the shareholder or management,* and *director* describe the relationships better.

Description of Transaction

26.11 A clear description of a related party transaction that sets out the significance of the transaction to the operations of the entity clarifies the effects of the transaction on the entity. Such a description includes information about the nature of the items exchanged and whether the exchange is in the normal course of operations.

26.12 An exchange of goods or services between related parties that has not been given accounting recognition is also a related party transaction. For example, an entity may provide a related party with management services or use of a patent or license in the normal course of operations without receiving consideration in exchange. An explanation of the nature of such a transaction and the fact that no consideration has been received or paid is useful to explain the effect of the transaction on the entity.

Amount of Transactions

26.13 To convey the extent of related party transactions, the recognized amounts of such transactions are disclosed. Disclosure of information aggregated by financial statement category (for example, revenue, purchases, major operating costs, interest expense or income, and management fee income or expense) and nature of relationship is more useful than disclosure of individual transactions with related parties, except for individually significant transactions.

Representations About Market Value

26.14 Representations that the exchange amount is equivalent to market value (or an arm's length equivalent value) should not be made unless they can be substantiated. When an entity has undertaken a related party transaction on the same terms as current transactions with unrelated parties with similar volumes, terms, and conditions, that fact should be disclosed. In many cases, a market value cannot be determined unless there are identical transactions, and the values of the items exchanged are determined by the market.

Additional Disclosures

26.15 Entities should comply with disclosure requirements in the following chapters:

    a. Chapter 11, "Equity, Debt, and Other Investments." See disclosures applicable to the equity method of accounting for investments.

    b. Chapter 17, "Contingencies." Some guarantees are issued to benefit entities that meet the definition of a related party, such as joint ventures and equity method investees. In those cases, the disclosures required in the "Guarantees" section of chapter 17 may be in addition to the disclosures required by this chapter.

    c. Chapter 28, "Business Combinations." See the requirements in the "Combinations of Entities Under Common Control" section of chapter 28.

    d. Chapter 18, "Equity." See the requirements in the "Limited Liability Entities" section of chapter 18.

Chapter 27

Subsequent Events

Purpose and Scope

27.01 This chapter establishes recognition and disclosure principles for events subsequent to the financial statement date.

27.02 Financial statements are prepared to reflect the financial position at a particular date and the operating results and cash flows for a period ended on that date. However, events occurring after the financial statement date may indicate a need to adjust amounts or make specific disclosures in those statements. Therefore, when preparing financial statements, the implications and financial effects of subsequent events should be considered.

27.03 In general, there are two types of subsequent events:

   a. Those that provide further evidence of conditions that existed at the financial statement date

   b. Those that are indicative of conditions that arose subsequent to the financial statement date

The extent to which, and the manner in which, the effect of a subsequent event is reflected in the financial statements will depend on its type.

27.04 The effect of subsequent events may be so pervasive, however, that the viability of the whole, or a part, of the business of the entity is brought into question. A rapid deterioration in operating results or financial position after the date of the financial statements may indicate a need to consider whether it is proper to use the going concern assumption.

Accounting Treatment

27.05 Financial statements should be adjusted when events occurring between the date of the financial statements and the date the financial statements are available to be issued provide additional evidence relating to conditions that existed at the date of the financial statements.

27.06 Subsequent events may provide additional information relating to items included in the financial statements and may reveal conditions existing at the financial statement date that affect the estimates involved in the preparation of financial statements. All such information that becomes available prior to the date the financial statements are available to be issued should be used when evaluating the estimates made, and the financial statements should be adjusted where necessary. For example, the institution of bankruptcy proceedings against a debtor subsequent to the date of the financial statements may be indicative of the underlying financial situation of the debtor at the date of the financial statements. If the provision for that debt was inadequate, adjustment of the financial statements is required.

27.07 Financial statements are available to be issued when

   a. a complete set of financial statements, including all required note disclosures, has been prepared (see paragraphs 2.10–.12);

FRF-SME 27.07

  b. all final adjusting journal entries have been reflected in the financial statements (for example, adjustments for income taxes and bonuses);

  c. no changes to the financial statements are planned or expected; and

  d. the financial statements meeting the preceding requirements have been approved in accordance with the entity's process to finalize its financial statements.

27.08 Financial statements should not be adjusted for those events occurring between the date of the financial statements and the date the financial statements are available to be issued that do not relate to conditions that existed at the date of the financial statements.

27.09 Adjustment of the financial statements for subsequent events is not appropriate if such events do not relate to conditions existing at the financial statement date. To reflect the effect of such events would not be consistent with the concept that a statement of financial position represents the financial position of an entity at the financial statement date.

Disclosure

27.10 Disclosure should be made of the date through which subsequent events have been evaluated and the fact that this is the date that the financial statements were available to be issued.

27.11 Disclosure should be made of those events occurring between the date of the financial statements and the date the financial statements are available to be issued that do not relate to conditions that existed at the date of the financial statements but are of such a nature that they should be disclosed to keep the financial statements from being misleading.

27.12 At a minimum, the disclosure required by paragraph 27.11 should include

  a. a description of the nature of the event and

  b. an estimate of the financial effect, when practicable, or a statement that such an estimate cannot be made.

27.13 Examples of events described in paragraph 27.11 include

  a. an event, such as a fire or flood, that results in a loss;

  b. a decline in the market value of investments;

  c. purchase of a business;

  d. commencement of litigation when the cause of action arose subsequent to the date of the financial statements;

  e. changes in foreign currency exchange rates; and

  f. the issue of capital stock or long-term debt.

Chapter 28

Business Combinations

Purpose and Scope

28.01 This chapter establishes principles and requirements for how the *acquirer*[1]

 a. recognizes and measures in its financial statements the *identifiable* assets acquired, the liabilities assumed, and any *noncontrolling interest* in the *acquiree*;

 b. recognizes and measures the goodwill acquired in the *business combination* or a gain from a bargain purchase; and

 c. determines what information to disclose to enable users of the financial statements to evaluate the nature and financial effects of the business combination.

28.02 This chapter applies to a transaction or other event that meets the definition of a business combination and to combinations of entities under common control. This chapter does not apply to

 a. the formation of a joint venture.

 b. the acquisition of an asset, or a group of assets, that does not constitute a *business*.

Identifying a Business Combination

28.03 Management should determine whether a transaction or other event is a business combination by applying the definition in this chapter, which requires that the assets acquired and liabilities assumed constitute a business. If the assets acquired are not a business, the reporting entity should account for the transaction or other event as an asset acquisition. In such cases, the acquirer should identify and recognize the individual identifiable assets acquired (including those assets that meet the definition of, and recognition criteria for, intangible assets in chapter 13, "Intangible Assets") and liabilities assumed. The transaction cost should be allocated to the individual identifiable assets and liabilities on the basis of their relative market values at the date of purchase. Such a transaction or event does not give rise to goodwill.

The Acquisition Method

28.04 Management should account for each business combination by applying the acquisition method.

28.05 Applying the acquisition method requires

 a. identifying the acquirer;

 b. determining the *acquisition date*;

---

[1] Italicized terms are defined in the glossary.

c. recognizing and measuring the identifiable assets acquired, the liabilities assumed, and any noncontrolling interest in the acquiree; and

d. recognizing and measuring goodwill or a gain from a bargain purchase.

Identifying the Acquirer

28.06 For each business combination, one of the combining entities should be identified as the acquirer.

Determining the Acquisition Date

28.07 The acquirer should identify the acquisition date, which is the date it obtains *control* of the acquiree.

28.08 The date the acquirer obtains control of the acquiree is generally the date the acquirer legally transfers the consideration, acquires the assets, and assumes the liabilities of the acquiree—the closing date. However, the acquirer might obtain control on a date that is either earlier or later than the closing date. For example, the acquisition date precedes the closing date if a written agreement provides that the acquirer obtains control of the acquiree on a date before the closing date. An acquirer should consider all pertinent facts and circumstances when identifying the acquisition date.

Recognizing and Measuring the Identifiable Assets Acquired, Liabilities Assumed, and Any Noncontrolling Interest in the Acquiree

Recognition Principle

28.09 As of the acquisition date, the acquirer should recognize, separately from goodwill, the identifiable assets acquired, the liabilities assumed, and any noncontrolling interest in the acquiree. Recognition of identifiable assets acquired and liabilities assumed is subject to the conditions specified in paragraphs 28.10–.11.

Recognition Conditions

28.10 To qualify for recognition, the identifiable assets acquired and liabilities assumed must meet the definitions of assets and liabilities in chapter 1, "Financial Statement Concepts," at the acquisition date. For example, costs the acquirer expects, but is not obliged to incur in the future, to effect its plan to exit an activity of an acquiree or terminate the employment of or relocate an acquiree's employees are not liabilities at the acquisition date. Therefore, the acquirer does not recognize those costs as part of applying the acquisition method. Instead, the acquirer recognizes those costs in its postcombination financial statements in accordance with other chapters.

Business Combinations

28.11 In addition, to qualify for recognition, the identifiable assets acquired and liabilities assumed must be part of what the acquirer and the acquiree (or its former owners) exchanged in the business combination transaction, rather than the result of separate transactions. The acquirer should apply the guidance in paragraphs 28.47–.48 to determine which assets acquired or liabilities assumed are part of the exchange for the acquiree and which, if any, are the result of separate transactions to be accounted for in accordance with their nature and the applicable chapters.

28.12 The acquirer's application of the recognition principle and conditions may result in recognizing some assets and liabilities that the acquiree had not previously recognized as assets and liabilities in its financial statements. For example, the acquirer may recognize the acquired identifiable intangible assets, such as a brand name, a patent, or a customer relationship, that the acquiree did not recognize as assets in its financial statements because it developed them internally and charged the related costs to expense.

Classifying or Designating Identifiable Assets Acquired and Liabilities Assumed in a Business Combination

28.13 At the acquisition date, the acquirer should classify or designate the identifiable assets acquired and liabilities assumed as necessary to apply other chapters subsequently. The acquirer should make those classifications or designations on the basis of the contractual terms, economic conditions, its operating or accounting policies, and other pertinent conditions as they exist at the acquisition date.

28.14 In some situations, other chapters provide for different accounting, depending on how an entity classifies or designates a particular asset or liability.

Measurement Principle

28.15 The acquirer should measure the identifiable assets acquired and the liabilities assumed at their acquisition-date market values.

28.16 For each business combination, the acquirer should measure any noncontrolling interest in the acquiree at the noncontrolling interest's proportionate share of the acquiree's identifiable net assets.

Exceptions to the Recognition and Measurement Principles

28.17 This chapter provides limited exceptions to its recognition and measurement principles. Paragraphs 28.18–.27 specify both the particular items for which exceptions are provided and the nature of those exceptions. The acquirer should account for those items by applying the requirements in paragraphs 28.18–.27, which will result in some items being

    a. recognized either by applying recognition conditions in addition to those in paragraphs 28.09–.10 or by applying the requirements of other chapters, with results that differ from applying the recognition principle and conditions and

    b. measured at an amount other than their acquisition-date market values.

Exceptions to Both the Recognition and Measurement Principles

Intangible Assets

28.18 An entity should make an accounting policy choice to account for intangible assets acquired in a business combination either by

   a. separately recognizing the intangible asset as an identifiable asset or

   b. not separately recognizing the intangible asset as an identifiable asset and subsuming into goodwill the value of the intangible asset.

28.19 For an intangible asset to be separately recognized as an identifiable asset, its acquisition-date market value should be measured reliably. The acquirer should assign a useful life to the recognized identifiable intangible asset. When the precise length of an intangible asset's useful life is not known, the acquirer should estimate its useful life. Guidance for determining the useful life of an intangible asset is provided in paragraph 13.58. If the acquirer cannot reliably measure the acquisition-date market value of the intangible asset or cannot estimate its useful life, then separate recognition of the intangible asset as an identifiable asset is not permitted and the value of the intangible asset should be subsumed into goodwill.

28.20 The accounting policy option in paragraph 28.18 may be made on an individual intangible asset basis. Once made, the accounting policy chosen for a specific intangible asset cannot be subsequently reversed.

Asset Retirement Obligations

28.21 The acquirer should recognize and measure an asset retirement obligation associated with the assets acquired in a business combination in accordance with the section, "Asset Retirement Obligations," in chapter 17, "Contingencies."

Income Taxes

28.22 If the acquirer uses the deferred income taxes method of accounting for income taxes, then it should recognize and measure a deferred income tax asset or liability arising from the assets acquired and liabilities assumed in a business combination in accordance with chapter 21, "Income Taxes."

28.23 If the acquirer uses the deferred income taxes method of accounting for income taxes, then it should account for the potential tax effects of temporary differences and carryforwards of an acquiree that exist at the acquisition date or arise as a result of the acquisition in accordance with chapter 21.

Employee Benefits

28.24 The accrued benefit obligation is calculated using best estimate assumptions consistent with those that will be used on a going-forward basis in accordance with chapter 20, "Retirement and Other Postemployment Benefits." Similarly, plan assets are valued at market value in accordance with chapter 20. Any previously existing, unamortized net actuarial gain (loss), unamortized prior service cost, unamortized transitional obligation, or unamortized transitional asset is eliminated with the result that the accrued benefit asset or accrued benefit liability is the difference between the accrued benefit obligation and the market value of plan assets. The carrying amount of an accrued benefit asset in the acquired entity's financial statements may need to be reduced when the acquirer expects limitations on its ability to access a plan excess as a result of existing regulations of the relevant jurisdiction and the plan.

Indemnification Assets

28.25 The seller in a business combination may contractually indemnify the acquirer for the outcome of a contingency or uncertainty related to all or part of a specific asset or liability. For example, the seller may indemnify the acquirer against losses above a specified amount on a liability arising from a particular contingency; in other words, the seller will guarantee that the acquirer's liability will not exceed a specified amount. As a result, the acquirer obtains an indemnification asset. The acquirer should recognize an indemnification asset at the same time it recognizes the indemnified item measured on the same basis as the indemnified item. Therefore, if the indemnification relates to an asset or liability that is recognized at the acquisition date and measured at its acquisition-date market value, the acquirer should recognize the indemnification asset at the acquisition date measured at its acquisition-date market value.

28.26 In some circumstances, the indemnification may relate to an asset or a liability that is an exception to the recognition or measurement principles. In those circumstances, the indemnification asset should be recognized and measured using assumptions consistent with those used to measure the indemnified item, subject to management's assessment of the collectability of the indemnification asset and any contractual limitations on the indemnified amount. Paragraph 28.51 provides guidance on the subsequent accounting for an indemnification asset.

Exceptions to the Measurement Principle

Assets Held for Sale

28.27 The acquirer should measure an acquired noncurrent asset (or disposal group) that is classified as held for sale at the acquisition date in accordance with chapter 15, "Disposal of Long-Lived Assets and Discontinued Operations."

Recognizing and Measuring Goodwill or a Gain From a Bargain Purchase

28.28 The acquirer should recognize goodwill[2] as of the acquisition date measured as the excess of (a) over (b) as follows:

    a. The aggregate of

        i. the consideration transferred, measured in accordance with this chapter, which generally requires acquisition-date market value (see paragraph 28.33);

---

[2] For guidance on the subsequent accounting and amortization of goodwill, see paragraphs 13.59–.61.

ii. the amount of any noncontrolling interest in the acquiree measured in accordance with this chapter; and

iii. in a business combination achieved in stages (see paragraphs 28.37–.38), the acquisition-date market value of the acquirer's previously held equity interest in the acquiree

b. The net of the acquisition-date amounts of the identifiable assets acquired and the liabilities assumed measured in accordance with this chapter.

28.29 In a business combination in which the acquirer and the acquiree (or its former owners) exchange only equity interests, the acquisition-date market value of the acquiree's *equity interests* may be more reliably measurable than the acquisition-date market value of the acquirer's equity interests. If so, the acquirer should determine the amount of goodwill by using the acquisition-date market value of the acquiree's equity interests instead of the acquisition-date market value of the equity interests transferred. To determine the amount of goodwill in a business combination in which no consideration is transferred, the acquirer should use the acquisition-date market value of the acquirer's interest in the acquiree, determined using a valuation technique in place of the acquisition-date market value of the consideration transferred.

Bargain Purchases

28.30 Occasionally, an acquirer will make a bargain purchase, which is a business combination in which the amount in paragraph 28.28(b) exceeds the aggregate of the amounts specified in paragraph 28.28(a). If that excess remains after applying the requirements in paragraph 28.32, the acquirer should recognize the resulting gain in net income on the acquisition date. The gain should be attributed to the acquirer.

28.31 A bargain purchase might happen, for example, in a business combination that is a forced sale in which the seller is acting under compulsion. However, the recognition or measurement exceptions for particular items discussed in paragraphs 28.18–.27 may also result in recognizing a gain (or change the amount of a recognized gain) on a bargain purchase.

28.32 Before recognizing a gain on a bargain purchase, the acquirer should reassess whether it has correctly identified all the assets acquired and all the liabilities assumed and should recognize any additional assets or liabilities that are identified in that review. The acquirer should then review the procedures used to measure the amounts this chapter requires to be recognized at the acquisition date for all of the following:

a. The identifiable assets acquired and liabilities assumed

b. The noncontrolling interest in the acquiree, if any

c. For a business combination achieved in stages, the acquirer's previously held equity interest in the acquiree

d. The consideration transferred

The objective of the review is to ensure that the measurements appropriately reflect consideration of all available information as of the acquisition date.

Consideration Transferred

28.33 The consideration transferred in a business combination should be measured at market value, which should be calculated as the sum of the acquisition-date market values of the assets transferred by the acquirer, the liabilities incurred by the acquirer to former owners of the acquiree, and the equity interests issued by the acquirer.

28.34 The consideration transferred may include assets or liabilities of the acquirer that have carrying amounts that differ from their market values at the acquisition date (for example, nonmonetary assets or a business of the acquirer). If so, the acquirer should remeasure the transferred assets or liabilities to their market values as of the acquisition date and recognize the resulting gains or losses, if any, in net income. However, sometimes the transferred assets or liabilities remain within the combined entity after the business combination (for example, because the assets or liabilities were transferred to the acquiree rather than to its former owners) and, therefore, the acquirer retains control of them. In that situation, the acquirer should measure those assets and liabilities at their carrying amounts immediately before the acquisition date and should not recognize a gain or loss in net income on assets or liabilities it controls both before and after the business combination.

Contingent Consideration

28.35 The consideration the acquirer transfers in exchange for the acquiree includes any asset or liability resulting from a contingent consideration arrangement. The acquirer should recognize *contingent consideration* when its payment or receipt is probable and reasonably estimable.

28.36 The acquirer should classify an obligation to pay contingent consideration as a liability or as equity on the basis of the definitions of an equity instrument and a financial liability. The acquirer should classify as an asset a right to the return of previously transferred consideration.

Additional Guidance for Applying the Acquisition Method to Particular Types of Business Combinations

A Business Combination Achieved in Stages

28.37 An acquirer sometimes obtains control of an acquiree in which it held an equity interest immediately before the acquisition date. For example, on December 31, 20X1, entity A holds a 35-percent noncontrolling equity interest in entity B. On that date, entity A purchases an additional 40-percent interest in entity B, which gives it control of entity B. This chapter refers to such a transaction as a *business combination achieved in stages*, sometimes also referred to as a *step acquisition*.

28.38 In a business combination achieved in stages, the acquirer should remeasure its previously held equity interest in the acquiree at its acquisition-date market value and recognize the resulting gain or loss, if any, in net income.

A Business Combination Achieved Without the Transfer of Consideration

28.39 An acquirer sometimes obtains control of an acquiree without transferring consideration. The acquisition method of accounting for a business combination applies to those combinations. Such circumstances include the following:

   a. The acquiree repurchases a sufficient number of its own shares for an existing investor (the acquirer) to obtain control.

   b. Minority veto rights, which previously kept the acquirer from controlling an acquiree in which the acquirer held the majority voting rights, lapse.

   c. The acquirer and acquiree agree to combine their businesses by contract alone. The acquirer transfers no consideration in exchange for control of an acquiree and holds no equity interests in the acquiree, either on the acquisition date or previously.

28.40 In a business combination achieved by contract alone, the acquirer should attribute to the owners of the acquiree the amount of the acquiree's net assets recognized in accordance with this chapter. In other words, the equity interests in the acquiree held by parties other than the acquirer are a noncontrolling interest in the acquirer's postcombination financial statements, even if the result is that all the equity interests in the acquiree are attributed to the noncontrolling interest.

Measurement Period

28.41 If the initial accounting for a business combination is incomplete by the end of the reporting period in which the combination occurs, the acquirer should report in its financial statements provisional amounts for the items for which the accounting is incomplete. During the *measurement period*, the acquirer should retrospectively adjust the provisional amounts recognized at the acquisition date to reflect new information obtained about facts and circumstances that existed as of the acquisition date and, if known, would have affected the measurement of the amounts recognized as of that date. During the measurement period, the acquirer should also recognize additional assets or liabilities if new information is obtained about facts and circumstances that existed as of the acquisition date and, if known, would have resulted in the recognition of those assets and liabilities as of that date. The measurement period ends as soon as the acquirer receives the information it was seeking about facts and circumstances that existed as of the acquisition date or learns that more information is not obtainable. However, the measurement period should not exceed one year from the acquisition date.

28.42 The measurement period is the period after the acquisition date during which the acquirer may adjust the provisional amounts recognized for a business combination. The measurement period provides the acquirer with a reasonable time to obtain the information necessary to identify and measure the following, as of the acquisition date, in accordance with the requirements of this chapter:

   a. The identifiable assets acquired, liabilities assumed, and any noncontrolling interest in the acquiree

Business Combinations

    b. The consideration transferred for the acquiree (or the other amount used in measuring goodwill)

    c. In a business combination achieved in stages, the equity interest in the acquiree previously held by the acquirer

    d. The resulting goodwill or gain on a bargain purchase

28.43 The acquirer should consider all pertinent factors when determining whether information obtained after the acquisition date should result in an adjustment to the provisional amounts recognized or whether that information results from events that occurred after the acquisition date. Pertinent factors include the date when additional information is obtained and whether the acquirer can identify a reason for a change to provisional amounts. Information that is obtained shortly after the acquisition date is more likely to reflect circumstances that existed at the acquisition date than is information obtained several months later. For example, unless an intervening event that changed its market value can be identified, the sale of an asset to a third party shortly after the acquisition date for an amount that differs significantly from its provisional market value determined at that date is likely to indicate an error in the provisional amount.

28.44 The acquirer recognizes an increase (decrease) in the provisional amount recognized for an identifiable asset (liability) by means of a decrease (increase) in goodwill. However, new information obtained during the measurement period may sometimes result in an adjustment to the provisional amount of more than one asset or liability. For example, the acquirer might have assumed a liability to pay damages related to an accident in one of the acquiree's facilities, part or all of which are covered by the acquiree's liability insurance policy. If the acquirer obtains new information during the measurement period about the acquisition-date market value of that liability, the adjustment to goodwill resulting from a change to the provisional amount recognized for the liability should be offset (in whole or in part) by a corresponding adjustment to goodwill resulting from a change to the provisional amount recognized for the claim receivable from the insurer.

28.45 During the measurement period, the acquirer should recognize adjustments to the provisional amounts as if the accounting for the business combination had been completed at the acquisition date. Thus, the acquirer should revise comparative information for prior periods presented in financial statements as needed, including making any change in depreciation, amortization, or other income effects recognized in completing the initial accounting.

28.46 After the measurement period ends, the acquirer should revise the accounting for a business combination only to correct an error in accordance with chapter 9, "Accounting Changes, Changes in Accounting Estimates, and Correction of Errors."

Determining What Is Part of the Business Combination Transaction

28.47 The acquirer and the acquiree may have a preexisting relationship or other arrangement before negotiations for the business combination began, or they may enter into an arrangement during the negotiations that is separate from the business combination. In either situation, the acquirer should identify any amounts that are not part of what the acquirer and the acquiree (or its former owners) exchanged in the business combination (that is, amounts that are not part of the exchange for the acquiree). The acquirer should recognize as part of applying the acquisition method only the consideration transferred for the acquiree and the assets acquired and liabilities assumed in the exchange for the acquiree. Separate transactions should be accounted for in accordance with the relevant chapters.

28.48 A transaction entered into by, or on behalf of, the acquirer or primarily for the benefit of the acquirer or the combined entity, rather than primarily for the benefit of the acquiree (or its former owners) before the combination, is likely to be a separate transaction. The following are examples of separate transactions that are not to be included when applying the acquisition method:

a. A transaction that, in effect, settles preexisting relationships between the acquirer and acquiree

b. A transaction that remunerates employees or former owners of the acquiree for future services

c. A transaction that reimburses the acquiree or its former owners for paying the acquirer's acquisition-related costs

Acquisition-Related Costs

28.49 *Acquisition-related costs* are costs the acquirer incurs to effect a business combination. Those costs include finder's fees; advisory, legal, accounting, valuation, and other professional or consulting fees; general administrative costs, including the costs of maintaining an internal acquisitions department; and costs of registering and issuing debt and equity securities. The acquirer should account for acquisition-related costs as expenses in the periods in which the costs are incurred and the services are received, with one exception: The costs to issue equity securities should be recognized in accordance with chapter 18, "Equity."

Subsequent Measurement and Accounting

28.50 In general, an acquirer should subsequently measure and account for assets acquired, liabilities assumed or incurred, and equity instruments issued in a business combination in accordance with other applicable chapters for those items, depending on their nature. However, this chapter provides guidance on subsequently measuring and accounting for indemnification assets.

Indemnification Assets

28.51 At the end of each subsequent reporting period, the acquirer should measure an indemnification asset that was recognized at the acquisition date on the same basis as the indemnified liability or asset, subject to any contractual limitations on its amount and, for an indemnification asset that is not subsequently measured at its market value, management's assessment of the collectability of the indemnification asset. The acquirer should derecognize the indemnification asset only when it collects the asset, sells it, or otherwise loses the right to it.

Combinations of Entities Under Common Control

28.52 This section applies to combinations between entities under common control. The following are examples of those types of transactions:

    a. An entity charters a newly formed entity and then transfers some or all of its net assets to that newly chartered entity.

    b. A parent transfers the net assets of a wholly-owned subsidiary into the parent and liquidates the subsidiary. That transaction is a change in legal organization but not a change in the reporting entity.

    c. A parent transfers its controlling interest in several partially owned subsidiaries to a new, wholly-owned subsidiary. That also is a change in legal organization but not in the reporting entity.

    d. A parent exchanges its ownership interests or the net assets of a wholly-owned subsidiary for additional shares issued by the parent's less-than-wholly-owned subsidiary, thereby increasing the parent's percentage of ownership in the less-than-wholly-owned subsidiary but leaving all the existing, noncontrolling interest outstanding.

    e. A parent's less-than-wholly-owned subsidiary issues its shares in exchange for shares of another subsidiary previously owned by the same parent, and the noncontrolling shareholders are not party to the exchange. That is not a business combination from the perspective of the parent.

    f. A limited liability company is formed by combining entities under common control.

Recognition

28.53 When accounting for a transfer of assets or exchange of shares between entities under common control, the entity that receives the net assets or the equity interests should initially recognize the assets and liabilities transferred at the date of transfer.

Measurement

28.54 When accounting for a transfer of assets or exchange of shares between entities under common control, the entity that receives the net assets or equity interests should initially measure the recognized assets and liabilities transferred at their carrying amounts in the accounts of the transferring entity at the date of transfer.

28.55 In some instances, the entity that receives the net assets or equity interests (the receiving entity) and the entity that transferred the net assets or equity interests (the transferring entity) may account for similar assets and liabilities using different accounting methods. In such circumstances, the carrying amounts of the assets and liabilities transferred may be adjusted to the basis of accounting used by the receiving entity if the change would provide reliable and more relevant information about the effects of transactions, other events, or conditions on the entity's financial position, financial performance, or cash flows. Any such change in accounting method should be applied retrospectively, and financial statements presented for prior periods should be adjusted unless it is impracticable to do so.

Financial Statement Presentation in Period of Transfer

28.56 The receiving entity's financial statements should report results of operations for the period in which the transfer occurs as though the transfer of net assets or exchange of equity interests had occurred at the beginning of the period. Thus, results of operations for that period will comprise those of the previously separate entities combined from the beginning of the period to the date the transfer is completed and those of the combined operations from that date to the end of the period. By eliminating the effects of intraentity transactions when determining the results of operations for the period before the combination, those results will be on substantially the same basis as the results of operations for the period after the date of combination. The effects of intraentity transactions on current assets, current liabilities, revenue, and cost of sales for periods presented and on retained earnings at the beginning of the periods presented should be eliminated to the extent possible.

28.57 Similarly, the receiving entity should present the statement of financial position and other financial information as of the beginning of the period as though the assets and liabilities had been transferred at that date.

Comparative Financial Statement Presentation for Prior Years

28.58 Financial statements and financial information presented for prior years also should be retrospectively adjusted to furnish comparative information. All adjusted financial statements and financial summaries should indicate clearly that financial data of previously separate entities are combined. However, the comparative information in prior years should only be adjusted for periods during which the entities were under common control.

Disclosure

28.59 The acquirer should disclose information that enables users of its financial statements to evaluate the nature and financial effect of a business combination that occurs either

  a. during the current reporting period or

  b. after the end of the reporting period but before the financial statements are available to be issued.

28.60 To meet the objective in paragraph 28.59, the acquirer should disclose the following information for each material business combination:

  a. The name and a description of the acquiree

  b. The acquisition date

  c. The percentage of voting equity interests acquired

  d. The acquisition-date market value of the total consideration transferred and the acquisition-date market value of each major class of consideration, such as

Business Combinations

      i. cash;

      ii. liabilities incurred (for example, a liability for contingent consideration); and

      iii. equity interests of the acquirer, including the number of instruments or interests issued or issuable

e. A description of the arrangement and the basis for determining the amount of the payment for contingent consideration arrangements and indemnification assets

f. A condensed statement of financial position showing the amounts recognized as of the acquisition date for each major class of assets acquired and liabilities assumed

g. The amount of any gain recognized in a bargain purchase in accordance with paragraph 28.28 and the line item in the statement of operations in which the gain is recognized

h. The amount of the noncontrolling interest in the acquiree recognized at the acquisition date and the measurement basis for that amount

i. The accounting policy related to intangible assets acquired and those intangible assets recognized separately, including their amounts and useful lives

j. In a business combination achieved in stages

      i. the acquisition-date market value of the equity interest in the acquiree held by the acquirer immediately before the acquisition date and

      ii. the amount of any gain or loss recognized as a result of remeasuring to market value the equity interest in the acquiree held by the acquirer before the business combination (see paragraph 28.38) and the line item in the statement of operations in which that gain or loss is recognized

28.61 For individually immaterial business combinations occurring during the reporting period that are material collectively, the acquirer should disclose the following information:

a. The number of entities acquired and a brief description of those entities

b. The acquisition-date market value of the total consideration transferred

c. The number of equity instruments or interests of the acquirer issued or issuable

d. A description of the arrangement and the basis for determining the amount of the payment for contingent consideration arrangements and indemnification assets

28.62 If the acquisition date of a business combination is after the end of the reporting period but before the financial statements are available to be issued, the acquirer should disclose the information required by paragraphs 28.60–.61, unless the initial accounting for the business combination is incomplete at the time the financial statements are available to be issued. In that situation, the acquirer should describe which disclosures could not be made and the reasons why they cannot be made.

FRF-SME 28.62

Combinations of Entities Under Common Control

28.63 The notes to financial statements of the receiving entity should disclose the following for the period in which the transfer of assets and liabilities or exchange of equity interests occurred:

　　a. The name and brief description of the entity included in the reporting entity as a result of the net asset transfer or exchange of equity interests

　　b. The method of accounting for the transfer of net assets or exchange of equity interests

Chapter 29

New Basis (Push-Down) Accounting

Purpose and Scope

29.01 This chapter establishes recognition, measurement, and disclosure principles dealing with the comprehensive revaluation of assets and liabilities by entities in order to establish a new cost basis.

Recognition

29.02 Assets and liabilities may be comprehensively revalued by means of push-down accounting when an acquirer gains control of an entity. *Control*[1] of an entity is gained when more than 50 percent of the outstanding residual equity interests in the entity have been acquired, in one or more transactions between nonrelated parties, by an acquirer. The acquirer may be a corporation, an individual, or other type of entity permitted by law or a group of individuals or entities that act together to acquire control of an entity. When an acquirer gains control of an entity (acquisition of an entity), a new cost basis for a continuing entity may be established.

29.03 In the case of an acquisition of an entity, the application of *push-down accounting* results in comparable accounting to what would have resulted had the acquirer either purchased the assets and assumed the liabilities of the entity directly or established a new legal entity to hold the assets and assume the liabilities of the acquired entity and continue its operations.

29.04 A comprehensive revaluation is only appropriate when the acquirer, representing an individual or group's collective interest, controls the entity.

29.05 When one or more transactions take place between nonrelated parties, it is presumed that the transaction or transactions have been bargained in an arm's length manner between knowledgeable, willing parties who are under no compulsion to act and, therefore, that values determined in that process represent market value. However, transactions between related parties are not an appropriate basis for a comprehensive revaluation. (For purposes of this chapter, *related parties* are as defined in chapter 26, "Related Party Transactions.") When an individual or entity already owns an equity interest in an entity, the revaluation or market value is proportionate to that owner's increase in ownership. For example, if a 10-percent owner acquires the equity interest of a 90-percent owner, the revaluation is stepped up for the 90 percent that represents the new ownership.

29.06 When new costs are not reasonably determinable for individual assets and liabilities, comprehensive revaluation is not appropriate. An example of when new costs are not reasonably determinable is in an acquisition when an entity is acquired as part of a group purchase (that is, when a group of assets and liabilities is acquired for a single amount), and the entity does not have, and cannot obtain, from the acquirer details of the purchase price and its allocation among assets and liabilities.

---

[1] Italicized terms are defined in the glossary.

29.07 Comprehensive revaluation of assets and liabilities through the application of push-down accounting is not required when the condition in paragraph 29.02 is met as a result of the acquisition of an entity. Application of push-down accounting is based on the presumption that the acquirer would find the new costs more useful when evaluating investment returns and entity performance. In situations in which the acquirer prefers to retain old cost basis financial statements (either for its own purposes or the purposes of other financial statement users, such as holders of outstanding public debt), push-down accounting is not required.

Acquisition of an Entity—Push-Down Accounting

Measurement

29.08 When a comprehensive revaluation of an entity's assets and liabilities is undertaken as a result of a transaction or transactions as described in paragraph 29.02, push-down accounting may be applied.

29.09 The application of push-down accounting provides symmetry between the carrying amounts of assets and liabilities reported in the acquired entity's financial statements and the carrying amounts of assets and liabilities reported in the consolidated financial statements of the parent.

29.10 When applying push-down accounting, the values used are those resulting from accounting for the acquisition(s) in accordance with chapter 28, "Business Combinations."

29.11 When an acquisition is financed by debt, in whole or in part, it is not considered appropriate for the acquired entity to record the debt, unless it is a liability of the acquired entity.

Retained Earnings and the Revaluation Adjustment

29.12 When a comprehensive revaluation of an entity's assets and liabilities is undertaken as a result of a transaction or transactions as described in paragraph 29.02, the transaction should be accounted for as a capital transaction, and the portion of retained earnings that has not been included in the consolidated retained earnings of the acquirer or is not related to any continuing, noncontrolling interests in the entity should be reclassified to either capital stock, additional paid-in capital, or a separately identified account within shareholders' equity.

29.13 Shareholders' equity is also restated to reflect the purchase transaction or transactions.

29.14 The treatment accorded to retained earnings is also applied to other shareholders' equity accounts that arose prior to the purchase transaction or transactions and that are not specifically related to capital invested.

29.15 The purpose of the revaluation of assets and liabilities is to provide information for assessing returns that reflect the investment of the controlling shareholder in the entity. It is consistent with this purpose that the revaluation adjustment (the net effect of the revaluation of the entity's assets and liabilities) is accounted for as capital of the acquired entity. The revaluation adjustment is included in either capital stock, additional paid-in capital, or a separately identified account within shareholders' equity.

New Basis (Push-Down) Accounting

Income Tax Benefits

29.16 Under the deferred income taxes method, deferred income tax assets are appropriately recognized as part of a comprehensive revaluation to the extent that they are more likely than not to be realized (see chapter 21, "Income Taxes"). Deferred income tax assets that are not considered to be more likely than not to be realized at the time of the comprehensive revaluation should be excluded from the revaluation. If such an unrecognized deferred income tax asset were recognized subsequent to the application of push-down accounting, the benefit should be recognized in net income (or, if chapter 21 so requires, outside net income).

Disclosure

29.17 In the period that push-down accounting has been first applied, the financial statements should disclose the following:

a. The date push-down accounting was applied and the date or dates of the purchase transaction or transactions that led to the application of push-down accounting

b. A description of the situation resulting in the application of push-down accounting

c. The amount of the change in each major class of assets, liabilities, and shareholders' equity arising from the application of push-down accounting

29.18 In the fiscal period that push-down accounting has been applied and the following fiscal period, the financial statements should disclose

a. the date push-down accounting was applied;

b. the amount of the revaluation adjustment and the shareholders' equity account in which the revaluation adjustment was recorded; and

c. the amount of retained earnings reclassified and the shareholders' equity account to which it was reclassified.

Chapter 30

Nonmonetary Transactions

Purpose and Scope

30.01 This chapter establishes principles for the recognition, measurement, and disclosure of nonmonetary transactions. It defines when an exchange of assets is measured at market value and when an exchange of assets is measured at the *carrying amount*.[1]

30.02 This chapter applies to nonmonetary transactions except

   a. business combinations that are accounted for in accordance with chapter 28, "Business Combinations;"

   b. transactions involving retirement and other postemployment benefits that are accounted for in accordance with chapter 20, "Retirement and Other Postemployment Benefits;" and

   c. the replacement, through insurance or expropriation proceeds, of nonmonetary assets that are lost, destroyed, or expropriated. These items are monetary transactions.

Measurement

30.03 An entity should measure an asset exchanged or transferred in a nonmonetary transaction at the more reliably measurable of the market value of the asset given up and the market value of the asset received, unless

   a. the transaction lacks *commercial substance*;

   b. the transaction is an exchange of a product or property held for sale in the ordinary course of business for a product or property to be sold in the same line of business to facilitate sales to customers other than the parties to the exchange;

   c. neither the market value of the asset received nor the market value of the asset given up is reliably measurable;

   d. the transaction is a nonmonetary nonreciprocal transfer to owners to which paragraph 30.10 applies; or

   e. the transaction is between related parties and is not in the normal course of operations. Usually, a related party transaction that is in the normal course of operations occurs within a normal business relationship and on terms and conditions that are similar to those of transactions with unrelated parties.

30.04 An entity should measure an asset exchanged or transferred in a nonmonetary transaction that is not measured at market value in accordance with paragraph 30.03 at the carrying amount of the asset given up, adjusted by the market value of any monetary consideration received or given.

---

[1] Italicized terms are defined in the glossary.

30.05 When an exchange described in paragraph 30.04 involves partial monetary consideration, the carrying amount of the asset given up is adjusted by the market value of the monetary consideration. The entity paying the monetary consideration measures the nonmonetary asset received at the carrying amount of the asset given up, plus the market value of the monetary consideration paid. The entity receiving the monetary consideration measures the nonmonetary asset received at the carrying amount of the nonmonetary asset given up less the market value of the monetary consideration received, unless the monetary consideration exceeds the carrying amount, in which case, a gain is recognized for the amount of such excess.

Measurement Criteria

30.06 When an entity is able to reliably determine the market value of both the asset received and the asset given up, the market value of the asset given up is used to measure the asset received unless the market value of the asset received is more reliably measurable. If market value is not reliably measureable, then the transaction is based on the carrying amounts.

Commercial Substance

30.07 A nonmonetary transaction has commercial substance when the entity's future cash flows are expected to change significantly as a result of the transaction. The entity's future cash flows are expected to change significantly when

   a. the configuration of the future cash flows of the asset received differs significantly from the configuration of the cash flows of the asset given up (see paragraph 30.08) or

   b. the *entity-specific value* of the asset received differs from the entity-specific value of the asset given up, and the difference is significant relative to the market value of the assets exchanged.

In some cases, a qualitative assessment will be conclusive when determining that the estimated cash flows of the entity are expected to change significantly as a result of the transaction.

30.08 The configuration of future cash flows is composed of the risk, timing, and amount of the cash flows. A change in any one of these considerations is a change in the configuration.

30.09 Entity-specific value, resulting from entity-specific measurement, differs from market value. It attempts to capture the value of an item in the context of the reporting entity. The entity uses its expectations about its use of the asset rather than the use assumed by marketplace participants.

Restructuring or Liquidation

30.10 An entity should measure a nonmonetary nonreciprocal transfer to owners that represents a spin-off or other form of restructuring or liquidation at the carrying amount of the nonmonetary assets or liabilities transferred.

Recognition of Gains and Losses

30.11 An entity should recognize any gain or loss resulting from a nonmonetary transaction in net income for the period.

30.12 Transfers described in paragraph 30.10 do not give rise to a gain or loss in the financial statements of the transferor.

Disclosure

30.13 An entity should disclose the following information in the period in which a nonmonetary transaction occurs to enable users of the financial statements to understand the effects of a nonmonetary transaction on the financial statements:

    a. The nature of the transaction

    b. Its basis of measurement (market value or carrying amount) and the method for determining that amount

    c. The amount

    d. Related gains and losses

Chapter 31

Foreign Currency Translation

Purpose and Scope

31.01 This chapter establishes principles for the translation of transactions of a reporting entity that are denominated in a foreign currency (*foreign currency transactions*[1]).

31.02 This chapter assumes that the *reporting entity* prepares its financial statements in U.S. dollars. If another currency (such as the Canadian dollar) is used for reporting purposes, all references to U.S. dollars in this chapter should be changed to that currency, and the U.S. dollar should be treated as a foreign currency.

31.03 For foreign currency transactions, the objective of translation is to express such transactions in a manner that achieves consistency with the accounting treatment for domestic transactions. Because domestic transactions are automatically measured in U.S. dollars, the U.S. dollar is the appropriate unit of measure for foreign currency transactions. Accordingly, the *temporal method* is used to translate foreign currency transactions.

Translation of Foreign Currency Transactions and Related Financial Statement Items of the Reporting Entity

31.04 When the reporting entity purchases or sells goods or services on credit, with settlement to be in a foreign currency, it gives rise to a payable or receivable in that foreign currency. Any subsequent change in exchange rate between the U.S. dollar and the foreign currency will affect the U.S. dollar equivalent of that payable or receivable.

31.05 Once foreign currency purchases and sales, or inventories, fixed assets, and other nonmonetary items obtained through foreign currency transactions have been translated and recorded, any subsequent changes in the exchange rate will not affect those recorded amounts.

31.06 At the transaction date, each asset, liability, revenue, or expense arising from a foreign currency transaction of the reporting entity should be translated into U.S. dollars by the use of the exchange rate in effect at that date.

31.07 If a transaction denominated in a foreign currency is not settled by the statement of financial position date and the exchange rate has changed, the receivable or payable should be translated at the equivalent amount of U.S. dollars that would be collected or paid at the statement of financial position date.

31.08 At each statement of financial position date, *monetary items* denominated in a foreign currency should be translated to reflect the exchange rate in effect at the statement of financial position date.

---

[1] Italicized terms are defined in the glossary.

31.09 At each statement of financial position date, for nonmonetary assets of the reporting entity that are carried at net realizable value or market value, the U.S. dollar equivalent should be determined by applying the exchange rate in effect at the statement of financial position date to the foreign currency market price.

31.10 An exchange gain or loss arises when a foreign currency-denominated monetary item is settled or translated at an exchange rate different from the one at which it was previously recorded or carried.

31.11 An exchange gain or loss of the reporting entity that arises on translation or settlement of a foreign currency-denominated monetary item or a nonmonetary item carried at net realizable value or market value should be included in the determination of net income for the current period.

Use of Averages or Other Methods of Approximation

31.12 Literal application of this chapter might require a degree of detail in record keeping and computations that would be burdensome, as well as unnecessary, to produce reasonable approximations of the results. Accordingly, it is acceptable to use averages or other methods of approximation. For example, translation of the numerous revenues, expenses, gains, and losses at the exchange rates at the dates such items are recognized is generally impractical, and an appropriately-weighted average exchange rate for the period would normally be used to translate such items.

Disclosure

31.13 The amount of an exchange gain or loss included in net income should be disclosed. An entity may exclude from this amount those exchange gains or losses arising on investments in securities that are measured at market value.

Glossary

accounting policies. The specific principles, bases, conventions, rules, and practices applied by an entity when preparing and presenting financial statements.

accretion expense. The increase in the carrying amount of an asset retirement obligation due to the passage of time.

accrued benefit obligation. The actuarial present value of benefits attributed to employee services rendered to a particular date. As of a particular date prior to an employee's full eligibility date, an entity's accrued benefit obligation in respect of the employee is the portion of the obligation for retirement and other postemployment benefits attributed to that employee's service rendered to that date. On and after the full eligibility date, the accrued benefit obligation and obligation for retirement and other postemployment benefits for an employee are the same.

acquiree. The business or businesses that the acquirer obtains control of in a business combination.

acquirer. The entity that obtains control of the acquiree.

acquisition date. The date on which the acquirer obtains control of the acquiree.

active employees. Active employees are those currently rendering service to the entity. For chapter 20, "Retirement and Other Postemployment Benefits," active, former, and inactive employees are referred to collectively as *employees*.

additional paid-in capital. Comprises amounts paid in by equity holders. Additional paid-in capital in the form of excess paid in by equity holders includes premiums on shares issued, any portion of the proceeds of issue of shares without par value not allocated to capital stock, gain on forfeited shares, proceeds arising from shares contributed by equity holders, credits resulting from redemption or conversion of shares at less than the amount set up as capital stock, and any other contribution by equity holders in excess of amounts allocated to capital stock.

amortizable amount. The cost of an asset, or other amount substituted for cost, less its residual value.

amortization. The systematic allocation of the *amortizable amount* of an intangible asset over its useful life.

amortized cost. The amount at which an asset or liability is measured at initial recognition, plus or minus the cumulative amortization of any difference between that initial amount and the maturity amount and minus any reduction (directly or through the use of an allowance account) for uncollectibility or write down.

asset retirement cost. The amount that is capitalized and increases the carrying amount of a long-lived asset when a liability for an asset retirement obligation is recognized.

asset retirement obligation. A legal obligation associated with the retirement of a tangible long-lived asset that an entity is required to settle as a result of an existing or enacted law, statute, ordinance, or written or oral contract or by legal construction of a contract under the doctrine of promissory estoppel.

available to be issued. Financial statements are available to be issued when

- a complete set of financial statements, including all required note disclosures, has been prepared (see paragraphs 2.10–.12);
- all final adjusting journal entries have been reflected in the financial statements (for example, adjustments for income taxes and bonuses);
- no changes to the financial statements are planned or expected; and
- the financial statements meeting the preceding requirements have been approved in accordance with the entity's process to finalize its financial statements.

bargain purchase option. A provision allowing the lessee, at its option, to purchase the leased property for a price that is sufficiently lower than the expected market value of the property, at the date the option becomes exercisable, such that exercise of the option appears, at the inception of the lease, to be reasonably assured.

bargain renewal option. A provision allowing the lessee, at its option, to renew the lease for a rental that is sufficiently lower than the expected fair rental of the property, at the date the option becomes exercisable, such that exercise of the option appears, at the inception of the lease, to be reasonably assured. *Fair rental* means the going rate for rental of equivalent property under similar terms and conditions.

business. An integrated set of activities and assets that is capable of being conducted and managed for the purpose of providing a return in the form of dividends, lower costs, or other economic benefits directly to investors or other owners, members, or participants.

business combination. A transaction or other event in which an acquirer obtains control of one or more businesses. Transactions sometimes referred to as *true mergers* or *mergers of equals* are also business combinations, as that term is used in the FRF for SMEs accounting framework.

capital lease. A lease that, from the point of view of the lessee, transfers substantially all the benefits and risks incident to ownership of property to the lessee.

carrying amount. The recorded amount of an asset or liability after adjustment, if any, for amortization or depreciation or any write-downs.

cash. Comprises cash on hand and demand deposits.

cash equivalents. Short-term (normally, a maturity of three months or less from the date of acquisition), highly liquid investments that are readily convertible to known amounts of cash and that are subject to an insignificant risk of changes in value.

cash flows. Inflows and outflows of cash and cash equivalents.

change in accounting estimate. An adjustment of the carrying amount of an asset or a liability, or the amount of the periodic consumption of an asset, that results from the assessment of the present status

Glossary

of, and expected future benefits and obligations associated with, assets and liabilities. Changes in accounting estimates result from new information or new developments and, accordingly, are not corrections of errors.

commercial substance. A transaction has commercial substance when the entity's future cash flows are expected to change significantly as a result of the transaction.

completed contract method. A method of accounting that recognizes revenue only when the sale of goods or the rendering of services under a contract is completed or substantially completed.

consolidated financial statements. Financial statements produced by aggregating the financial statements of one or more subsidiary companies, in which the parent company controls the subsidiary companies, on a line-by-line basis (that is, adding together corresponding items of assets, liabilities, revenues, and expenses) with the financial statements of the parent company, eliminating intercompany balances and transactions and providing for any noncontrolling interest in a subsidiary company.

contingency. An existing condition or situation involving uncertainty about possible gain or loss to an entity that will ultimately be resolved when one or more future events occur or fail to occur.

contingent consideration. Usually an obligation of the acquirer to transfer additional assets or equity interests to the former owners of an acquiree as part of the exchange for control of the acquiree if specified future events occur or conditions are met. However, contingent consideration also may give the acquirer the right to the return of previously transferred consideration if specified conditions are met.

contingent rental. A rental based on a factor other than the passage of time (for example, percentage of sales, amount of usage, prime interest rate, and price indexes).

control. For chapters 22, "Subsidiaries," 23, "Consolidated Financial Statements and Noncontrolling Interests," and 29, "New Basis (Push-Down) Accounting," control is defined as being indicated by the ownership of more than 50 percent of the outstanding residual equity interests, which is generally based on voting rights.

For chapters 28, "Business Combinations," 24, "Interests in Joint Ventures," and 26, "Related Party Transactions," control is defined as the continuing power to determine the strategic operating, investing, and financing policies related to an entity, assets, liabilities, or economic activities without the cooperation of others.

corporate joint venture. An investment in the stock of entities other than subsidiaries, owned and operated by a small group of entities (the joint venturers) as a separate and specific business or project for the mutual benefit of the members of the group.

cost. The amount of consideration given up to acquire, construct, develop, or improve an item of property, plant, and equipment and includes all costs directly attributable to the acquisition, construction, development, or improvement of the asset, including installing it at the location and in the condition necessary for its intended use. Cost includes any asset retirement cost accounted for in accordance with the section "Asset Retirement Obligations," in chapter 17, "Contingencies."

In the context of accounting for intangible assets, cost is defined as the amount of cash or cash equivalents paid or the market value of other consideration given to acquire an asset at the time of its acquisition or construction, or, when appropriate, the amount attributed to that asset when initially recognized in accordance with the requirements of other chapters.

cost (benefit) of current income taxes. The amount of income taxes payable (refundable) in respect of the period.

cost (benefit) of deferred income taxes. The change during the period in deferred income tax liabilities and deferred income tax assets.

cost method. A basis of accounting for investments whereby the investment is initially recorded at cost; earnings from such investments are recognized only to the extent received or receivable.

date of transition to the FRF for SMEs accounting framework. The beginning of the earliest period for which an entity presents financial statements under the FRF for SMEs accounting framework.

deferred income tax assets. The amounts of income tax benefits arising in respect of

- deductible temporary differences;
- the carryforward of unused tax losses; and
- the carryforward of unused income tax reductions, except for investment tax credits.

deferred income tax liabilities. The amounts of income taxes arising from taxable temporary differences.

deferred income taxes method. A method of accounting under which an entity reports as an expense (income) of the period the cost (benefit) of current income taxes and the cost (benefit) of deferred income taxes, determined in accordance with the rules established by taxation authorities.

defined benefit plan. A pension plan that defines the amount of pension benefit to be provided. The amount of the benefit is usually a function of one or more factors such as age, years of service, or compensation. Any pension plan that does not meet the definition of a defined contribution plan should be considered a defined benefit plan.

defined contribution plan. A plan that provides benefits for services rendered based solely on the amount contributed to each plan participant's account and the returns on the investment of those contributions. Each participant has his or her own account and, in many cases, directs the investment of the contribution. The plan specifies how the contribution amounts are to be determined.

depreciation. A method of allocating the cost of a tangible asset over its useful life and begins when the asset is placed in service.

derecognition. The removal of a previously recognized financial asset or financial liability from an entity's statement of financial position.

Glossary

derivative. A contract with all three of the following characteristics:

- Its value changes in response to the change in a specified interest rate, financial instrument price, commodity price, foreign exchange rate, index of prices or rates, a credit rating or credit index, or other variable (sometimes called the "underlying") provided in the case of a nonfinancial variable that the variable is not specific to a party to the contract.

- It requires no initial net investment or an initial net investment that is smaller than would be required for other types of contracts that would be expected to have a similar response to changes in market factors.

- It is settled at a future date.

development. The application of research findings or other knowledge to a plan or design for the production of new or substantially improved materials, devices, products, processes, systems, or services before the start of commercial production or use.

direct financing lease. A lease that, from the point of view of the lessor, transfers substantially all the benefits and risks incident to ownership of property to the lessee and, at the inception of the lease, the market value of leased property is the same as its carrying amount to the lessor (usually not a manufacturer or dealer). A lease is not precluded from being classified as a direct financing lease after it is renewed or extended, even though the carrying amount of the property at the end of the original lease term is different from its market value at that date.

disposal group. A group of assets to be disposed of, by sale or otherwise, together as a group in a single transaction, and liabilities directly associated with those assets that will be transferred in the transaction. (Examples of such liabilities include, but are not limited to, legal obligations that transfer with a long-lived asset, such as certain environmental obligations, and obligations that, for business reasons, a potential buyer would prefer to settle when assumed as part of a group, such as warranty obligations that relate to an acquired customer base.)

dividends. Distributions paid or payable in cash or other assets and do not include distributions of shares unless the effect is to change the equity interests of two or more classes of shares.

economic life of the leased property. The estimated remaining period during which the property is expected to be economically usable by one or more users, with normal repairs and maintenance, for the purpose for which it was intended at the inception of the lease and without limitation by the lease term.

entity-specific value. The present value of the cash flows an entity expects to arise from the continuing use of an asset and its disposal at the end of its useful life or expects to incur when settling a liability. Entity-specific value resulting from entity-specific measurement differs from market value. It attempts to capture the value of an item in the context of the reporting entity. The entity uses its expectations about its use of the asset, rather than the use assumed by marketplace participants.

equity. The residual interest in the assets of the entity after deducting all of its liabilities.

equity instrument. Any contract that evidences a residual interest in the assets of an entity after deducting all of its liabilities.

equity interests. Used broadly to mean ownership interests of investor-owned entities.

equity method. A basis of accounting for investments whereby the investment is initially recorded at cost and the carrying amount, adjusted thereafter to include the investor's pro rata share of postacquisition earnings of the investee. The amount of the adjustment is included in the determination of net income by the investor, and the investment account of the investor is also increased or decreased to reflect the investor's share of capital transactions and changes in accounting policies and corrections of errors relating to prior period financial statements applicable to postacquisition periods. Profit distributions received or receivable from an investee reduce the carrying amount of the investment.

executory costs. Costs related to the operation of the leased property (for example, insurance, maintenance cost, and property taxes).

financial asset. Any asset that is

- cash;
- a contractual right to receive cash or another financial asset from another party;
- a contractual right to exchange financial instruments with another party under conditions that are potentially favorable; or
- an equity instrument of another entity.

The cost incurred by an entity to purchase a right to reacquire its own equity instruments from another party is a deduction from its equity, not a financial asset.

financial instrument. A contract that creates a financial asset for one entity and a financial liability or equity instrument of another entity.

financial liability. Any liability that is a contractual obligation to

- deliver cash or another financial asset to another party or
- exchange financial instruments with another party under conditions that are potentially unfavorable to the entity.

financing activities. Activities that result in changes in the size and composition of the equity capital and borrowings of the entity.

financing fees and transaction costs. Financing fees are amounts that compensate the lender for the risk of providing funds to the borrower. Financing fees, sometimes referred to as *fees in lieu of interest, loan fees*, or *financing costs*, include

- fees charged to originate, arrange, or syndicate a loan or debt financing;
- commitment, standby, and guarantee fees; and
- refinancing, restructuring, and renegotiation fees.

Financing fees may be refundable or nonrefundable.

Transaction costs are incremental costs that are directly attributable to the acquisition, issue, or disposal of a financial asset or financial liability. Transaction costs include expenditures such as legal fees, reimbursement of the lender's administrative costs, and appraisal costs associated with a loan.

firm purchase commitment. An agreement with an unrelated party, binding on both parties and usually legally enforceable, that

- specifies all the significant terms, including the price and timing of the transaction and
- includes a disincentive for nonperformance that is sufficiently large to make performance probable.

foreign currency transactions. Transactions of the reporting entity whose terms are denominated in a currency other than its reporting currency.

former employees. Former employees are those who are retired, whose employment has been terminated, or who have left the entity. For chapter 20, active, former, and inactive employees are referred to collectively as *employees*.

goodwill. An asset representing the future economic benefits arising from other assets acquired in a business combination that are not individually identified and separately recognized.

identifiable. An asset is identifiable if it either

- is separable (that is, capable of being separated or divided from the entity and sold, transferred, licensed, rented, or exchanged, either individually or together with a related contract, identifiable asset, or liability, regardless of whether the entity intends to do so) or
- arises from contractual or other legal rights, regardless of whether those rights are transferable or separable from the entity or from other rights and obligations.

impracticable. A requirement is considered impracticable when the entity cannot apply it after making every reasonable effort to do so.

In the context of applying a change in an accounting policy, for a particular prior period, it is impracticable to apply a change in an accounting policy retrospectively if

- the effects of the retrospective application are not determinable;
- the retrospective application requires assumptions about what management's intent would have been in that period; or
- the retrospective application requires significant estimates of amounts, and it is impossible to distinguish objectively information about those estimates that
  — provides evidence of circumstances that existed on the date(s) at which those amounts are to be recognized, measured, or disclosed and
  — would have been available when the financial statements for that prior period were available to be issued.

inception of the lease. The earlier of the date of the lease agreement and the date of a commitment that is signed by the parties to the lease transaction and includes the principal terms of the lease (this is the effective date used for classification of the lease).

income taxes. Income taxes include
- all domestic and foreign taxes that are based on taxable income;
- taxes that are based on a measure of revenue less certain specified expenses;
- alternative minimum income taxes, including taxes based on measures other than income and that may be used to reduce income taxes of another period; and
- fees assessed on revenues if the entity does not pay taxes on profits.

initial direct costs. Those costs incurred by the lessor that are directly associated with negotiating and executing a specific leasing transaction. Such costs include commissions, legal fees, and costs of preparing and processing documents for new leases. Such costs do not include supervisory and administrative costs, promotion and lease design costs intended for recurring use, costs incurred in collection activities, and provisions for uncollectable rentals.

insurance contract. A contract under which one party (the insurer) accepts significant insurance risk from another party (the policyholder) by agreeing to compensate the policyholder if a specified uncertain future event (the insured event) adversely affects the policyholder. Insurance contracts include any contract based on climatic, geological, or other physical variables.

intangible asset. An identifiable, nonmonetary asset without physical substance that the entity controls and which embodies future economic benefits.

interest rate implicit in the lease. The discount rate that, at the inception of the lease, causes the aggregate present value of
- the minimum lease payments, from the standpoint of the lessor, excluding that portion of the payments representing executory costs to be paid by the lessor and any profit on such costs and
- the unguaranteed residual value accruing to the benefit of the lessor

to be equal to the market value of the leased property to the lessor at the inception of the lease.

inventories. Assets that are
- held for sale in the ordinary course of business;
- in the process of production for such sale; or
- in the form of materials or supplies to be consumed in the production process or in the rendering of services, or packaging supplies.

investing activities. The acquisition and disposal of long-term assets and other investments not included in cash equivalents.

joint control. Joint control of an economic activity is the contractually agreed sharing of the continuing power to determine its strategic operating, investing, and financing policies.

joint venture. An economic activity resulting from a contractual arrangement whereby two or more venturers participate, directly or indirectly, in the jointly-controlled economic activity.

lease. The conveyance, by a lessor to a lessee, of the right to use a tangible asset, usually for a specified period of time in return for rent.

lease inducements. Incentives for a lessee to sign a lease (for example, an upfront cash payment to the lessee, an initial rent-free period or reduced rent payments in early periods, the reimbursement of costs of the lessee such as moving costs or leasehold improvements, or the assumption by the lessor of the lessee's preexisting lease).

lease term. The fixed, noncancellable period of the lease plus

- all periods covered by *bargain renewal options*;
- all periods for which failure to renew would impose on the lessee a penalty sufficiently large that renewal appears, at the inception of the lease, reasonably assured;
- all periods covered by ordinary renewal options during which the lessee has undertaken to guarantee the lessor's debt related to the leased property;
- all periods covered by ordinary renewal options preceding the date on which a bargain purchase option is exercisable; and
- all periods representing renewals or extensions of the lease at the lessor's option

provided that the lease term does not extend beyond the date a bargain purchase option becomes exercisable.

The lease term is considered to be noncancellable if cancellation is possible only

- upon the occurrence of some remote contingency;
- with permission of the lessor;
- upon the lessee entering into a new lease for the same or equivalent property with the same lessor; or
- upon payment by the lessee of a penalty sufficiently large that continuation of the lease appears, at the inception of the lease, reasonably assured.

lessee's rate for incremental borrowing. The interest rate that, at the inception of the lease, the lessee would have incurred to borrow, over a similar term and with similar security for the borrowing, the funds necessary to purchase the leased asset.

long-lived asset. An asset that does not meet the definition of a current asset (see chapter 5, "Current Assets and Current Liabilities"). The term *long-lived asset* could include an asset group or disposal group.

market value. The amount of the consideration that would be agreed upon in an arm's length transaction between knowledgeable, willing parties who are under no compulsion to act.

Related to lease accounting:

- When the lessor is a manufacturer or dealer, the market value of the property at the inception of the lease will usually be its normal selling price, reflecting any volume or trade discounts that may be applicable. However, the determination of market value would be made in light of market conditions prevailing at the time, which may indicate that the market value of the property is less than the normal selling price.

- When the lessor is not a manufacturer or dealer, the market value of the property at the inception of the lease will usually be its cost to the lessor, reflecting any volume or trade discounts that may be applicable. However, when there has been a lapse of time between the date of acquisition of the property by the lessor and the inception of the lease, the determination of market value would be made in light of market conditions prevailing at the inception of the lease, which may indicate that the market value of the property is greater or less than its cost or carrying amount.

materiality. Materiality is the term used to describe the significance of financial statement information to users. An item of information, or an aggregate of items, is material if it is probable that its omission or misstatement would influence or change a decision. Materiality is a matter of professional judgment in the particular circumstances.

minimum lease payments.

- From the point of view of the lessee, minimum lease payments comprise

    — the minimum rental payments called for by the lease over the lease term;

    — any partial or full guarantee, by the lessee or a third party related to the lessee, of the residual value of the leased property at the end of the lease term (when the lessee agrees to make up a deficiency in the lessor's realization of the residual value below a stated amount, the guarantee to be included in the minimum lease payments is the stated amount rather than an estimate of the deficiency to be made up); and

    — any penalty required to be paid by the lessee for failure to renew or extend the lease at the end of the lease term

    provided that if the lease contains a bargain purchase option, only the total of the minimum rental payments over the lease term and the payment called for by the bargain purchase option is included in minimum lease payments. Lease payments that depend on factors measurable at the inception of the lease, such as the consumer price index or the prime interest rate, are not, in substance, contingent rentals in their entirety, and are included in the minimum lease payments based on the index or rate existing at the inception of the lease.

- From the point of view of the lessor, minimum lease payments comprise

    — minimum lease payments for the lessee as described previously and

Glossary

— any residual value or rental payments beyond the lease term guaranteed by a third party unrelated to either the lessee or lessor, provided that the guarantor is financially capable of discharging the obligations under the guarantee.

monetary items. Money, and claims to money, the value of which (in terms of the monetary unit, whether foreign or domestic) is fixed by contract or otherwise.

monetary assets and liabilities. Money, monetary assets to be received, or claims to future cash flows that are fixed or determinable in amounts and timing by contract or other arrangement. Examples are cash and accounts and notes receivable and payable in cash.

more likely than not. An event is more likely than not when the probability that it will occur is greater than 50 percent.

multiemployer plan. A defined benefit plan under which a single plan funds the benefits for employees of different unrelated companies. These types of plans are often set up as a result of union contracts. The plan assumes the liability for benefits to all participants without regard to the company. Although contributions are determined on an annual basis by a formula specified in the plan, if a company terminates its participation in the plan, it may be subject to a termination liability.

near term. A period of time not to exceed one year from the date of the financial statements.

net realizable value. The estimated selling price in the ordinary course of business less the estimated costs of completion and the estimated costs necessary to make the sale.

noncontrolling interest. The equity in a subsidiary not attributable, directly or indirectly, to a parent.

nonmonetary assets and liabilities. Assets and liabilities that are not monetary. Examples are inventories; investments in common stock; property, plant, and equipment; and liabilities for rent collected in advance. A contractual right to receive services in the future is a nonmonetary asset, and a contractual obligation to perform services in the future is a nonmonetary liability.

nonmonetary transactions. Nonmonetary transactions are either

- **nonmonetary exchanges**, which are exchanges of nonmonetary assets, liabilities, or services for other nonmonetary assets, liabilities, or services with little or no monetary consideration involved or

- **nonmonetary nonreciprocal transfers**, which are transfers of nonmonetary assets, liabilities, or services without consideration. Nonreciprocal transfers include, but are not limited to

  — donations of nonmonetary assets or services;

  — payments of dividends-in-kind;

  — stock dividends, when the shareholder has the option of receiving cash or shares; and

  — the distribution of assets to owners in the liquidation of all, or part, of an entity.

FRF-SME GLO

The issue of shares in a stock split and the payment of nonoptional stock dividends are not nonreciprocal transfers.

obligation for retirement and other postemployment benefits. The actuarial present value as of a particular date of benefits expected to be paid under a defined benefit plan. The obligation is measured on the basis of the expected amount and timing of future benefits, taking into consideration the expected future cost of providing the benefits and the extent to which the costs are shared by employees or others.

operating activities. The principal revenue-producing activities of the entity and all other activities that are not investing or financing activities.

operating lease. A lease in which the lessor does not transfer substantially all the benefits and risks incident to ownership of property.

owners. Used broadly to include holders of equity interests of investor-owned entities.

plan assets. Assets that have been segregated and restricted in a trust or other legal entity separate from a reporting entity to provide for retirement and other postemployment benefits under the following conditions:

- The assets of the separate entity are to be used only to settle the related accrued benefit obligation, are not available to the reporting entity's own creditors, and either cannot be returned to the reporting entity or can be returned to the reporting entity only if the remaining assets of the trust are sufficient to meet the plan's obligations.

- To the extent that sufficient assets are in the separate entity, the reporting entity will have no obligation to pay the related retirement and other postemployment benefits directly.

Plan assets include any financial instruments issued by the reporting entity and held by the trust or other legal entity. For the purposes of the FRF for SMEs accounting framework, plan assets do not include amounts held by the reporting entity and not yet paid into the trust or other legal entity. Plan assets may include certain arrangements with insurance entities.

percentage of completion method. A method of accounting that recognizes revenue proportionately with the degree of completion of the rendering of goods or services under a contract.

prior period errors. Omissions from, and misstatements in, the entity's financial statements for one or more prior periods arising from a failure to use, or the misuse of, reliable information that

- was available when financial statements for those periods were available to be issued and

- could reasonably be expected to have been obtained and taken into account in the preparation and presentation of those financial statements.

Such errors include the effects of mathematical mistakes, mistakes in applying accounting policies, oversights or misinterpretations of facts, and fraud.

Glossary

probable. The future event or events are likely to occur. Probable is a higher level of likelihood than "more likely than not." Probable does not mean virtually certain.

promissory estoppel. The legal principle that a promise or assurance made without consideration may, nonetheless, be enforced to prevent injustice, when the promise or assurance was intended to affect a contract or other legal relationship between the promisor and the promisee and be acted on, and the promisee acted on the promise or assurance or, in some way, changed its position.

property, plant, and equipment. Identifiable tangible assets that meet all the following criteria:

- Are held for use in the production or supply of goods and services, for administrative purposes, or for the development, construction, maintenance, or repair of other property, plant, and equipment
- Have been acquired, constructed, or developed with the intention of being used on a continuing basis
- Are not intended for sale in the ordinary course of business

proportionate consolidation. A method of accounting and reporting only applicable to unincorporated entities in which it is an established industry practice, whereby a venturer may account in its financial statements for its pro rata share of the assets, liabilities, revenues, and expenses that are subject to joint control. The venturer's pro rata share of the assets, liabilities, revenues, and expenses that are subject to joint control is combined on a line-by-line basis with similar items in the venturer's financial statements. This method of accounting differs from full consolidation in that only the venturer's portion of all assets, liabilities, revenues, and expenses is recognized rather than the full amount, offset by noncontrolling interests.

prospective application. A change in an accounting policy, and of recognizing the effect of a change in an accounting estimate, that consists of

- applying the new accounting policy to transactions, other events, and conditions occurring after the date the policy is changed and
- recognizing the effect of the change in the accounting estimate in the current and future periods affected by the change.

push-down accounting. A technique that attributes revised values to the assets and liabilities reported in the entity's financial statements based on a purchase transaction or transactions of its equity interests. Application of the technique results in the acquirer's cost being assigned to the assets and liabilities of the acquired entity.

reasonably possible. The chance of the occurrence (or nonoccurrence) of the future event(s) is more than remote but less than likely.

related parties. Related parties exist when one party has the ability to exercise, directly or indirectly, control, joint control, or significant influence over the other. Two or more parties are related when they are subject to common control, joint control, or common significant influence. Related parties also include management and immediate family members.

related party transaction. A transfer of economic resources or obligations between related parties, or the provision of services by one

FRF-SME GLO

party to a related party, regardless of whether any consideration is exchanged. The parties to the transaction are related prior to the transaction. When the relationship arises as a result of the transaction, the transaction is not one between related parties.

remote. The chance of the occurrence (or nonoccurrence) of the future event(s) is slight.

reporting entity. In the context of chapter 31, "Foreign Currency Translation," an entity whose financial statements include transactions entered into by the entity in a foreign currency.

research. Original and planned investigation undertaken with the prospect of gaining new scientific or technical knowledge and understanding.

residual value. The estimated net realizable value of an item of property, plant, and equipment at the end of its useful life to an entity. Residual value is entity-specific compared to salvage value.

In the context of intangible assets, residual value is defined as the estimated amount that an entity would currently obtain from disposal of the asset after deducting the estimated costs of disposal, if the asset were already of the age and in the condition expected at the end of its useful life.

residual value of the leased property. The estimated market value of the leased property at the end of the lease term.

retained earnings. Comprises the accumulated balance of income less losses arising from the operation of the business after taking into account dividends and other amounts that may properly be charged or credited thereto. When the accumulation is a negative figure, "accumulated deficit" is a suitable designation. As used in the FRF for SMEs accounting framework, the term *retained earnings* also refers to owners' capital accounts, depending upon the nature of the entity.

retirement. Retirement of a long-lived asset is its other-than-temporary removal from service, including its sale, abandonment, recycling, or disposal in some other manner, but not its temporary idling.

retrospective application. A type of application that applies a new accounting policy to transactions, other events, and conditions as if that policy had always been applied.

retrospective restatement. Correcting the recognition, measurement, and disclosure of amounts of elements of financial statements as if a prior period error had never occurred.

revenue. The inflow of cash, receivables, or other consideration arising in the course of the ordinary activities of an entity, normally from the sale of goods, the rendering of services, and the use by others of entity resources yielding interest, royalties, and dividends. Revenue is net of items such as trade or volume discounts, returns and allowances, claims for damaged goods, and certain excise and sales taxes. Excise and sales taxes to be netted against revenue would normally include those imposed at the time of sale and would normally exclude those imposed prior to the time of sale on either the goods or their constituents.

sale-leaseback transaction. The sale of property with the purchaser leasing the property back to the seller.

Glossary

sales-type lease. A lease that, from the point of view of the lessor, transfers substantially all the benefits and risks incident to ownership of property to the lessee and, at the inception of the lease, the market value of the leased property is greater or less than its carrying amount, thus, giving rise to a profit or loss to the lessor (usually a manufacturer or dealer).

salvage value. The estimated net realizable value of an item of property, plant, and equipment at the end of its useful life. Salvage value is normally negligible.

service potential. The output or service capacity of an item of property, plant, and equipment, normally determined by reference to attributes such as physical output capacity, associated operating costs, useful life, and quality of output.

severe impact. A significant financially disruptive effect on the normal functioning of the entity. Severe impact is a higher threshold than material. Matters that are important enough to influence a user's decisions are deemed to be material, yet they may not be so significant as to disrupt the normal functioning of the entity. The concept of severe impact, however, includes matters that are less than catastrophic.

significant influence. Significant influence over an entity is the ability to affect the strategic operating, investing, and financing policies of the entity.

subsidiary. An entity that another entity (parent) controls.

taxable income (tax loss). The amount for a period, determined in accordance with the rules established by taxation authorities, upon which income taxes are payable (refundable).

taxes payable method. A method of accounting under which an entity reports as an expense (income) of the period only the cost (benefit) of current income taxes for that period, determined in accordance with the rules established by taxation authorities.

temporal method. A method of translation that translates assets, liabilities, revenues, and expenses in a manner that retains their bases of measurement in terms of the U.S. dollar (that is, it uses the U.S. dollar as the unit of measure). In particular

- monetary items are translated at the exchange rate in effect at the statement of financial position date;

- nonmonetary items are translated at historical exchange rates, unless such items are carried at net realizable value or market value, in which case, they are translated at the exchange rate in effect at the statement of financial position date;

- revenue and expense items are translated at the exchange rate in effect on the dates they occur; and

- depreciation or amortization of assets translated at historical exchange rates is translated at the same exchange rates as the assets to which it relates.

temporary differences. Differences between the tax basis of an asset or liability and its carrying amount in the statement of financial position. Temporary differences may be either

FRF-SME GLO

- **deductible temporary differences**, which are temporary differences that will result in deductible amounts when determining taxable income of future periods when the carrying amount of the asset or liability is recovered or settled, or
- **taxable temporary differences**, which are temporary differences that will result in taxable amounts when determining taxable income of future periods when the carrying amount of the asset or liability is recovered or settled.

unguaranteed residual value. That portion of the residual value of leased property that is not guaranteed or is guaranteed solely by a party related to the lessor.

useful life. The period over which an asset, singly or in combination with other assets, is expected to contribute directly or indirectly to the future cash flows of an entity.

venturer. A party to a joint venture, who has joint control over that joint venture, has the right and ability to obtain future economic benefits from the resources of the joint venture, and is exposed to the related risks.

Implementation Resources

Notice to Readers

These implementation resources were developed by the staff of the AICPA and CPA professionals serving small- and medium-sized entities to assist in the implementation of the FRF for SMEs™ accounting framework. These implementation resources have not been approved, disapproved, or otherwise acted upon by any senior technical committee of the AICPA or the Financial Accounting Standards Board and has no official or authoritative status.

Acknowledgements

The AICPA greatly appreciates the invaluable work provided by J. Russell Madray, CPA, and Thomas A. Ratcliffe, Ph.D., CPA, CGMA, both of whom developed these implementation resources in conjunction with Robert J. Durak, CPA, CGMA, of the AICPA staff.

Overview

These implementation resources are intended to assist CPAs and others who are preparing financial statements in accordance with the AICPA's FRF for SMEs™. The FRF for SMEs accounting framework is a self-contained, special purpose framework intended for use by privately-held small- to medium-sized entities (SMEs) in preparing their financial statements.

The framework was developed to address transactions that are typically encountered by private, for-profit SMEs. If the FRF for SMEs accounting framework does not specifically address a transaction, other event, or condition, management is advised in the framework to use its judgment and apply the general principles, concepts, and criteria contained in the FRF for SMEs in developing accounting policies. As such, the FRF for SMEs accounting framework is intended as a principles-based framework. It de-emphasizes "bright line" rules, a dependence on interpretive guidance, and a need for extensive implementation materials. Rather, the framework emphasizes the use of professional judgment in applying overall principles.

Nonetheless, AICPA staff recognizes that owner-managers of SMEs, their outside CPAs, and those who use their financial statements, would benefit from certain implementation resources that will help them better understand the kind of financial statements that result from utilizing the FRF for SMEs accounting framework, and how the framework compares to other bases of accounting. In addition, AICPA staff recognizes that those preparing financial statements under the FRF for SMEs accounting framework would find a presentation and disclosure checklist and certain illustrative application examples helpful. Finally, CPAs reporting on financial statements prepared under the FRF for SMEs accounting framework would benefit from sample audit, compilation, and review reports.

Illustrative Financial Statements

This section of *Financial Reporting Framework for Small- and Medium-Sized Entities Implementation Resources* contains sample financial statements intended to illustrate financial statements prepared under the FRF for SMEs accounting framework. Two sets of sample financial statements, including notes to the financial statements, are presented. Each of the two sets also contains financial statements based on accounting principles generally accepted in the United States of America (U.S. GAAP). During the AICPA staff's outreach efforts related to the FRF for SMEs accounting framework, users of financial statements and other stakeholders asked for comparisons of financial statements prepared under the framework to those prepared under U.S. GAAP. These are presented for comparative purposes.

These sample financial statements are included for illustrative purposes and are not intended to establish reporting requirements. Furthermore, the dollar amounts shown are illustrative only and are not intended to indicate any customary relationship among accounts. The sample financial statements do not include all of the accounts and transactions that might be found in practice. The notes indicate the subject matter generally required to be disclosed, but should be expanded, reduced, or modified to suit individual circumstances and materiality considerations.

In the following illustrative financial statements based on the FRF for SMEs accounting framework, it is presumed that the management of both Acme Manufacturing, Inc. and affiliates and Alpha Contractors, Inc. and subsidiary evaluated the financial reporting needs and responsibilities of their businesses and determined that the FRF for SMEs accounting framework was a suitable accounting option to use in the preparation of their financial statements.

Acme Manufacturing Inc. and Affiliates
Consolidated Comparative Financial Statements
December 31, 2013 and 2012
Based on the FRF for SMEs Accounting Framework

Primary differences between the Acme illustrative financial statements based on the FRF for SMEs accounting framework and those based on U.S. GAAP are

- the FRF for SMEs accounting framework is unlike U.S. GAAP in that it does not include the concept of variable interest entities (VIEs). The U.S. GAAP presentation requires the consolidation of VIEs and related disclosures. The FRF for SMEs reporting option does not require consolidation of VIEs nor include disclosures about VIEs. The FRF for SMEs accounting framework does include disclosure about related parties.

- in the FRF for SMEs accounting framework, goodwill is amortized over 15 years, unlike the U.S. GAAP presentation, which requires impairment testing of goodwill and no amortization.

- in the U.S. GAAP presentation, Acme is required to comply with accounting guidance for uncertainty in income taxes and makes the related disclosures. The FRF for SMEs accounting framework does not contain similar requirements.

Independent Accountants' Review Report

To the Stockholders
Acme Manufacturing, Inc. and Affiliates

We have reviewed the accompanying consolidated statements of assets, liabilities, and equity of Acme Manufacturing, Inc. and Affiliates, as of December 31, 2013 and 2012, and the related consolidated statements of revenues and expenses and cash flows for the years then ended. A review includes primarily applying analytical procedures to management's financial data and making inquiries of company management. A review is substantially less in scope than an audit, the objective of which is the expression of an opinion regarding the financial statements taken as a whole. Accordingly, we do not express such an opinion.

Management is responsible for the preparation and fair presentation of financial statements in accordance with the *Financial Reporting Framework for Small- and Medium-Sized Entities* issued by the American Institute of Certified Public Accountants and for designing, implementing, and maintaining internal control relevant to the preparation and fair presentation of the financial statements.

Our responsibility is to conduct the reviews in accordance with Statements on Standards for Accounting and Review Services issued by the American Institute of Certified Public Accountants. Those standards require us to perform procedures to obtain limited assurance that there are no material modifications that should be made to the financial statements. We believe that the results of our procedures provide a reasonable basis for our report.

FRF-SME

Based on our reviews, we are not aware of any material modifications that should be made to the accompanying financial statements in order for them to be in conformity with the *Financial Reporting Framework for Small- and Medium-Sized Entities*, described in Note 1.

[*Signature of Accounting Firm*]
Boise, Idaho
April 26, 2014

Acme Manufacturing, Inc. and Affiliates
Consolidated Statements of Assets, Liabilities, and Equity
(FRF for SMEs Accounting Framework Basis)
December 31, 2013 and 2012

Assets

	2013	2012
Current assets		
Cash and cash equivalents	$ 319,979	$ 232,479
Accounts receivable	1,094,291	899,337
Employee receivables	5,739	4,867
Inventories	26,461	28,820
Prepaid expenses	13,177	6,697
Total current assets	1,459,647	1,172,200
Investments		
Land held for investment	7,570	8,397
Total investments	7,570	8,397
Property and equipment		
Land	10,711	7,849
Buildings	19,058	13,743
Leasehold improvements	8,748	8,748
Furniture, fixtures, and equipment	27,550	26,944
Automobiles and trucks	155,626	154,165
Shop tools and equipment	115,829	111,009
	337,522	322,458
Less accumulated depreciation	269,486	257,736
Net property and equipment	68,036	64,722
Other assets		
Goodwill	1,159	1,304
Loan costs	170	218
Cash surrender value of life insurance	59,841	56,416
Total other assets	61,170	57,938
Total assets	$1,596,423	$1,303,257

See independent accountants' review report and notes to consolidated financial statements.

(continued)

FRF-SME

Liabilities and equity

	2013	2012
Current liabilities		
Accounts payable	$ 609,732	$ 494,729
Current maturities of long-term debt	1,218	127,737
Employee withholdings and payroll taxes	6,939	9,831
Accrued liabilities:		
Interest	13	520
Bonuses	30,213	20,584
Salaries	29,869	31,160
Taxes other than income taxes	—	5,856
Total current liabilities	677,984	690,417
Noncurrent liabilities		
Noncurrent maturities of long-term debt	—	1,218
Total liabilities	677,984	691,635
Equity		
Acme, Inc. equity:		
Common stock—$10 par value, 285 shares authorized, issued and outstanding	2,850	2,850
Additional paid-in capital	24,604	24,604
Retained earnings	890,985	584,168
Total equity	918,439	611,622
Total liabilities and equity	$1,596,423	$1,303,257

See independent accountants' review report and notes to consolidated financial statements.

Acme Manufacturing, Inc. and Affiliates
Consolidated Statements of Revenues and Expenses
(FRF for SMEs Accounting Framework Basis)
For the Years Ended December 31, 2013 and 2012

	2013	2012
Net sales	$5,825,504	$4,157,067
Cost of sales	5,242,891	3,978,145
Gross profit	582,613	178,922
Operating expenses		
Selling, general, and administrative	229,650	228,216
Interest	5,765	17,686
Total operating expenses	235,415	245,902
Operating income (loss)	347,198	(66,980)
Other income		
Interest	1,020	2,217
Gain (loss) on sale of assets	1,774	(1,340)
Miscellaneous income	10,528	15,598
Total other income	13,322	16,475
Net income (loss)	$ 360,520	$ (50,505)

See independent accountants' review report and notes to consolidated financial statements.

FRF-SME

Acme Manufacturing, Inc. and Affiliates
Consolidated Statements of Cash Flows
(FRF for SMEs Accounting Framework Basis)
For the Years Ended December 31, 2013 and 2012

	2013	2012
Cash flows from operating activities		
Cash received from operations	$ 5,820,408	$ 4,424,128
Cash paid for operating expenses	(5,522,788)	(4,291,484)
Interest received	1,020	2,217
Interest paid	(6,272)	(17,395)
Net cash provided by operating activities	292,368	117,466
Cash flows from investing activities		
Capital expenditures	(17,677)	(20,613)
Principal receipts on notes receivable	—	227
Proceeds from sale of assets	1,773	—
Net cash used by investing activities	(15,904)	(20,386)
Cash flows from financing activities		
Principal payments on long-term debt	(135,088)	(629,704)
Payment of loan costs	(173)	—
Distributions to stockholders	(53,703)	(40,712)
Net cash used by financing activities	(188,964)	(670,416)
Net increase (decrease) in cash and cash equivalents	87,500	(573,336)
Cash and cash equivalents at beginning of year	232,479	805,815
Cash and cash equivalents at end of year	$ 319,979	$ 232,479
Reconciliation of net income (loss) to net cash provided by operating activities		
Net income (loss)	$ 360,520	$ (50,505)
Adjustments to reconcile net income (loss) to net cash provided by operating activities		
Depreciation and amortization	22,905	25,759
(Gain) loss on sale of assets	(1,774)	1,340

	2013	2012
Changes in assets and liabilities:	—	—
Accounts receivable	(179,085)	320,550
Inventories	2,359	(3,498)
Prepaid expenses	(6,480)	27,171
Cash surrender value of life insurance	(3,425)	(12,434)
Accounts payable and accrued liabilities	97,348	(190,917)
Total adjustments	(68,152)	167,971
Net cash provided by operating activities	$ 292,368	$ 117,466

See independent accountants' review report and notes to consolidated financial statements.

Acme Manufacturing, Inc. and Affiliates
Notes to Consolidated Financial Statements
December 31, 2013 and 2012

1. SUMMARY OF SIGNIFICANT ACCOUNTING POLICIES

Basis of Accounting

The accompanying financial statements have been prepared in accordance with the *Financial Reporting Framework for Small- and Medium-Sized Entities* issued by the American Institute of Certified Public Accountants, which is a special purpose framework and not U.S. generally accepted accounting principles (U.S. GAAP). The accounting principles that compose the framework are appropriate for the preparation and presentation of small- and medium-sized entity financial statements, based on the needs of the financial statement users and cost and benefit considerations. This special purpose framework, unlike U.S. GAAP, does not require the consolidation of VIEs, which is a term and concept found in GAAP. In addition, this special purpose framework requires the amortization of goodwill, unlike GAAP, which requires impairment testing of goodwill and no amortization.

Nature of Organization

Acme Manufacturing, Inc. (the Company) is primarily involved in the manufacturing and sales of irrigation systems to commercial customers. Outdoor Lighting Concepts, Inc. primarily sells lighting fixtures and parts to individuals.

Most of the Company's business activity is with customers located within the geographical area of the state of Idaho.

Principles of Consolidation

The accompanying consolidated financial statements include the accounts of Acme Manufacturing, Inc. and its wholly-owned subsidiary, Outdoor Lighting Concepts, Inc. All significant intercompany transactions have been eliminated.

Accounts Receivable

The Company reports all receivables at gross amounts due from customers. Because historical losses related to these receivables have been insignificant, management uses the direct write-off method to account for bad debts. On a continuing basis, management analyzes delinquent receivables and, once these receivables are determined to be uncollectible, they are written off through a charge against earnings.

Inventories

Inventory of irrigation supplies and parts is stated at the lower of cost or net realizable value, on a first-in, first-out basis.

Property and Equipment

Property and equipment are recorded at cost and are depreciated using the straight-line method over the estimated useful lives of the assets, which is 40 years for buildings; 15 years for leasehold improvements; 7 years for furniture, fixtures, and equipment; 6 years for automobiles and trucks; and 7 years for shop tools and equipment.

Maintenance and repairs are charged to expense when incurred and the cost of additions, replacements, and improvements is capitalized.

Income Taxes

The Company and its wholly-owned subsidiary have elected to be treated as S corporations under applicable federal and state income tax laws. In lieu of corporate income taxes, the owners are taxed on their proportionate share of the respective Company's taxable income. Therefore, no provision or liability for federal or state income taxes has been included in the financial statements.

With few exceptions, the Company is no longer subject to U.S. federal, state, and local income tax examinations by tax authorities for years before 2010.

Cash and Cash Equivalents

For purposes of the consolidated statements of cash flows, the Company considers all highly liquid debt instruments purchased with an original maturity of three months or less to be cash equivalents.

Use of Estimates in the Preparation of Financial Statements

The preparation of financial statements in conformity with the *Financial Reporting Framework for Small and Medium-Sized Entities* requires management to make estimates and assumptions that affect the reported amounts of assets and liabilities and the disclosure of contingent assets and liabilities at the date of the financial statements and the reported amounts of revenues and expenses during the reporting period. Actual results could differ from those estimates.

Goodwill

Goodwill represents the excess of the purchase price over market value of the Company's ownership in Outdoor Lighting Concepts, Inc., and is amortized over 15 years.

Evaluation of Subsequent Events

The Company has evaluated subsequent events through April 26, 2014, which is the date the financial statements were available to be issued.

2. CONCENTRATION OF CREDIT RISK

The Company maintains its cash in bank deposit accounts which, at times, may exceed federally insured limits. The balances are insured by the Federal Deposit Insurance Corporation (FDIC) up to $250,000. At December 31, 2013, the Company had balances in excess of insured limits totaling $159,795. The Company has not experienced any losses in such accounts.

3. RELATED PARTY TRANSACTIONS

In 2009, the stockholders of the Company entered into an agreement whereby the majority stockholder sold his interest to the remaining stockholders. In connection with this transaction, distributions were made that were in turn loaned back to the Company in the form of unsecured notes payable. The balances on these notes payable were paid in full during 2012.

FRF-SME

4. LONG-TERM DEBT

The details concerning long-term debt for the years ended December 31, 2013 and 2012, follow.

	2013	2012
Note payable to First Commerce Bank, with interest at 6.15%, monthly payments of principal and interest of $729, secured by equipment, due February 2014	1,218	6,574
Note payable to County Bank, with variable interest between 4.2% and 8%, secured by real estate, due January 2014	—	122,381
Total	1,218	128,955
Less current maturities of long-term debt	1,218	127,737
Noncurrent maturities of long-term debt	$ —	$ 1,218

5. CHANGES IN EQUITY

The following table summarizes changes in Company equity accounts during 2013 and 2012.

	Common Stock	Additional Paid-in Capital	Retained Earnings
Balance at January 1, 2013	$2,850	$24,604	$584,168
Net income	—	—	360,520
Distributions	—	—	(53,703)
Balance at December 31, 2013	$2,850	$24,604	$890,985

	Common Stock	Additional Paid-in Capital	Retained Earnings
Balance at January 1, 2012	$2,850	$24,604	$675,385
Net loss	—	—	(50,505)
Distributions	—	—	(40,712)
Balance at December 31, 2012	$2,850	$24,604	$584,168

See independent accountants' review report.

FRF-SME

Acme Manufacturing Inc. and Affiliates
Consolidated Comparative Financial Statements
December 31, 2013 and 2012
Based on U.S. GAAP

Primary differences between the Acme illustrative financial statements based on the FRF for SMEs accounting framework and those based on U.S. GAAP are

- the FRF for SMEs accounting framework is unlike U.S. GAAP in that it does not include the concept of VIEs. The U.S. GAAP presentation requires the consolidation of VIEs and related disclosures. The FRF for SMEs reporting option does not require consolidation of VIEs nor include disclosures about VIEs. The FRF for SMEs accounting framework does include disclosure about related parties.
- in the FRF for SMEs accounting framework, goodwill is amortized over 15 years, unlike the U.S. GAAP presentation, which requires impairment testing of goodwill and no amortization.
- in the U.S. GAAP presentation, Acme is required to comply with accounting guidance for uncertainty in income taxes and makes the related disclosures. The FRF for SMEs accounting framework does not contain similar requirements.

Independent Accountants' Review Report

To the Stockholders
Acme Manufacturing, Inc. and Affiliates

We have reviewed the accompanying consolidated balance sheets of Acme Manufacturing, Inc. and Affiliates, as of December 31, 2013 and 2012, and the related consolidated statements of income and cash flows for the years then ended. A review includes primarily applying analytical procedures to management's financial data and making inquiries of company management. A review is substantially less in scope than an audit, the objective of which is the expression of an opinion regarding the financial statements taken as a whole. Accordingly, we do not express such an opinion.

Management is responsible for the preparation and fair presentation of financial statements in accordance with accounting principles generally accepted in the United States of America and for designing, implementing, and maintaining internal control relevant to the preparation and fair presentation of the financial statements.

Our responsibility is to conduct the reviews in accordance with Statements on Standards for Accounting and Review Services issued by the American Institute of Certified Public Accountants. Those standards require us to perform procedures to obtain limited assurance that there are no material modifications that should be made to the financial statements. We believe that the results of our procedures provide a reasonable basis for our report.

Based on our reviews, we are not aware of any material modifications that should be made to the accompanying financial statements in order for them to be in conformity with accounting principles generally accepted in the United States of America.

[*Signature of Accounting Firm*]
Boise, Idaho
March 27, 2014

Acme Manufacturing, Inc. and Affiliates
Consolidated Balance Sheets
December 31, 2013 and 2012

Assets

	2013	2012
Current assets		
Cash and cash equivalents	$ 319,979	$ 232,479
Accounts receivable	1,094,291	899,337
Employee receivables	5,739	4,867
Inventories	26,461	28,820
Prepaid expenses	13,177	6,697
Total current assets	1,459,647	1,172,200
Investments		
Land held for investment	7,570	8,397
Total investments	7,570	8,397
Property and equipment		
Land	43,551	43,551
Buildings	80,046	80,046
Leasehold improvements	8,748	8,748
Furniture, fixtures, and equipment	27,550	26,944
Automobiles and trucks	155,626	154,165
Shop tools and equipment	115,829	111,009
	431,350	424,463
Less accumulated depreciation	269,487	257,737
Net property and equipment	161,863	166,726
Other assets		
Goodwill	1,449	1,449
Loan costs	170	218
Cash surrender value of life insurance	59,841	56,416
Total other assets	61,460	58,083
Total assets	**$1,690,540**	**$1,405,406**

See independent accountants' review report and notes to consolidated financial statements.

Liabilities and equity

	2013	2012
Current liabilities		
Accounts payable	$ 609,732	$ 494,729
Current maturities of long-term debt	8,233	134,455
Employee withholdings and payroll taxes	6,939	9,831
Accrued liabilities:		
Interest	13	520
Bonuses	30,213	20,584
Salaries	29,869	31,160
Taxes other than income taxes	—	5,856
Total current liabilities	684,999	697,135
Noncurrent liabilities		
Noncurrent maturities of long-term debt	158,312	44,754
Total liabilities	843,311	741,889
Equity		
Acme, Inc. equity:		
Common stock—$10 par value, 285 shares authorized, issued and outstanding	2,850	2,850
Additional paid-in capital	24,604	24,604
Retained earnings	891,274	584,310
Total Acme, Inc. equity	918,728	611,764
Noncontrolling interest	(71,499)	51,753
Total equity	847,229	663,517
Total liabilities and equity	$1,690,540	$1,405,406

See independent accountants' review report and notes to consolidated financial statements.

Acme Manufacturing, Inc. and Affiliates
Consolidated Statements of Income
For the Years Ended December 31, 2013 and 2012

	2013	2012
Net sales	$5,834,171	$4,159,783
Cost of sales	5,242,891	3,978,145
Gross profit	591,280	181,638
Operating expenses		
Selling, general and administrative	229,505	228,071
Interest	5,765	17,686
Total operating expenses	235,270	245,757
Operating income (loss)	356,010	(64,119)
Other income		
Interest	1,020	2,217
Gain (loss) on sale of assets	1,774	(1,340)
Miscellaneous income	10,528	15,598
Total other income	13,322	16,475
Net income (loss)	369,332	(47,644)
Income attributed to noncontrolling interest	(8,667)	(2,716)
Net income (loss) attributable to Acme Manufacturing, Inc.	$ 360,665	$ (50,360)

See independent accountants' review report and notes to consolidated financial statements.

Acme Manufacturing, Inc. and Affiliates
Consolidated Statements of Cash Flows
For the Years Ended December 31, 2013 and 2012

	2013	2012
Cash flows from operating activities		
Cash received from operations	$ 5,829,074	$ 4,424,128
Cash paid for operating expenses	(5,522,788)	(4,291,484)
Interest received	1,020	2,217
Interest paid	(6,272)	(17,395)
Net cash provided by operating activities	301,034	117,466
Cash flows from investing activities		
Capital expenditures	(10,573)	(21,179)
Principal receipts on notes receivable	—	227
Proceeds from sale of assets	1,773	—
Net cash used by investing activities	(8,800)	(20,952)
Cash flows from financing activities		
Principal payments on long-term debt	(301,101)	(629,704)
Proceeds from notes payable	288,438	—
Payment of loan costs	(173)	—
Contributions from noncontrolling owners	380	—
Distributions to stockholders	(192,278)	(40,146)
Net cash used by financing activities	(204,734)	(669,850)
Net increase (decrease) in cash and cash equivalents	87,500	(573,336)
Cash and cash equivalents at beginning of year	232,479	805,815
Cash and cash equivalents at end of year	$ 319,979	$ 232,479
Reconciliation of net income (loss) to net cash provided by operating activities		
Net income (loss)	$ 369,332	$ (47,644)
Adjustments to reconcile net income (loss) to net cash provided by operating activities		
Depreciation and amortization	22,760	25,614
(Gain) loss on sale of assets	(1,774)	1,340

(continued)

	2013	2012
Changes in assets and liabilities:	—	—
Accounts receivable	(195,825)	317,834
Inventories	2,359	(3,498)
Prepaid expenses	(6,480)	27,171
Cash surrender value of life insurance	(3,425)	(12,434)
Accounts payable and accrued liabilities	114,087	(190,917)
Total adjustments	(68,298)	165,110
Net cash provided by operating activities	$ 301,034	$ 117,466

See independent accountants' review report and notes to consolidated financial statements.

Acme Manufacturing, Inc. and Affiliates
Notes to Consolidated Financial Statements
December 31, 2013 and 2012

1. SUMMARY OF SIGNIFICANT ACCOUNTING POLICIES

Nature of Organization

Acme Manufacturing, Inc. (the Company) is primarily involved in the manufacturing and sales of irrigation systems to commercial customers. Outdoor Lighting Concepts, Inc. primarily sells lighting fixtures and parts to individuals.

Most of the Company's business activity is with customers located within the geographical area of the state of Idaho.

Principles of Consolidation

The accompanying consolidated financial statements include the accounts of Acme Manufacturing, Inc. and its wholly-owned subsidiary, Outdoor Lighting Concepts, Inc., as well as variable interest entities (VIEs) for which the Company is considered the primary beneficiary. See note 6 for a discussion of VIEs.

All significant intercompany transactions have been eliminated.

Accounts Receivable

The Company reports all receivables at gross amounts due from customers. Because historical losses related to these receivables have been insignificant, management uses the direct write-off method to account for bad debts. On a continuing basis, management analyzes delinquent receivables and, once these receivables are determined to be uncollectible, they are written off through a charge against earnings.

Inventories

Inventory of irrigation supplies and parts is stated at the lower of cost or market, on a first-in, first-out basis.

Property and Equipment

Property and equipment are recorded at cost and are depreciated using the straight-line method over the estimated useful lives of the assets.

Maintenance and repairs are charged to expense when incurred and the cost of additions, replacements, and improvements is capitalized.

Advertising

Advertising costs are expensed as incurred. Advertising expense was $4,006 and $4,883 for the years ended December 31, 2013 and 2012, respectively.

Income Taxes

The Company and its wholly-owned subsidiary have elected to be treated as S corporations under applicable federal and state income tax laws. Other consolidated affiliates, as described in note 6, were organized as partnerships. In lieu of corporate income taxes, the owners are taxed on their proportionate share of the respective Company's taxable income. Therefore, no provision or liability for federal or state income taxes has been included in the financial statements.

Effective January 1, 2009, the Company implemented the accounting guidance for uncertainty in income taxes using the provisions of

FRF-SME

Financial Accounting Standards Board (FASB) *Accounting Standards Codification* (ASC) 740, *Income Taxes*. Using that guidance, tax positions initially need to be recognized in the financial statements when it is more-likely-than-not the positions will be sustained upon examination by the tax authorities.

As of December 31, 2013, the Company had no uncertain tax positions, or interest and penalties, that qualify for either recognition or disclosure in the financial statements.

With few exceptions, the Company is no longer subject to U.S. federal, state, and local income tax examinations by tax authorities for years before 2010.

Cash and Cash Equivalents

For purposes of the consolidated statements of cash flows, the Company considers all highly liquid debt instruments purchased with an original maturity of three months or less to be cash equivalents.

Use of Estimates in the Preparation of Financial Statements

The preparation of financial statements in conformity with U.S GAAP requires management to make estimates and assumptions that affect the reported amounts of assets and liabilities and the disclosure of contingent assets and liabilities at the date of the financial statements and the reported amounts of revenues and expenses during the reporting period. Actual results could differ from those estimates.

Goodwill

Goodwill represents the excess of the purchase price over fair value of the Company's ownership in Outdoor Lighting Concepts, Inc. In accordance with FASB ASC 350, *Intangibles—Goodwill and Other*, the Company evaluates goodwill on an annual basis for potential impairment.

Evaluation of Subsequent Events

The Company has evaluated subsequent events through March 27, 2014, which is the date the financial statements were available to be issued.

2. CONCENTRATION OF CREDIT RISK

The Company maintains its cash in bank deposit accounts which, at times, may exceed federally insured limits. The balances are insured by the FDIC up to $250,000. At December 31, 2013, the Company had balances in excess of insured limits totaling $159,795. The Company has not experienced any losses in such accounts.

3. RELATED PARTY TRANSACTIONS

In 2009, the stockholders of the Company entered into an agreement whereby the majority stockholder sold his interest to the remaining stockholders. In connection with this transaction, distributions were made that were, in turn, loaned back to the Company in the form of unsecured notes payable. The balances on these notes payable were paid in full during 2012.

4. LONG-TERM DEBT

The details concerning long-term debt for the years ended December 31, 2013 and 2012 follow.

Implementation Resources

	2013	2012
Note payable to Stone Bank, with variable interest at 1.75% plus 5-year U.S. Treasury rate, monthly payments of principal and interest of $1,360, secured by property, due November 2019	$ —	$ 13,830
Note payable to Lakeside Bank, with interest at 6.89%, monthly payments of principal and interest of $892, secured by certain vehicles, due December 2015	1,238	5,064
Note payable to River Bank, with variable interest at 1.75% plus 5-year U.S. Treasury rate, monthly payments of principal and interest of $1,225, secured by property, due November 2019	—	12,817
Note payable to First Commerce Bank, with interest at 6.15%, monthly payments of principal and interest of $729, secured by equipment, due February 2014	1,218	6,574
Note payable to Sun Valley Bank, with interest at 7.5%, monthly payments of principal and interest of $750, secured by property, due November 2024	—	17,369
Note payable to Stone Bank, with interest at 3%, monthly principal payments of $348, secured by a vehicle, due April 2015	652	1,174
Note payable to County Bank, with variable interest between 4.2% and 8%, secured by real estate, due January 2014	—	122,381
Note payable to SunTech Bank, with interest at 4%, secured by property, due December 2018	163,437	—
Total	166,545	179,209
Less current maturities of long-term debt	8,233	134,455
Noncurrent maturities of long-term debt	$158,312	$ 44,754

The aggregate amounts of principal maturities for the next five years follow.

2014	$ 8,233
2015	5,945
2016	5,813
2017	6,053
2018	140,501

FRF-SME

5. CHANGES IN EQUITY

The following table summarizes changes in Company equity accounts during 2013 and 2012.

	Common Stock	Additional Paid-in Capital	Retained Earnings	Noncontrolling Interest	Total
Balance at January 1, 2013	$2,850	$24,604	$584,310	$51,753	$663,517
Net income	—	—	360,665	8,667	369,332
Contributions	—	—	—	6,658	6,658
Distributions	—	—	(53,701)	(138,577)	(192,278)
Balance at December 31, 2013	$2,850	$24,604	$891,274	$(71,499)	$847,229

	Common Stock	Additional Paid-in Capital	Retained Earnings	Noncontrolling Interest	Total
Balance at January 1, 2012	$2,850	$24,604	$674,816	$49,037	$751,307
Net income (loss)	—	—	(50,360)	2,716	(47,644)
Distributions	—	—	(40,146)	—	(40,146)
Balance at December 31, 2012	$2,850	$24,604	$584,310	$51,753	$663,517

FRF-SME

6. VARIABLE INTEREST ENTITIES

Management performs an analysis of the Company's variable interests to determine if those type interests are held in other entities. The analysis primarily is based on a qualitative review, but also includes quantitative considerations in evaluating the variable interests. Qualitative analyses are performed based on an evaluation of the design by the entity, its organizational structure (to include decision-making ability), and financial arrangements. When used to supplement qualitative analyses, quantitative analyses are based on forecasted cash flows of the entity.

U.S. GAAP require reporting entities to consolidate VIEs when they have variable interests that provide a controlling financial interest in VIEs. Entities that consolidate VIEs are referred to as primary beneficiaries.

Coyote Leasing Company and Sun Valley Real Estate Partnership (both are partnerships) each owned certain land and buildings leased to the Company under month-to-month operating leases and used for manufacturing operations. During 2013, Coyote Leasing Company merged with Sun Valley Real Estate Partnership.

The consolidated entity is the owner and lessor of the real estate in which the Company is the sole lessee of the assets under single-lease arrangements. The leases of each entity were evaluated to determine if the arrangements gave the Company a variable interest in a VIE, and to determine whether the Company was the primary beneficiary that would result in consolidating the VIEs. The Company is considered to be the primary beneficiary as a result of an obligation to absorb losses that could be significant to the VIEs. Additionally, because the Company operates the assets being leased from the VIEs, the Company directs activities that most significantly affect economic performance of each of the VIEs.

The following is summarized financial data for each VIE that is included in the Company's consolidated financial statements as of and for the years ended December 31, 2013 and 2012.

2013	Coyote Leasing Company	Sun Valley Real Estate Partnership
Assets	$ 93,828	$ —
Liabilities	$165,327	$ —
Equity	$ (71,499)	$ —
2012		
Assets	$ 84,160	$17,845
Liabilities	$ 37,360	$12,892
Equity	$ 46,800	$ 4,953

See independent accountants' review report.

FRF-SME

Alpha Contractors, Inc. and Subsidiary
Comparative Financial Statements
December 31, 2013 and 2012
Based on the FRF for SMEs Accounting Framework

Primary differences between the Alpha Contractors illustrative financial statements based on the FRF for SMEs accounting framework and those based on U.S. GAAP are

- in the financial statements based on the FRF for SMEs accounting framework, Alpha Contractors adopts the taxes payable method for accounting for income taxes. In the U.S. GAAP presentation, Alpha Contractors is required to follow the deferred taxes method, including the accounting guidance for uncertainty in income taxes, and makes the related disclosures.
- the financial statements based on the FRF for SMEs accounting framework do not include the "Impairment of Long-Lived Assets" disclosure in the summary of significant accounting policies that is contained in the U.S. GAAP-based financial statements. The FRF for SMEs accounting framework does not require impairment testing of long-lived assets.

Note: Supplemental schedules, which are commonly prepared to accompany or supplement the basic financial statements, have not been prepared as part of this illustration.

Independent Auditor's Report

To the Stockholders
Alpha Contractors, Inc. and Subsidiary

We have audited the accompanying consolidated financial statements of Alpha Contractors, Inc. and Subsidiary, which comprise the consolidated statements of assets, liabilities, and equity as of December 31, 2013 and 2012, and the related consolidated statements of revenues, expenses, and retained earnings, and cash flows for the years then ended, and the related notes to the consolidated financial statements.

Management's Responsibility for the Financial Statements
Management is responsible for the preparation and fair presentation of these financial statements in accordance with the *Financial Reporting Framework for Small- and Medium-Sized Entities* issued by the American Institute of Certified Public Accountants, described in Note 1; this includes determining that the *Financial Reporting Framework for Small- and Medium-Sized Entities* is an acceptable basis for the preparation of the financial statements in the circumstances. Management is also responsible for the design, implementation, and maintenance of internal control relevant to the preparation and fair presentation of financial statements that are free from material misstatement, whether due to fraud or error.

Auditor's Responsibility
Our responsibility is to express an opinion on these financial statements based on our audits. We conducted our audits in accordance with auditing standards generally accepted in the United States of America. Those standards require that we plan and perform the audits to obtain reasonable assurance about whether the financial statements are free from material misstatement.

An audit involves performing procedures to obtain audit evidence about the amounts and disclosures in the financial statements. The procedures selected depend on the auditor's judgment, including the assessment of the risks of material misstatement of the financial statements, whether due to fraud or error. In making those risk assessments, the auditor considers internal control relevant to the Company's preparation and fair presentation of the financial statements in order to design audit procedures that are appropriate in the circumstances, but not for the purpose of expressing an opinion on the effectiveness of the Company's internal control. Accordingly, we express no such opinion. An audit also includes evaluating the appropriateness of accounting policies used and the reasonableness of significant accounting estimates made by management, as well as evaluating the overall presentation of the financial statements.

We believe that the audit evidence we have obtained is sufficient and appropriate to provide a basis for our audit opinion.

Opinion

In our opinion, the financial statements referred to above present fairly, in all material respects, the financial position of Alpha Contractors, Inc. and Subsidiary, as of December 31, 2013 and 2012, and the results of its operations and its cash flows for the years then ended in accordance with the *Financial Reporting Framework for Small- and Medium-Sized Entities*, described in Note 1.

Basis of Accounting

We draw attention to Note 1 of the financial statements, which describes the basis of accounting. The financial statements are prepared in accordance with the *Financial Reporting Framework for Small- and Medium-Sized Entities*, which is a basis of accounting other than accounting principles generally accepted in the United States of America. Our opinion is not modified with respect to this matter.

[*Signature of Accounting Firm*]
Greenville, South Carolina
February 18, 2014

Alpha Contractors, Inc.
Consolidated Statements of Assets, Liabilities, and Equity
(FRF for SMEs Accounting Framework Basis)
December 31, 2013 and 2012

Assets	2013	2012
Cash and cash equivalents	$ 304,400	$ 221,300
Contracts receivables	3,789,200	3,334,100
Costs and estimated earnings in excess of billings on uncompleted contracts	156,900	100,600
Inventory	89,700	99,100
Prepaid charges and other assets	118,400	83,200
Total current assets	4,458,600	3,838,300
Advances to and equity in joint venture	205,600	130,700
Note receivable, related company	175,000	150,000
Property and equipment, net of accumulated depreciation and amortization	976,400	1,019,200
Total long term assets	1,357,000	1,299,900
Total assets	$5,815,600	$5,138,200

Liabilities and Shareholders' Equity

Liabilities	2013	2012
Current maturities of notes payable	$ 110,300	$ 110,300
Current portion of lease obligations payable	62,250	57,250
Accounts and retentions payable	2,543,100	2,588,500
Billings in excess of costs and estimated earnings on uncompleted contracts	242,000	221,700
Accrued loss on uncompleted contract	76,700	
Other accrued liabilities	88,600	114,600
Total current liabilities	3,122,950	3,092,350
Notes payable, less current maturities	357,800	468,100
Lease obligations payable, less current portion	135,350	194,050
Long-term accrued liabilities	154,200	26,200
Total long term liabilities	647,350	688,350
Total liabilities	3,770,300	3,780,700

FRF-SME

	2013	2012
Shareholders' equity		
Common stock—$1 par value, 500,000 authorized shares, 300,000 issued and outstanding shares	300,000	300,000
Retained earnings	1,745,300	1,057,500
Total shareholders' equity	2,045,300	1,357,500
Total liabilities and shareholders' equity	$5,815,600	$5,138,200

Alpha Contractors, Inc.
Consolidated Statements of Revenues, Expenses, and Retained Earnings
(FRF for SMEs Accounting Framework Basis)
Years Ended December 31, 2013 and 2012

	2013	2012
Contract revenues earned	$9,630,800	$6,225,400
Cost of revenues earned	7,436,100	4,951,300
Gross profit	2,194,700	1,274,100
Selling, general, and administrative expense	895,600	755,600
Income from operations	1,299,100	518,500
Other income (expense)		
Equity in earnings from unconsolidated joint venture	49,900	5,700
Gain on sale of equipment	10,000	2,000
Interest expense (net of interest income of $8,800 in 2013 and $6,300 in 2012)	(69,500)	(70,800)
Total other expense	(9,600)	(63,100)
Income before current year tax expense	1,289,500	455,400
Income tax expense	451,700	300,900
Net income	837,800	154,500
Retained earnings, beginning of year	1,057,500	1,053,000
	1,895,300	1,207,500
Less: Dividends paid (per share $.50 [2013]; $.50 [2012])	150,000	150,000
Retained earnings, end of year	$1,745,300	$1,057,500

FRF-SME

Alpha Contractors, Inc.
Consolidated Statements of Cash Flows
(FRF for SMEs Accounting Framework Basis)
Years Ended December 31, 2013 and 2012

	2013	2012
Cash flows from operating activities:		
Net income	$837,800	$154,500
Adjustments to reconcile net income to net cash provided by operating activities:		
Depreciation and amortization	167,800	153,500
Provision for losses on contract receivables	6,300	1,100
Gain on sale of equipment	(10,000)	(2,000)
Equity earnings from unconsolidated joint venture	(49,900)	(5,700)
Increase in long-term accrued liabilities	128,000	26,200
Increase in contract receivables	(461,400)	(10,200)
Increase in costs and estimated earnings in excess of billings on uncompleted contracts	(56,300)	(8,000)
Increase in billings in excess of costs and estimated earnings on uncompleted contracts	20,300	18,500
Decrease (increase) in inventory	9,400	(3,600)
(Increase) decrease in prepaid charges and other assets	(35,200)	16,100
(Decrease) increase in accounts and retentions payable	(45,400)	113,200
Increase in accrued loss on uncompleted contract	76,700	
(Decrease) increase in other accrued liabilities	(26,000)	18,800
Net cash provided by operating activities	562,100	472,400
Cash flows from investing activities:		
Proceeds of equipment sold	25,000	5,000
Acquisition of equipment	(140,000)	(175,000)
Advances to joint venture	(25,000)	(9,700)
Advances to related company	(25,000)	(50,000)
Net cash used in investing activities	(165,000)	(229,700)

(continued)

FRF-SME

	2013	2012
Cash flows from financing activities:		
Principal payments on notes payable	(110,300)	(90,300)
Principal payments under capital lease obligations	(53,700)	(9,700)
Cash dividends paid	(150,000)	(150,000)
Net cash used in financing activities	(314,000)	(250,000)
Net increase (decrease) in cash and cash equivalents	83,100	(7,300)
Cash and cash equivalents at beginning of year	221,300	228,600
Cash and cash equivalents at end of year	$304,400	$221,300

Implementation Resources

Alpha Contractors, Inc.
Notes to Consolidated Financial Statements
December 31, 2013 and 2012

1. SUMMARY OF SIGNIFICANT ACCOUNTING POLICIES

Basis of Accounting

The accompanying financial statements have been prepared in accordance with the *Financial Reporting Framework for Small- and Medium-Sized Entities* issued by the American Institute of Certified Public Accountants, which is a special purpose framework and not U.S. generally accepted accounting principles (U.S. GAAP). The accounting principles that compose the framework are appropriate for the preparation and presentation of small- and medium-sized entity financial statements, based on the needs of the financial statement users and cost and benefit considerations. This special purpose framework, unlike U.S. GAAP, does not require the recognition of deferred taxes. We have chosen the option to recognize only current income tax assets and liabilities.

Nature of Operations

The Company is engaged in the construction of industrial and commercial buildings primarily in the southeastern region of the United States. The Company's work is performed under cost-plus-fee contracts, fixed-price contracts, and fixed-price contracts modified by incentive and penalty provisions. These contracts are undertaken by the Company or its wholly owned subsidiary alone or in partnership with other contractors through joint ventures. The length of the Company's contracts varies but is typically about two years. The Company follows the practice of filing statutory liens on all construction projects when collection problems are anticipated. The liens serve as collateral for contracts receivable.

Use of Estimates

The preparation of financial statements in conformity with the *Financial Reporting Framework for Small and Medium-Sized Entities* requires management to make estimates and assumptions that affect the reported amounts of assets and liabilities and the disclosure of contingent assets and liabilities at the date of the financial statements and the reported amounts of revenues and expenses during the reporting period. Actual results could differ from those estimates.

Statement of Assets, Liabilities, and Equity Classification

The Company includes in current assets and liabilities retainage amounts receivable and payable under construction contracts, which may extend beyond one year. A one-year time period is used as the basis for classifying all other current assets and liabilities.

Principles of Consolidation

The consolidated financial statements include the Company's majority-owned entity, a wholly owned corporate subsidiary (Beta Building). All significant intercompany transactions are eliminated. Income from Beta Building was $212,300 in 2013 and $35,900 in 2013. The Company has a noncontrolling interest in a joint venture (partnership), which is reported on the equity method.

FRF-SME

Cash and Cash Equivalents

For purposes of the consolidated statements of cash flows, the Company considers all highly liquid debt instruments purchased with an original maturity of three months or less to be cash equivalents.

Contracts Receivable

Contracts receivable from performing construction of industrial and commercial buildings are based on contracted prices. The Company provides an allowance for doubtful collections, which is based upon a review of outstanding receivables, historical collection information, and existing economic conditions. Normal contracts receivable are due 30 days after the issuance of the invoice. Contract retentions are due 30 days after completion of the project and acceptance by the owner. Receivables past due more than 120 days are considered delinquent. Delinquent receivables are written off based on individual credit evaluation and specific circumstances of the customer.

Inventory

Inventory consisting of building materials is stated at the lower of cost (first in, first out method) or net realizable value.

Property and Equipment

Property and equipment are stated at cost. Depreciation is computed primarily using the straight-line method over the estimated useful lives of the assets, which range from 5 to 39 years. Leasehold improvements are amortized over the shorter of the useful life of the related assets or the lease term. Expenditures for repairs and maintenance are charged to expense as incurred. For assets sold or otherwise disposed of, the cost and related accumulated depreciation are removed from the accounts, and any related gain or loss is reflected in income for the period.

Revenue and Cost Recognition

Revenues from fixed price construction contracts are recognized on the percentage of completion method, measured on the basis of incurred costs to estimated total costs for each contract. This cost to cost method is used because management considers it to be the best available measure of progress on these contracts. Revenues from cost-plus fee contracts are recognized on the basis of costs incurred during the period plus the fee earned, measured by the cost to cost method.

The financial statements include some amounts that are based on management's best estimates and judgments. The most significant estimates relate to costs to complete long-term contracts. These estimates may be adjusted as more current information becomes available, and any adjustment could be significant.

Contract costs include all direct material and labor costs and those indirect costs related to contract performance, such as indirect labor, supplies, tools, repairs, and depreciation costs. Selling, general, and administrative costs are charged to expense as incurred. Provisions for estimated losses on uncompleted contracts are made in the period in which such losses are determined. Changes in job performance, job conditions, and estimated profitability, including those arising from contract penalty provisions, and final contract settlements may result in revisions to costs and income and are recognized in the period in which the revisions are determined. Profit incentives are included in revenues when their realization is reasonably assured. An amount equal to contract costs attributable to claims is included in revenues when realization is probable and the amount can be reliably estimated.

The asset, "costs and estimated earnings in excess of billings on uncompleted contracts," represents revenues recognized in excess of amounts billed. The liability, "billings in excess of costs and estimated earnings on uncompleted contracts," represents billings in excess of revenues recognized.

Union-Sponsored Pension Plan

The Company participates in a union-sponsored pension plan (ABC Pension Fund), which is a defined benefit plan, that covers union employees. Contributions to the plan are based on a fixed rate per hour worked. Pension expense under this plan was $550,000 and $500,000 for the years ended December 31, 2013 and 2012, respectively.

Income Taxes

For financial reporting purposes, the Company has elected to use the taxes payable method. Under that method, income tax expense represents the amount of income tax the Company expects to pay based on the Company's current year taxable income.

Current year taxable income varies from income before current year tax expense primarily due to the use of the completed-contract method and the use of an accelerated depreciation method for tax reporting purposes.

Business tax credits are applied as a reduction to the provision for federal income taxes using the flow-through method.

Evaluation of Subsequent Events

The Company has evaluated subsequent events through February 18, 2014, which is the date the financial statements were available to be issued.

2. CONTRACTS RECEIVABLE[1]

	December 31, 2013	December 31, 2012
Billed		
Completed contracts	$ 621,100	$ 500,600
Contracts in progress	2,146,100	1,931,500
Retained	976,300	866,200
Unbilled	121,600	105,400
	3,865,100	3,403,700
Less: Allowances for doubtful collections	75,900	69,600
	$3,789,200	$3,334,100

---

[1] This disclosure is not explicitly required by the FRF for SMEs accounting framework. However, as the FRF for SMEs framework is principles based, it requires the presentation of sufficient information for a fair presentation. As such, management of Alpha Contractors has decided to include this disclosure in the financial statements as necessary to provide sufficient information to the financial statement users.

FRF-SME

Analysis of the changes in the allowance for doubtful collections.

	2013	2012
Balance at January 1	$69,600	$68,000
Additions charged to operations	6,300	1,100
Direct write-downs	—	500
Recoveries	—	—
Balance at December 31	$75,900	$69,600

Contracts receivable at December 31, 2013, include a claim, expected to be collected within one year, for $290,600 arising from a dispute with the owner over design and specification changes in a building currently under construction. The changes were made at the request of the owner to improve the thermal characteristics of the building and, in the opinion of counsel, gave rise to a valid claim against the owner.

The retained and unbilled contracts receivable at December 31, 2013, included $38,600 that was not expected to be collected within one year.

Contracts receivable include approximately $800,000 due under one contract.

3. COSTS AND ESTIMATED EARNINGS ON UNCOMPLETED CONTRACTS[2]

The following is a summary of contracts in progress at December 31, 2013 and 2012.

	2013	2012
Costs incurred on uncompleted contracts	$4,346,500	$3,165,400
Estimated earnings	651,600	506,100
	4,998,100	3,671,500
Less: Billings to date	5,083,200	3,792,600
	$ (85,100)	$ (121,100)
These amounts are included in accompanying consolidated statements of assets, liabilities, and equity under the following captions:		
Costs and estimated earnings in excess of billings on uncompleted contracts	$ 156,900	$ 100,600
Billings in excess of costs and estimated earnings on uncompleted contracts	(242,000)	(221,700)
	$ (85,100)	$ (121,100)

---

[2] See footnote 1.

4. ADVANCES TO AND EQUITY IN JOINT VENTURE

The Company has a noncontrolling interest (one-third) in a general partnership joint venture (XYZ Venture) formed to construct an office building. All of the partners participate in construction, which is under the general management of the Company. Summary information on the joint venture follows.

	December 31, 2013	December 31, 2012
Current assets	$ 483,100	$280,300
Construction and other assets	220,500	190,800
	703,600	471,100
Less: Liabilities	236,800	154,000
Net assets	$ 466,800	$317,100
Revenue	$3,442,700	$299,400
Net income	$ 149,700	$ 17,100
Company's interest		
Share of net income	$ 49,900	$ 5,700
Advances to joint venture	$ 50,000	$ 25,000
Equity in net assets	155,600	105,700
Total advances and equity	$ 205,600	$130,700

5. TRANSACTIONS WITH RELATED PARTY

The note receivable, related company, is an installment note bearing annual interest at 9 percent, payable quarterly, with the principal payable in annual installments of $25,000, commencing October 1, 2015.

The major shareholder of the Company owns the majority of the outstanding common stock of this related company, whose principal activity is leasing land and buildings. Alpha Contractors, Inc., rents land and office facilities from the related company on a 10-year lease ending September 30, 2021, for an annual rental of $19,000.

6. PROPERTY AND EQUIPMENT

	December 31, 2013	December 31, 2012
Assets		
Land	$ 57,500	$ 57,500
Buildings	262,500	262,500
Shop and construction equipment	827,600	727,600
Automobiles and trucks	104,400	89,100
Leased equipment under capital leases	300,000	300,000
	1,552,000	1,436,700
Accumulated depreciation and amortization	575,600	417,500
Net property and equipment	$ 976,400	$1,019,200

Depreciation expense related to property, plant, and equipment was $158,000 in 2013 and $148,800 for 2012.

7. FINANCING ACTIVITIES

Line of Credit

The Company has a line of credit agreement with a bank of $1,500,000. There were no borrowings against the line at December 31, 2013 and 2012. The line bears interest at the bank's prime lending rate. The line is reviewed annually and is due on demand. Under terms of the line of credit, the Company is required to maintain a specified debt service coverage ratio and debt to tangible net worth ratio, as those terms are defined.

Notes Payable

The following is a summary of all notes payable.

	December 31, 2013	December 31, 2012
Unsecured note payable to Aztec Bank, due in quarterly installments of $22,575 plus interest at 1% over prime through June 2018	$388,100	$478,400
Note payable to State Bank collateralized by equipment[3] (carrying amount of $150,000), due in monthly installments of $1,667 plus interest at 10% through January 2018	80,000	100,000
	$468,100	$578,400
Current maturities	110,300	110,300
	$357,800	$468,100

Principal payments on note payables are due as follows.

Year ending December 31,

2014	$110,300
2015	$110,300
2016	$110,300
2017	$110,300
2018	$ 26,900

8. LEASE OBLIGATIONS PAYABLE

The Company leases certain specialized construction equipment under leases classified as capital leases. The leased equipment is amortized on a straight line basis over 6 years. Total accumulated amortization related to the leased equipment is $100,000 and $50,000 at December 31, 2013, and 2012, respectively. The following is a schedule showing the future minimum lease payments under capital leases by years and the present value of the minimum lease payments as of December 31, 2013. The interest rate related to the lease obligation is 9.3 percent and the maturity date is January 2016.

---

[3] *Note:* Terms and conditions related to the pledge of collateral should be disclosed as appropriate.

Year ending December 31

2014	$ 76,500
2015	76,500
2016	76,500
Total minimum lease payments	229,500
Less: Amount representing interest	31,900
Present value of minimum lease payments	$197,600

At December 31, 2013, the present value of minimum lease payments due within one year is $62,250.

Total rental expense, excluding payments on capital leases, totaled $86,300 in 2013 and $74,400 in 2012.

9. SURETY BONDS

The Company, as a condition for entering into some of its construction contracts, had outstanding surety bonds as of December 31, 2013 and 2012. The surety bonds are collateralized by the contracts receivable and personally guaranteed by the stockholders of the Company.

10. CONTINGENCIES

From time to time, the Company is involved in routine litigation that arises in the ordinary course of business. There are no pending significant legal proceedings to which the Company is a party for which management believes the ultimate outcome would have a material adverse effect on the Company's financial position.

The Company is contingently liable to a surety company under a general indemnity agreement. The Company agrees to indemnify the surety for any payments made on contracts of surety ship, guaranty, or indemnity. The Company believes that all contingent liabilities will be satisfied by their performance on the specific bonded contracts.

11. BACKLOG[4]

The following schedule shows a reconciliation of backlog representing the amount of revenue the Company expects to realize from work to be performed on uncompleted contracts in progress at December 31, 2013 and 2012, and from contractual agreements on which work has not yet begun.

---

[4] This disclosure is not explicitly required by the FRF for SMEs accounting framework. However, as the FRF for SMEs framework is principles based, it requires the presentation of sufficient information for a fair presentation. As such, management of Alpha Contractors has decided to include this disclosure in the financial statements as necessary to provide sufficient information to the financial statement users. Management may have also chosen to provide qualitative information about backlog and omit a quantitative reconciliation. Backlog information for the year ending December 31, 2012, may also need to be disclosed depending upon the circumstances of a contractor and the needs of the financial statement users.

Contract revenues on uncompleted contracts at December 31, 2012	$ 9,779,900
Contract adjustments	430,600
Contract revenues for new contracts, 2013	1,502,700
	11,713,200
Less: Contract revenue earned, 2013	9,630,800
Backlog at December 31, 2013	$2,082,400

In addition, between January 1, 2014, and February 18, 2014, the Company entered into additional construction contracts with revenues of $332,800.

Alpha Contractors, Inc. and Subsidiary
Comparative Financial Statements
December 31, 2013 and 2012
Based on U.S. GAAP

Primary differences between the Alpha Contractors illustrative financial statements based on the FRF for SMEs accounting framework and those based on U.S. GAAP are

- in the financial statements based on the FRF for SMEs accounting framework, Alpha Contractors adopts the taxes payable method for accounting for income taxes. In the U.S. GAAP presentation, Alpha Contractors is required to follow the deferred taxes method, including the accounting guidance for uncertainty in income taxes, and makes the related disclosures.

- the financial statements based on the FRF for SMEs accounting framework do not include the "Impairment of Long-Lived Assets" disclosure in the summary of significant accounting policies that is contained in the U.S. GAAP-based financial statements. The FRF for SMEs accounting framework does not require impairment testing of long-lived assets.

Note: Supplemental schedules, which are commonly prepared to accompany or supplement the basic financial statements, have not been prepared as part of this illustration.

Independent Auditor's Report

To the Stockholders
Alpha Contractors, Inc. and Subsidiary

We have audited the accompanying consolidated financial statements of Alpha Contractors, Inc. and Subsidiary, which comprise the consolidated balance sheets as of December 31, 2013 and 2012, and the related consolidated statements of income and retained earnings, and cash flows for the years then ended, and the related notes to the consolidated financial statements.

Management's Responsibility for the Financial Statements

Management is responsible for the preparation and fair presentation of these financial statements in accordance with accounting principles generally accepted in the United States of America; this includes the design, implementation, and maintenance of internal control relevant to the preparation and fair presentation of financial statements that are free from material misstatement, whether due to fraud or error.

Auditor's Responsibility

Our responsibility is to express an opinion on these financial statements based on our audits. We conducted our audits in accordance with auditing standards generally accepted in the United States of America. Those standards require that we plan and perform the audits to obtain reasonable assurance about whether the financial statements are free from material misstatement.

An audit involves performing procedures to obtain audit evidence about the amounts and disclosures in the financial statements. The procedures selected depend on the auditor's judgment, including the assessment of the risks of material misstatement of the financial statements, whether due to fraud or error. In making those risk assessments, the auditor considers internal control relevant to the Company's preparation and fair presentation of the financial statements in order to design audit procedures that are appropriate in the circumstances, but not for the purpose of expressing an opinion on the effectiveness of the Company's internal control. Accordingly, we express no such opinion. An audit also includes evaluating the appropriateness of accounting policies used and the reasonableness of significant accounting estimates made by management, as well as evaluating the overall presentation of the financial statements.

We believe that the audit evidence we have obtained is sufficient and appropriate to provide a basis for our audit opinion.

Opinion

In our opinion, the consolidated financial statements referred to above present fairly, in all material respects, the financial position of Alpha Contractors, Inc. and Subsidiary as of December 31, 2013 and 2012, and the results of its operations and its cash flows for the years then ended in accordance with accounting principles generally accepted in the United States of America.

[Signature of Accounting Firm]
Greenville, South Carolina
February 18, 2014

Alpha Contractors, Inc.
Consolidated Balance Sheets
December 31, 2013 and 2012

Assets	2013	2012
Cash and cash equivalents	$ 304,400	$ 221,300
Contracts receivables	3,789,200	3,334,100
Costs and estimated earnings in excess of billings on uncompleted contracts	156,900	100,600
Inventory	89,700	99,100
Prepaid charges and other assets	118,400	83,200
Total current assets	4,458,600	3,838,300
Advances to and equity in joint venture	205,600	130,700
Note receivable, related company	175,000	150,000
Property and equipment, net of accumulated depreciation and amortization	976,400	1,019,200
Total long term assets	1,357,000	1,299,900
Total assets	$5,815,600	$5,138,200

Liabilities and Shareholders' Equity

Liabilities	2013	2012
Current maturities of notes payable	$ 110,300	$ 110,300
Current portion of lease obligations payable	62,250	57,250
Accounts and retentions payable	2,543,100	2,588,500
Billings in excess of costs and estimated earnings on uncompleted contracts	242,000	221,700
Accrued loss on uncompleted contract	76,700	
Current deferred tax liability	594,000	389,800
Other accrued liabilities	88,600	114,600
Total current liabilities	3,716,950	3,482,150
Notes payable, less current maturities	357,800	468,100
Lease obligations payable, less current portion	135,350	194,050
Long-term accrued liabilities	154,200	26,200
Deferred tax liability	25,200	18,200
Total long term liabilities	672,550	706,550
Total liabilities	4,389,500	4,188,700

FRF-SME

	2013	2012
Shareholders' equity		
Common stock—$1 par value, 500,000 authorized shares, 300,000 issued and outstanding shares	300,000	300,000
Retained earnings	1,126,100	649,500
Total shareholders' equity	1,426,100	949,500
Total liabilities and shareholders' equity	$5,815,600	$5,138,200

Alpha Contractors, Inc.
Consolidated Statements of Income and Retained Earnings
Years Ended December 31, 2013 and 2012

	2013	2012
Contract revenues earned	$9,630,800	$6,225,400
Cost of revenues earned	7,436,100	4,951,300
Gross profit	2,194,700	1,274,100
Selling, general, and administrative expense	895,600	755,600
Income from operations	1,299,100	518,500
Other income (expense)		
Equity in earnings from unconsolidated joint venture	49,900	5,700
Gain on sale of equipment	10,000	2,000
Interest expense (net of interest income of $8,800 in 2013 and $6,300 in 2012)	(69,500)	(70,800)
Total other expense	(9,600)	(63,100)
Income before provision of income taxes	1,289,500	455,400
Provision for income taxes	662,900	225,000
Net income	626,600	230,400
Retained earnings, beginning of year	649,500	569,100
	1,276,100	799,500
Less: Dividends paid (per share $.50 [2013]; $.50 [2012])	150,000	150,000
Retained earnings, end of year	$1,126,100	$ 649,500

Alpha Contractors, Inc.
Consolidated Statements of Cash Flows
Years Ended December 31, 2013 and 2012

	2013	2012
Cash flows from operating activities:		
Net income	$626,600	$230,400
Adjustments to reconcile net income to net cash provided by operating activities:		
Depreciation and amortization	167,800	153,500
Provision for losses on contract receivables	6,300	1,100
Gain on sale of equipment	(10,000)	(2,000)
Increase (decrease) in deferred taxes	211,200	(75,900)
Equity earnings from unconsolidated joint venture	(49,900)	(5,700)
Increase in long-term accrued liabilities	128,000	26,200
Increase in contract receivables	(461,400)	(10,200)
Net (decrease) increase in billings related to costs and estimated earnings on uncompleted contracts	(36,000)	10,500
Decrease (increase) in inventory	9,400	(3,600)
(Increase) decrease in prepaid charges and other assets	(35,200)	16,100
(Decrease) increase in accounts and retentions payable	(45,400)	113,200
Increase in accrued loss on uncompleted contract	76,700	
(Decrease) increase in other accrued liabilities	(26,000)	18,800
Net cash provided by operating activities	562,100	472,400
Cash flows from investing activities:		
Proceeds of equipment sold	25,000	5,000
Acquisition of equipment	(140,000)	(175,000)
Advances to joint venture	(25,000)	(9,700)
Advances to related company	(25,000)	(50,000)
Net cash used in investing activities	(165,000)	(229,700)

(continued)

FRF-SME

	2013	2012
Cash flows from financing activities:		
Principal payments on notes payable	(110,300)	(90,300)
Principal payments under capital lease obligations	(53,700)	(9,700)
Cash dividends paid	(150,000)	(150,000)
Net cash used in financing activities	(314,000)	(250,000)
Net increase (decrease) in cash and cash equivalents	83,100	(7,300)
Cash and cash equivalents at beginning of year	221,300	228,600
Cash and cash equivalents at end of year	$304,400	$221,300

Supplemental data:
Interest paid—2013, $73,500; 2012, $75,100
Income taxes paid—2013, $478,300; 2012, $313,200

Alpha Contractors, Inc.
Notes to Consolidated Financial Statements
December 31, 2013 and 2012

1. SUMMARY OF SIGNIFICANT ACCOUNTING POLICIES

Nature of Operations

The Company is engaged in the construction of industrial and commercial buildings primarily in the southeastern region of the United States. The Company's work is performed under cost-plus-fee contracts, fixed-price contracts, and fixed-price contracts modified by incentive and penalty provisions. These contracts are undertaken by the Company or its wholly owned subsidiary alone or in partnership with other contractors through joint ventures. The length of the Company's contracts varies but is typically about two years. The Company follows the practice of filing statutory liens on all construction projects when collection problems are anticipated. The liens serve as collateral for contracts receivable.

Use of Estimates

The preparation of financial statements in conformity with U.S. GAAP requires management to make estimates and assumptions that affect the reported amounts of assets and liabilities and the disclosure of contingent assets and liabilities at the date of the financial statements and the reported amounts of revenues and expenses during the reporting period. Actual results could differ from those estimates.

Balance Sheet Classification

The Company includes in current assets and liabilities retainage amounts receivable and payable under construction contracts, which may extend beyond one year. A one-year time period is used as the basis for classifying all other current assets and liabilities.

Principles of Consolidation

The consolidated financial statements include the Company's majority-owned entity, a wholly owned corporate subsidiary. All significant intercompany transactions are eliminated. The Company has a noncontrolling interest in a joint venture (partnership), which is reported on the equity method.

Cash and Cash Equivalents

For purposes of the consolidated statements of cash flows, the Company considers all highly liquid debt instruments purchased with an original maturity of three months or less to be cash equivalents.

Contracts Receivable

Contracts receivable from performing construction of industrial and commercial buildings are based on contracted prices. The Company provides an allowance for doubtful collections, which is based upon a review of outstanding receivables, historical collection information, and existing economic conditions. Normal contracts receivable are due 30 days after the issuance of the invoice. Contract retentions are due 30 days after completion of the project and acceptance by the owner. Receivables past due more than 120 days are considered delinquent. Delinquent receivables are written off based on individual credit evaluation and specific circumstances of the customer.

FRF-SME

Inventory

Inventory consisting of building materials is stated at the lower of cost (first in, first out method) or market.

Property and Equipment

Property and equipment are stated at cost. Depreciation is computed primarily using the straight-line method over the estimated useful lives of the assets, which range from 5 to 39 years. Leasehold improvements are amortized over the shorter of the useful life of the related assets or the lease term. Expenditures for repairs and maintenance are charged to expense as incurred. For assets sold or otherwise disposed of, the cost and related accumulated depreciation are removed from the accounts, and any related gain or loss is reflected in income for the period.

Impairment of Long-Lived Assets

The Company reviews long-lived assets for impairment whenever events or changes in circumstances indicate that the carrying amount of such assets may not be recoverable. Recoverability of these assets is determined by comparing the forecasted undiscounted net cash flows of the operation to which the assets relate to the carrying amount. If the operation is determined to be unable to recover the carrying amount of its assets, then assets are written down first, followed by other long-lived assets of the operation to fair value. Fair value is determined based on discounted cash flows or appraised values, depending on the nature of the assets. As of December 31, 2013, and 2012, there were no impairment losses recognized for long-lived assets.

Revenue and Cost Recognition

Revenues from fixed price construction contracts are recognized on the percentage of completion method, measured on the basis of incurred costs to estimated total costs for each contract. This cost to cost method is used because management considers it to be the best available measure of progress on these contracts. Revenues from cost-plus fee contracts are recognized on the basis of costs incurred during the period plus the fee earned, measured by the cost to cost method.

The financial statements include some amounts that are based on management's best estimates and judgments. The most significant estimates relate to costs to complete long-term contracts. These estimates may be adjusted as more current information becomes available, and any adjustment could be significant.

Contract costs include all direct material and labor costs and those indirect costs related to contract performance, such as indirect labor, supplies, tools, repairs, and depreciation costs. Selling, general, and administrative costs are charged to expense as incurred. Provisions for estimated losses on uncompleted contracts are made in the period in which such losses are determined. Changes in job performance, job conditions, and estimated profitability, including those arising from contract penalty provisions, and final contract settlements may result in revisions to costs and income and are recognized in the period in which the revisions are determined. Profit incentives are included in revenues when their realization is reasonably assured. An amount equal to contract costs attributable to claims is included in revenues when realization is probable and the amount can be reliably estimated.

The asset, "costs and estimated earnings in excess of billings on uncompleted contracts," represents revenues recognized in excess of amounts billed. The liability, "billings in excess of costs and estimated earnings on uncompleted contracts," represents billings in excess of revenues recognized.

Income Taxes

Provisions for income taxes are based on taxes payable or refundable for the current year and deferred taxes on temporary differences between the amount of taxable income and pretax financial income and between the tax bases of assets and liabilities and their reported amounts in the financial statements. Deferred tax assets and liabilities are included in the consolidated financial statements at currently enacted income tax rates applicable to the period in which the deferred tax assets and liabilities are expected to be realized or settled as prescribed in FASB ASC 740. As changes in tax laws or rate are enacted, deferred tax assets and liabilities are adjusted through the provision for income taxes.

Current year taxable income varies from income before current year tax expense primarily due to the use of the completed-contract method and the use of an accelerated depreciation method for tax reporting purposes.

Business tax credits are applied as a reduction to the current provision for federal income taxes using the flow-through method.

Effective January 1, 2009, the Company implemented the accounting guidance for uncertainty in income taxes using the provisions of FASB ASC 740. Using that guidance, tax positions initially need to be recognized in the financial statements when it is more-likely-than-not the positions will be sustained upon examination by the tax authorities.

As of December 31, 2013, the Company had no uncertain tax positions, or interest and penalties, that qualify for either recognition or disclosure in the financial statements.

With few exceptions, the Company is no longer subject to U.S. federal, state, and local income tax examinations by tax authorities for years before 2010.

Evaluation of Subsequent Events

The Company has evaluated subsequent events through February 18, 2014, which is the date the financial statements were available to be issued.

2. CONTRACTS RECEIVABLE

	December 31, 2013	December 31, 2012
Billed		
Completed contracts	$ 621,100	$ 500,600
Contracts in progress	2,146,100	1,931,500
Retained	976,300	866,200
Unbilled	121,600	105,400
	3,865,100	3,403,700
Less: Allowances for doubtful collections	75,900	69,600
	$3,789,200	$3,334,100

FRF-SME

The total recorded investment in impaired contracts receivable recognized in accordance with FASB ASC 310, *Receivables*, was $125,000 in 2013 and $103,000 in 2012. These amounts also approximate the average recorded investment in impaired contracts receivable during the related periods. The allowance for credit losses associated with these receivables was $41,000 in 2013 and $38,000 in 2012. It is management's policy not to accrue interest income on impaired contracts receivable given past difficulties in collecting such amounts. Interest income on impaired contracts receivable of $1,452 and $1,107 was recognized for cash payments received in 2013 and 2012, respectively. For impairment recognized in conformity with of FASB ASC 310, the entire change in present value of expected cash flows is reported as bad debt expense in the same manner in which impairment initially was recognized or as a reduction in the amount of bad debt expense that otherwise would be reported.

Analysis of the changes in the allowance for doubtful collections.

	2013	2012
Balance at January 1	$69,600	$68,000
Additions charged to operations	6,300	1,100
Direct write-downs	—	500
Recoveries	—	—
Balance at December 31	$75,900	$69,600

Contracts receivable at December 31, 2013, include a claim, expected to be collected within one year, for $290,600 arising from a dispute with the owner over design and specification changes in a building currently under construction. The changes were made at the request of the owner to improve the thermal characteristics of the building and, in the opinion of counsel, gave rise to a valid claim against the owner.

The retained and unbilled contracts receivable at December 31, 2013, included $38,600 that was not expected to be collected within one year.

Contracts receivable include approximately $800,000 due under one contract.

3. COSTS AND ESTIMATED EARNINGS ON UNCOMPLETED CONTRACTS

Following is a summary of contracts in progress at December 31, 2013 and 2012:

	2013	2012
Costs incurred on uncompleted contracts	$4,346,500	$3,165,400
Estimated earnings	651,600	506,100
	4,998,100	3,671,500
Less: Billings to date	5,083,200	3,792,600
	$ (85,100)	$ (121,100)

These amounts are included in accompanying consolidated balance sheets under the following captions:

	2013	2012
Costs and estimated earnings in excess of billings on uncompleted contracts	$ 156,900	$ 100,600
Billings in excess of costs and estimated earnings on uncompleted contracts	(242,000)	(221,700)
	$ (85,100)	$ (121,100)

4. ADVANCES TO AND EQUITY IN JOINT VENTURE

The Company has a noncontrolling interest (one-third) in a general partnership joint venture formed to construct an office building. All of the partners participate in construction, which is under the general management of the Company. Summary information on the joint venture follows.

	December 31, 2013	December 31, 2012
Current assets	$ 483,100	$280,300
Construction and other assets	220,500	190,800
	703,600	471,100
Less: Liabilities	236,800	154,000
Net assets	$ 466,800	$317,100
Revenue	$3,442,700	$299,400
Net income	$ 149,700	$ 17,100
Company's interest		
Share of net income	$ 49,900	$ 5,700
Advances to joint venture	$ 50,000	$ 25,000
Equity in net assets	155,600	105,700
Total advances and equity	$ 205,600	$130,700

FRF-SME

5. TRANSACTIONS WITH RELATED PARTY

The note receivable, related company, is an installment note bearing annual interest at 9 percent, payable quarterly, with the principal payable in annual installments of $25,000, commencing October 1, 2015.

The major shareholder of the Company owns the majority of the outstanding common stock of this related company, whose principal activity is leasing land and buildings. Alpha Contractors, Inc., rents land and office facilities from the related company on a 10-year lease ending September 30, 2021, for an annual rental of $19,000.

6. PROPERTY AND EQUIPMENT

	December 31, 2013	December 31, 2012
Assets		
Land	$ 57,500	$ 57,500
Buildings	262,500	262,500
Shop and construction equipment	827,600	727,600
Automobiles and trucks	104,400	89,100
Leased equipment under capital leases	300,000	300,000
	1,552,000	1,436,700
Accumulated depreciation and amortization		
Buildings	140,000	130,000
Shop and construction equipment	265,600	195,500
Automobiles and trucks	70,000	42,000
Leased equipment under capital leases	100,000	50,000
	575,600	417,500
Net property and equipment	$ 976,400	$1,019,200

7. ACCOUNTS PAYABLE

Accounts payable include amounts due to subcontractors, totaling $634,900 at December 31, 2013, and $560,400 at December 31, 2012, which have been retained pending completion and customer acceptance of jobs. Accounts payable at December 31, 2013, include $6,500 that is not expected to be paid within one year.

8. FINANCING ACTIVITIES

Line of Credit

The Company has a line of credit agreement with a bank of $1,500,000. There were no borrowings against the line at December 31, 2013 and 2012. The line bears interest at the bank's prime lending rate. The line is reviewed annually and is due on demand. Under terms of the line of credit, the Company is required to maintain a specified debt service coverage ratio and debt to tangible net worth ratio, as those terms are defined.

Notes Payable

Following is a summary of all notes payable:

	December 31, 2013	December 31, 2012
Unsecured note payable to Aztec Bank, due in quarterly installments of $22,575 plus interest at 1% over prime through June 2018	$388,100	$478,400
Note payable to State Bank collateralized by equipment[5] (carrying amount of $150,000), due in monthly installments of $1,667 plus interest at 10% through January 2018	80,000	100,000
	$468,100	$578,400
Current maturities	110,300	110,300
	$357,800	$468,100

Principal payments on note payables are due as follows.

Year ending December 31,	
2014	$110,300
2015	$110,300
2016	$110,300
2017	$110,300
2018	$ 26,900

9. LEASE OBLIGATIONS PAYABLE

The Company leases certain specialized construction equipment under leases classified as capital leases. The following is a schedule showing the future minimum lease payments under capital leases by years and the present value of the minimum lease payments as of December 31, 2013. The interest rate related to the lease obligation is 9.3 percent and the maturity date is January 2016.

---

[5] See footnote 3.

Year ending December 31

2014	$ 76,500
2015	76,500
2016	76,500
Total minimum lease payments	229,500
Less: Amount representing interest	31,900
Present value of minimum lease payments	$197,600

At December 31, 2013, the present value of minimum lease payments due within one year is $62,250.

Total rental expense, excluding payments on capital leases, totaled $86,300 in 2013 and $74,400 in 2012.

10. SURETY BONDS

The Company, as a condition for entering into some of its construction contracts, had outstanding surety bonds as of December 31, 2013 and 2012. The surety bonds are collateralized by certain contracts receivable and personally guaranteed by the stockholders of the Company.

11. INCOME TAXES AND DEFERRED INCOME TAXES

The provision for taxes on income consists of the following.

	December 31, 2013	*December 31, 2012*
Current	$451,700	$300,900
Deferred	211,200	(75,900)
Total	$662,900	$225,000

The following represents the approximate tax effect of each significant type of temporary difference giving rise to the deferred income tax liability.

	December 31, 2013	*December 31, 2012*
Deferred tax asset:		
Employee benefits	$ 44,300	$ 38,100
Other	10,100	10,600
Total	$ 54,400	$ 48,700
Deferred tax liability:		
Earnings on uncompleted contracts	$594,000	$389,800

FRF-SME

	December 31, 2013	December 31, 2012
Property, plant, and equipment	64,300	54,100
Other	15,300	12,800
Total	$673,600	$456,700
Deferred tax liability, net	$619,200	$408,000

12. CONTINGENCIES

From time to time, the Company is involved in routine litigation that arises in the ordinary course of business. There are no pending significant legal proceedings to which the Company is a party for which management believes the ultimate outcome would have a material adverse effect on the Company's financial position.

The Company is contingently liable to a surety company under a general indemnity agreement. The Company agrees to indemnify the surety for any payments made on contracts of surety ship, guaranty, or indemnity. The Company believes that all contingent liabilities will be satisfied by their performance on the specific bonded contracts.

13. BACKLOG[6]

The following schedule shows a reconciliation of backlog representing the amount of revenue the Company expects to realize from work to be performed on uncompleted contracts in progress at December 31, 2013 and 2012, and from contractual agreements on which work has not yet begun.

Contract revenues on uncompleted contracts at December 31, 2012	$9,779,900
Contract adjustments	430,600
Contract revenues for new contracts, 2013	1,502,700
	11,713,200
Less: Contract revenue earned, 2013	9,630,800
Backlog at December 31, 2013	$2,082,400

In addition, between January 1, 2014, and February 18, 2014, the Company entered into additional construction contracts with revenues of $5,332,800.

---

[6] A reconciliation for the year ending December 31, 2012, may also need to be disclosed depending upon the circumstances of a contractor and the needs of the financial statement users.

FRF-SME

14. UNION-SPONSORED PENSION PLAN

The Company participates in a union-sponsored multiemployer defined benefit pension plan (ABC Pension Fund) that covers union employees. Contributions to the plan are based on a fixed rate per hour worked. The risks of participating in a multiemployer plan are different from single-employer plans in the following aspects:

a. Assets contributed to the multiemployer plan by one employer may be used to provide benefits to employees of other participating employers.

b. If a participating employer stops contributing to the plan, the unfunded obligations of the plan may be borne by the remaining participating employers.

c. If the Company chooses to stop participating in the multiemployer plan, the Company may be required to pay those plans an amount based on the underfunded status of the plan, referred to as a *withdrawal liability*.

The Company's participation in the multiemployer plan for the annual periods ended December 31, 2013, and 2012 is outlined in the following table. The "EIN/Pension Plan Number" column provides the employer identification number (EIN) and the three-digit plan number. Unless otherwise noted, the most recent Pension Protection Act zone status available in 2013 and 2012 is for the plan's year-end at December 31, 2012, and December 31, 2011, respectively. The zone status is based on information that the Company received from the plan and is certified by the plan's actuary. Among other factors, plans in the green zone are at least 80 percent funded. The last column lists the expiration date of the collective-bargaining agreement to which the plan is subject.

Implementation Resources

Pension Fund	EIN/Pension Plan Number	Pension Protection Act Zone Status		Contributions of Company		Expiration Date of Collective Bargaining Agreement
		2013	2012	2013	2012	
ABC	52-5599999-002	Green	Green	$550,000	$500,000	12/31/2016

Illustrative CPA Reports

To assist CPAs in reporting on financial statements prepared under the FRF for SMEs accounting framework, sample compilation, review, and audit reports are presented in this section.

When issuing a report on financial statements prepared in accordance with the FRF for SMEs accounting framework, the following requirements from the AICPA's *Professional Standards* should be complied with, depending on the nature of the service:

- Compilation of financial statements: AR section 80, *Compilation of Financial Statements*
- Review of financial statements: AR section 90, *Review of Financial Statements*
- Audit of financial statements: AU-C section 800, *Special Considerations—Audits of Financial Statements Prepared in Accordance With Special Purpose Frameworks*

These examples are for illustrative purposes only and are nonauthoritative. CPAs should refer directly to the applicable authoritative pronouncements for reporting requirements.

Standard Compilation Report

Accountant's Compilation Report

Board of Directors
XYZ Company

We have compiled the accompanying statements of financial position of XYZ Company, as of December 31, 2013, and the related statements of operations and cash flows for the year then ended. We have not audited or reviewed the accompanying financial statements and, accordingly, do not express an opinion or provide any assurance about whether the financial statements are in accordance with the *Financial Reporting Framework for Small- and Medium-Sized Entities*, issued by the American Institute of Certified Public Accountants.

Management is responsible for the preparation and fair presentation of financial statements in accordance with the *Financial Reporting Framework for Small- and Medium-Sized Entities* and for designing, implementing, and maintaining internal control relevant to the preparation and fair presentation of the financial statements.

Our responsibility is to conduct the compilation in accordance with Statements on Standards for Accounting and Review Services issued by the American Institute of Certified Public Accountants. The objective of a compilation is to assist management in presenting financial information in the form of financial statements without undertaking to obtain or provide any assurance that there are no material modifications that should be made to the financial statements.

[*Signature of accounting firm or accountant, as appropriate*]
[*Date*]

Standard Review Report

<u>Independent Accountant's Review Report</u>

Board of Directors
XYZ Company

We have reviewed the accompanying statements of financial position of XYZ Company, as of December 31, 2013, and the related statements of operations and cash flows for the year then ended. A review includes primarily applying analytical procedures to management's financial data and making inquiries of company management. A review is substantially less in scope than an audit, the objective of which is the expression of an opinion regarding the financial statements taken as a whole. Accordingly, we do not express such an opinion.

Management is responsible for the preparation and fair presentation of financial statements in accordance with the *Financial Reporting Framework for Small- and Medium-Sized Entities* issued by the American Institute of Certified Public Accountants and for designing, implementing, and maintaining internal control relevant to the preparation and fair presentation of the financial statements.

Our responsibility is to conduct the review in accordance with Statements on Standards for Accounting and Review Services issued by the American Institute of Certified Public Accountants. Those standards require us to perform procedures to obtain limited assurance that there are no material modifications that should be made to the financial statements. We believe that the results of our procedures provide a reasonable basis for our report.

Based on our review, we are not aware of any material modifications that should be made to the accompanying financial statements in order for them to be in conformity with *Financial Reporting Framework for Small- and Medium-Sized Entities*, as described in Note 1.

[Signature of accounting firm or accountant, as appropriate]
[Date]

Single Year Prepared in Accordance With the FRF for SMEs Accounting Framework

<u>Independent Auditor's Report</u>

To the Stockholders
ABC, Inc.

We have audited the accompanying financial statements of ABC, Inc., which comprise the statement of financial position as of December 31, 2013, and the related statements of operations and cash flows for the year then ended, and the related notes to the financial statements.

Management's Responsibility for the Financial Statements
Management is responsible for the preparation and fair presentation of these financial statements in accordance with the *Financial Reporting Framework for Small- and Medium-Sized Entities* issued by the American Institute of Certified Public Accountants described in Note 1; this includes determining that the *Financial Reporting Framework for*

Small- and Medium-Sized Entities is an acceptable basis for the preparation of the financial statements in the circumstances. Management is also responsible for the design, implementation, and maintenance of internal control relevant to the preparation and fair presentation of financial statements that are free from material misstatement, whether due to fraud or error.

Auditor's Responsibility

Our responsibility is to express an opinion on these financial statements based on our audit. We conducted our audit in accordance with auditing standards generally accepted in the United States of America. Those standards require that we plan and perform the audit to obtain reasonable assurance about whether the financial statements are free from material misstatement.

An audit involves performing procedures to obtain audit evidence about the amounts and disclosures in the financial statements. The procedures selected depend on the auditor's judgment, including the assessment of the risks of material misstatement of the financial statements, whether due to fraud or error. In making those risk assessments, the auditor considers internal control relevant to the company's preparation and fair presentation of the financial statements in order to design audit procedures that are appropriate in the circumstances but not for the purpose of expressing an opinion on the effectiveness of the company's internal control. Accordingly, we express no such opinion. An audit also includes evaluating the appropriateness of accounting policies used and the reasonableness of significant accounting estimates made by management, as well as evaluating the overall presentation of the financial statements.

We believe that the audit evidence we have obtained is sufficient and appropriate to provide a basis for our audit opinion.

Opinion

In our opinion, the financial statements referred to above present fairly, in all material respects, the financial position of ABC, Inc., as of December 31, 2013, and the results of its operations and its cash flows for the year then ended in accordance with *Financial Reporting Framework for Small- and Medium-Sized Entities* described in Note 1.

Basis of Accounting

We draw attention to Note 1 of the financial statements, which describes the basis of accounting. The financial statements are prepared in accordance with *Financial Reporting Framework for Small- and Medium-Sized Entities*, which is a basis of accounting other than accounting principles generally accepted in the United States of America. Our opinion is not modified with respect to this matter.

[Auditor's signature]
[Auditor's city and state]
[Date of the auditor's report]

Comparisons of the FRF for SMEs Reporting Framework to Other Bases of Accounting

Introduction

Owner-managers of SMEs, CPAs serving SMEs, users of SME financial statements, and other stakeholders are often familiar with the tax basis of accounting and U.S. GAAP. Also, many stakeholders are following the implementation of the International Financial Reporting Standard for Small- and Medium-Sized Entities (IFRS for SMEs) around the world as its use continues to expand and its implications for the U.S. marketplace continue to grow. As such, these stakeholders are interested in understanding how the principles and criteria included in the FRF for SMEs accounting framework compare to those other bases of accounting.

To assist those stakeholders, comparisons of the FRF for SMEs accounting framework to (1) the tax basis, (2) U.S. GAAP, and (3) IFRS for SMEs are presented on the following pages. These comparisons are not all inclusive. Rather, the following comparisons are made at a high level and are intended to draw attention to differences between the FRF for SMEs accounting framework and the other bases of accounting on certain accounting and financial reporting matters.

Comparison of the FRF for SMEs Accounting Framework With Tax Basis Accounting (May 2013)

The FRF for SMEs accounting framework draws upon a blend of traditional methods of accounting and accrual income tax accounting. One of its key features is that adjustments needed to reconcile tax return income with book income are reduced. The following is a comparative discussion of the FRF for SMEs accounting framework and tax basis accounting for certain topics considered significant for most users of the framework. This presentation does not describe all of the differences between the FRF for SMEs accounting framework and the tax basis of accounting. Rather, the presentation highlights areas that AICPA staff believes would be of particular interest to stakeholders.

Overview of Tax Basis Financial Statements

The *tax basis* is defined as "a basis of accounting that the entity uses to file its income tax return for the period covered by the financial statements." It is typically based on federal income tax laws found in the Internal Revenue Code (IRC), along with related regulations, revenue rulings, and procedures. These laws and regulations generally deal with the determination of taxable income and, therefore, focus on the measurement of revenues and expenses (and in some cases, on the determination of the basis of assets and liabilities). However, income tax laws generally do not address financial statement presentation or disclosure considerations.

IRS Accounting Methods

The tax basis of accounting covers a range of alternative bases, from cash to full accrual, depending on the nature of the reporting entity and, in some cases, the entity's elections. In general, the IRC allows two overall methods of accounting: the cash method and the accrual method.

FRF-SME

- Under the cash method (used by many small businesses)
  — income includes all items actually or constructively received during the year, and
  — expenses are generally deducted in the year they are actually paid or the property is transferred.
- Under the accrual method
  — income is generally reported in the year earned.
  — expenses are generally deducted in the year incurred.
  — Generally, the IRC requires that businesses that use inventories (they produce or purchase merchandise and sell it to produce income) use the accrual method for inventory purchases and sales.

Entities may select an accounting method based on the following rules.

C Corporations	• Generally, C corporations are required to use the accrual method of accounting.
	• However, the Internal Revenue Code (IRC) allows the use of the cash method if the corporation's average gross receipts are $5 million or less for the prior 3 years.
	• The IRC allows qualified personal service corporations to use the cash method.
S Corporations	• S corporations generally are eligible to use either the cash or accrual.
	• However, S corporations that allocate more than 35 percent of their losses to shareholders who do not actively participate in the management of the business cannot use the cash method.
Partnerships	• Partnerships are generally eligible to use either cash or accrual.
	• However, limited partnerships generally cannot use the cash method if they allocate more than 35 percent of their tax losses to limited partners.
	• If general or limited partnerships have C corporation partners, they cannot use the cash method if the partnerships have average gross receipts of more than $5 million for the three preceding tax years.
Sole Proprietorships	• Generally, sole proprietorships are eligible to use either cash or accrual.
	• A sole proprietor may use the accrual method for the business and the cash method for nonbusiness income and deductions.

FRF-SME

Key Differences Between the FRF for SMEs Accounting Framework and the Tax Basis of Accounting

Although the FRF for SMEs accounting framework largely parallels the accrual method under the tax basis of accounting, the FRF for SMEs reporting option provides a more comprehensive and consistent financial reporting and accounting basis than the tax basis. This leads to a more complete presentation of the entity's financial position, results of operations, and cash flows, as well as more informative disclosures.

Revenue and Expense Recognition

Generally, revenue and expense recognition does not differ between the FRF for SMEs accounting framework and the accrual method for income tax reporting purposes.

Revenue	Under the tax basis, income is generally reported in the year earned.
	• Entities using the tax basis generally include an amount as gross income for the tax year in which — all events that fix the entity's right to receive the amount have occurred, and — the entity can determine the amount with reasonable accuracy.
	Under this rule, an amount is included in gross income on the earliest of the following dates:
	• When payment is received
	• When the income amount is due to the entity
	• When the income is earned
Expenses	Expenses are generally deducted or capitalized when all of the following conditions are met:
	• All events necessary to establish the fact of liability or deduction have occurred.
	• The amount of the liability or deduction is determinable with reasonable accuracy.
	• Economic performance has occurred. — Generally, economic performance occurs when property or services are provided to (or by) another party, or when the property is used.

FRF-SME

Special Revenue Situations

As stated previously, generally, revenue recognition does not differ between the FRF for SMEs accounting framework and the accrual method for income tax reporting purposes. However, special rules may apply to the following.

Topic	FRF for SMEs Accounting Framework	Tax Basis
Installment Sales	• Revenue is ordinarily recognized at the time a sale is made, even if the sales price will be collected in installments.	• Income from an installment sale is recognized when it is fixed and determinable and all events have occurred. • Deductions are permitted later if the sale becomes uncollectible.
Sales Returns	• Recognition of probable returns in the period the sale is recognized.	• No allowance for returns is permitted—returns cannot be recorded until they occur.
Advance Payments	• Advance payments are generally recorded as deferred revenue and recognized when earned.	• Advance payments for services to be performed in a later tax year are generally recognized as income in the year the payment is received. • However, if the services are to be performed by the end of the next tax year, the entity can elect to postpone recognizing the advance payment until the next tax year.

Implementation Resources

Topic	FRF for SMEs Accounting Framework	Tax Basis

Long-Term Contracts	• Performance should be determined using one of the following methods:
	— Percentage-of-completion method
	— Completed-contract method
	   • Used when the entity cannot reasonably estimate the extent of progress toward completion
	   • May also be used if the following conditions are met:
	     — The completed contract method is used for income tax reporting purposes.
	     — The financial position and results of operations of the entity would not vary materially from those resulting from use of the percentage-of-completion method (for example, in circumstances in which an entity has primarily short-term contracts).
		• Generally, entities must report earnings from long-term contracts for tax purposes using the percentage-of-completion method.
		• However, entities with average gross receipts of $10 million or less for the 3 taxable years preceding the contract year and that perform only real property contracts that will be completed within 2 years or manufacturing contracts that will be completed within 1 year may use the completed-contract method.

Rental Income and Expense	• Lessees and lessors generally recognize rent under noncancelable operating leases on a straight-line method over the period the lessee controls the use of the leased property.	• Accrual method lessors usually recognize rental income under operating leases when earned. • Accrual method lessees generally recognize rent expense under operating leases when payments are due.

FRF-SME

Statement of Financial Position Measurement and Presentation Issues

Topic	FRF for SMEs Accounting Framework	Tax Basis
Receivables	• Allows entities to provide an allowance for receivables for which collection is doubtful.	• Must use the specific charge-off method to deduct bad debt losses related to trade notes and accounts receivable. Receivables are not charged to expense until all collection efforts have been exhausted and they are deemed worthless.
Inventories	• Inventory is measured at the lower of cost or net realizable value. • Cost is determined by any of the conventional cost flow assumptions. • Charging all overhead costs to expense is not permitted. • Abnormal amounts of production costs, wasted materials, and labor are to be charged to expense in the year they are incurred. • Overhead costs are allocated based on normal production capacity. This might create differences between inventory calculated under the framework and under tax laws. • Inventory losses are essentially recorded when they are probable and estimable, whether they result from obsolescence, damage, or declining prices.	• Inventory is generally valued using the cost method, lower of cost or market method, or retail method. • Cost is determined by any of the conventional cost flow assumptions. • Charging all overhead costs to expense is not permitted. • Inventory losses are generally not recognized until the inventory is actually offered for sale at lower prices or until the inventory is actually sold or discarded.

FRF-SME

Topic	FRF for SMEs Accounting Framework	Tax Basis
Investments	• Equity and debt instruments held for sale are accounted for at market value, which results in unrealized gains and losses being recognized in some cases. • The equity method is used to account for investments when the investor can exercise significant influence over the investee. Generally, significant influence exists when the ownership interest is 20% or more.	• In general, investments in debt and equity securities are carried at cost for income tax reporting purposes. Accordingly, gains and losses under the income tax basis generally are recognized only when realized. • For tax purposes, the equity method of accounting does not exist. Instead, dividend income is included in income. • A pro rata share of the investee income or loss is not recorded by the investor.
Prepaid Expenses	• Recorded as an asset and amortized to expense	• Expenses paid in advance are deductible only in the year to which the expense applies, unless the expense qualifies for the "12-month rule." • Under the 12-month rule, the entity is not required to capitalize amounts paid to create certain rights or benefits that do not extend beyond the earlier of the following: — 12 months after the right or benefit begins — The end of the tax year after the tax year in which payment is made

(continued)

FRF-SME

Topic	FRF for SMEs Accounting Framework	Tax Basis
Property and Equipment	• Requires depreciation to be recognized in a rational and systematic manner over the useful life of the asset. Depreciation expense is calculated on the cost less any expected *residual value*. • Assets contributed by an owner are valued at market value. • Does not recognize an expense similar to the IRC Section 179 deduction for costs incurred to acquire certain property and equipment during the year within specified limitations.	• Most property and equipment is depreciated under the Modified Accelerated Cost Recovery System, often resulting in more rapid depreciation over shorter lives than would be used under the FRF for SMEs accounting framework. • Internal Revenue Code (IRC) Section 179 permits taxpayers to deduct the cost incurred to acquire certain property and equipment during the year within specified limitations. • Assets contributed by an owner may be valued at the owner's tax basis. • Tax laws pertaining to capital leases are less explicit than under the FRF for SMEs accounting framework. Generally, for tax purposes, an equipment lease is not considered to be a capital lease unless it contains a bargain-purchase option.
Intangible Assets	• Goodwill is amortized over a 15 year period. • A recognized intangible asset is amortized over the best estimate of its useful life.	• Intangible assets (including goodwill) acquired after August 10, 1993 (or July 25, 1991, if elected), are referred to as IRC Section 197 intangibles and may be amortized over a 15-year life beginning with the month the assets were acquired.

FRF-SME

Topic	FRF for SMEs Accounting Framework	Tax Basis
Consolidation	• Consolidation is based on a threshold of more than 50% ownership. • The framework provides more explicit guidance on accounting for a business combination, as well as subsequent consolidation.	• The threshold for consolidation under the IRC is 80% ownership.

Comparison of the FRF for SMEs Accounting Framework With U.S. GAAP—Major Areas (May 2013)

The following table presents a high-level comparison of the FRF for SMEs accounting framework with U.S. GAAP for certain key topics. This presentation does not describe all of the differences between the FRF for SMEs accounting framework and U.S. GAAP. Rather, the presentation highlights areas that AICPA staff believes would be of particular interest to stakeholders.

Topic	FRF for SMEs Accounting Framework	U.S. GAAP
Fair Value	• Uses the term *market value*. It is defined as "the amount of the consideration that would be agreed upon in an arm's length transaction between knowledgeable, willing parties who are under no compulsion to act." • Market value measurement used only in very limited circumstances, such as business combinations, certain nonmonetary transactions, and marketable equity and debt securities that are held for sale.	• *Fair value* is defined as "the price that would be received to sell an asset or paid to transfer a liability in an orderly transaction between market participants at the measurement date." • Provides an overall framework to measuring fair value (for example, fair value hierarchy, valuation techniques). • Standardized disclosure requirements for fair value measurements. • Nonpublic entities are exempt from certain fair value disclosures.

(continued)

Topic	FRF for SMEs Accounting Framework	U.S. GAAP
Going Concern	• Requires management assessment of whether the going concern basis of accounting is appropriate. • When management becomes aware of material uncertainties relating to events or conditions and concludes that a known event or condition is probable of having a severe impact on the entity's ability to realize its assets and discharges its liabilities in the ordinary course of business, the entity should disclose those uncertainties along with its plans for dealing with the adverse effects of the conditions and events.	• No requirement for management assessment of whether the going concern basis of accounting is appropriate. • No requirement for specific disclosures.
Impairment	• No assessment of impairments for long-lived assets. • A depreciated or amortized cost approach is followed. Assets no longer used are written off.	• Long-lived assets are tested for impairment upon a triggering event. • Goodwill and indefinite-lived intangible assets are subject to an impairment test annually. An impairment test is also required upon a triggering event. Optional qualitative assessment is permitted (Step 0).[7]
Comprehensive Income	• No concept of comprehensive income or items of other comprehensive income (OCI).	• Certain items are classified as OCI and displayed as such.

---

[7] The Private Company Council (PCC) tentatively decided to provide private companies an alternative to (1) amortize goodwill, (2) only test goodwill for impairment upon a triggering event, and (3) to further simplify the goodwill impairment test.

FRF-SME

Topic	FRF for SMEs Accounting Framework	U.S. GAAP
Industry-Specific Guidance	• Framework does not contain industry-specific guidance.	• Extensive industry-specific guidance. • The Financial Accounting Standards Board is in the process of finalizing a broad principles-based revenue recognition model that will replace industry-specific revenue guidance.
Consolidation/ Subsidiaries	• Policy choice to either consolidate subsidiaries or account for subsidiaries using the equity method. • *Subsidiary* defined as an entity in which another entity owns more than 50 percent of the outstanding residual equity interests. • No concept of variable interest entities (VIEs).	• Consolidation is required for reporting entity with controlling financial interest in another entity. • VIE model is used when controlling financial interest is achieved through arrangements that do not involve voting interests.[8]
Income Taxes	• Policy choice to account for income taxes using either the taxes payable method or the deferred income taxes method. • No evaluation or accrual of uncertain tax positions.	• Income taxes accounted for using a deferred income tax method. • Uncertain income tax positions must be evaluated and accrual made if certain conditions are met.

(continued)

---

[8] The PCC currently has an ongoing project to consider the application of variable interest entity guidance to common control leasing arrangements.

Topic	FRF for SMEs Accounting Framework	U.S. GAAP
Leases	• Traditional accounting approach blended with some accrual income tax accounting methods. • Lessee classifies leases as either operating or capital leases. • Lessor accounts for leases as sales type, direct financing, or operating.	• Lessee classifies leases as either operating or capital leases. • Lessor accounts for leases as sales type, direct financing, or operating.[9]
Push-Down Accounting	• New basis (push-down) accounting guidance provided. • Specific guidance provided on comprehensive revaluation of assets and liabilities under certain conditions.	• No requirement to apply push-down accounting.
Intangible Assets	• All intangible assets are considered to have a finite useful life and are amortized over their estimated useful lives. • In accounting for expenditures on internally-generated intangible assets during the development phase, management should make an accounting policy choice to either expense such expenditures as incurred or capitalize such expenditures as an intangible asset, provided the criteria are met.	• A recognized intangible asset is amortized over its useful life unless that life is determined to be indefinite. • Intangible assets subject to amortization are tested for impairment upon a triggering event. • Indefinite-lived intangible assets are subject to an impairment test annually. An impairment test is also required upon a triggering event. Optional qualitative assessment is permitted.

---

[9] The Financial Accounting Standards Board (FASB) has an ongoing project to revamp its current lease accounting model and adopt a right-of-use (ROU) model. The lessee would recognize a ROU asset and liability for all lease contracts (other than short-term leases). The lessor would account for a lease under either the type A approach (receivable and residual) or the type B approach (operating lease) on the basis of the nature of the underlying asset and the terms and conditions of the lease.

Implementation Resources

Topic	*FRF for SMEs Accounting Framework*	U.S. GAAP
Goodwill	• Amortized over the same period as that used for federal income tax purposes or 15 years. • No impairment testing.	• No amortization. • Tested for impairment at least annually. • An impairment test is also required upon a triggering event. Optional qualitative assessment is permitted (Step 0).[10]
Revenue	• Broad, principle-based guidance on revenue recognition. • Revenue should be recognized when performance is achieved and ultimate collection is reasonably assured. • For goods: Performance is achieved when the entity transfers the risks and rewards associated with the goods to a customer. • For services: Performance should be determined using either the percentage of completion method or the completed contract method. Performance should be regarded as having been achieved when reasonable assurance exists regarding the measurement of the consideration that will be derived from rendering the service or performing the long-term contract.	• Revenue is realized or realizable when all of the following criteria are met:[11] — Persuasive evidence of an arrangement exists. — Delivery has occurred or services have been rendered. — The seller's price to the buyer is fixed or determinable. — Collectability is reasonable assured. • Construction and production contracts are accounted for using the percentage-of-completion method or completed contract method. • Industry-specific guidance.

(continued)

---

[10] See footnote 4.

[11] FASB is in the process of finalizing a new revenue recognition model. The core principle of the new model is that an entity should recognize revenue when promised goods or services are transferred to customers. The amount of revenue recognized reflects the consideration that is expected in exchange for those goods or services. The new revenue guidance will be effective for nonpublic entities with an annual reporting period beginning after December 15, 2017.

FRF-SME

Topic	FRF for SMEs Accounting Framework	U.S. GAAP
Investments/ Financial Assets and Liabilities	• Historical cost approach. • Market value measurement required only for investments being held for sale. • Changes in market value included in net income.	• Classification required based on management intent and ability. • Securities classified as "available for sale" or "trading" measured at fair value. • Debt securities classified as "held-to-maturity" measured at amortized cost. • Accounting for changes in fair value depends upon classification.
Derivatives	• Disclosure approach. • Recognition at settlement (cash basis). • No hedge accounting.	• All derivatives recognized as either assets or liabilities.[12] • Measured at fair value. • Accounting for changes in fair value depends on the use of the derivative. • Hedge accounting permitted.
Stock-Based Compensation	• Disclosure only.	• Stock-based compensation is classified as liability or equity. • Accounting for stock-based compensation expense depends upon classification. • Measurement of stock-based compensation is fair-value based.

---

[12] The PCC tentatively decided to provide private companies alternatives to account for interest rate swaps entered only for the purpose of economically converting its variable-rate borrowing to a fixed-rate borrowing if certain criteria are met. The PCC also tentatively decided to provide private companies a simplified shortcut method to make it easier to qualify for hedge accounting on such swaps.

Topic	*FRF for SMEs Accounting Framework*	U.S. GAAP
Stock-Based Compensation *(continued)*		• Nonpublic entities permitted to measure stock-based compensation under calculated-value method. When it is not possible to reasonably estimate fair value or calculated value, intrinsic value is permitted.
Defined Benefit Plans	• Policy choice to account for plans using either a current contribution payable method or one of the accrued benefit obligation methods.	• Plans accounted for using a projected benefit obligation model.
Business Combinations	• As of the acquisition date, the acquirer should recognize, separately from goodwill, the identifiable assets acquired, the liabilities assumed, and any noncontrolling interest in the acquiree. Identifiable assets acquired and liabilities assumed are measured at their acquisition-date market values. Certain exceptions exist.	• As of the acquisition date, the acquirer should recognize, separately from goodwill, the identifiable assets acquired, the liabilities assumed, and any noncontrolling interest in the acquiree. Identifiable assets acquired and liabilities assumed are measured at their acquisition-date fair values. Certain exceptions exist.[13]

(continued)

---

[13] The PCC tentatively decided to provide private companies an alternative to only recognize intangible assets arising from noncancellable contractual terms or those arising from other legal rights. This would likely result in fewer intangible assets being separately recognized.

Topic	FRF for SMEs Accounting Framework	U.S. GAAP
Business Combinations *(continued)*	• An entity should make an accounting policy choice to account for an intangible asset acquired in a business combination either by separately recognizing the intangible asset as an identifiable asset or by not separately recognizing the intangible asset as an identifiable asset and subsuming into goodwill the value of the intangible asset.	
Inventories	• Valued at lower of cost or net realizable value.	• Valued at lower of cost or market, with market generally considered to be replacement cost; however, market is not permitted to exceed net realizable value or be less than net realizable value less a normal profit margin.

Comparison of the FRF for SMEs Accounting Framework With IFRS for SMEs—Major Areas (May 2013)

In general, the FRF for SMEs reporting option is similar in many ways to IFRS for SMEs. Both are intended to be simplified, relevant, and cost-effective financial reporting frameworks for SMEs. In addition, both contain targeted financial statement disclosures and contain less prescriptive guidance. However, the IFRS for SMEs is GAAP whereas the FRF for SMEs reporting option is a special purpose framework (an other comprehensive basis of accounting). Also, the parameters defining what kinds of entities are intended to utilize the framework and IFRS for SMEs are different, with IFRS for SMEs having a more prescribed scope. The following table presents a high-level comparison of the FRF for SMEs accounting framework with IFRS for SMEs for certain key topics. This presentation does not describe all of the differences between the FRF for SMEs accounting framework and IFRS for SMEs. Rather, the presentation highlights areas that AICPA staff believes would be of particular interest to stakeholders.

Topic	FRF for SMEs Accounting Framework	IFRS for SMEs
Comparative Financial Statements	• Comparative financial statements are not required.	• Requires comparative information in respect of the previous comparable period for all amounts presented in the current period's financial statements. • An entity shall include comparative information for narrative and descriptive information when it is relevant to an understanding of the current period's financial statements.
Comprehensive Income	• No concept of comprehensive income or items of other comprehensive income.	• Provides an accounting policy choice between presenting total comprehensive income in a single statement or in two separate statements. • Certain items are classified as other comprehensive income and displayed as such.
Fair Value	• Uses the term *market value*. It is defined as "the amount of the consideration that would be agreed upon in an arm's length transaction between knowledgeable, willing parties who are under no compulsion to act." • Market value measurement used only in very limited circumstances, such as business combinations, certain nonmonetary transactions, and marketable equity and debt securities held-for-sale.	• Use the term *fair value*. It is the amount for which an asset could be exchanged, or a liability settled, between knowledgeable, willing parties in an arm's length transaction. • Wider use of fair value measurements compared to the FRF for SMEs accounting framework.

(continued)

FRF-SME

Topic	FRF for SMEs Accounting Framework	IFRS for SMEs
Inventories	• Last in, first out (LIFO) is permitted.	• LIFO is not permitted. • Inventory is assessed at the end of each reporting period for impairment or for recovery of previously recognized impairment.
Subsidiaries	• *Subsidiary* defined as an entity in which another entity owns more than 50 percent of the outstanding residual equity interests. • Policy choice to either consolidate subsidiaries or account for subsidiaries using the equity method. • No concept of special purpose entities (SPEs) or variable interest entities.	• *Subsidiary* defined as an entity that is controlled by the parent. • Control is the power to govern the financial and operating policies of an entity so as to obtain benefits from its activities. • If an entity has created a SPE to accomplish a narrow and well-defined objective, the entity shall consolidate the SPE when the substance of the relationship indicates that the SPE is controlled by that entity.
Investments/ Financial Assets and Liabilities	• Historical cost approach for investments and financial assets and liabilities. • Market value measurement required only for investments being held for sale, with changes in market value included in net income. • Investees over which the investor has significant influence are accounted for under the equity method.	• There are two classification categories for financial instruments: amortized cost and fair value through earnings. • Basic financial instruments are measured at amortized cost except for investments in nonconvertible and nonputtable preference shares and nonputtable ordinary shares that are publicly traded or whose fair value can be measured reliably.

FRF-SME

Topic	FRF for SMEs Accounting Framework	IFRS for SMEs
Investments/ Financial Assets and Liabilities *(continued)*		• All instruments other than basic debt instruments (including instruments with embedded derivatives) are measured at fair value through earnings. • Investments in associates (*associates* are entities in which the investor has the ability to exercise significant influence) are accounted for using one of the following methods: the cost method (if there is no published price quotation), equity method, or fair-value-through-earnings method.
Derivatives	• Disclosure approach. • Recognition at settlement (cash basis). • No hedge accounting.	• Derivatives are recognized and measured at fair value through earnings. • Hedge accounting prescribed.
Stock-Based Compensation	• Disclosure only.	• Compensation expense is recognized. • Specific accounting depends on terms and type of instrument.
Leases	• The criteria for determining whether a lease is a capital lease to a lessee generally are similar to IFRS for SMEs. Unlike IFRS for SMEs, however, the FRF for SMEs accounting framework provides specific quantitative thresholds for determining certain criteria.	• See the FRF for SMEs Accounting Framework column.

(continued)

Topic	FRF for SMEs Accounting Framework	IFRS for SMEs
Leases (continued)	• Under the FRF for SMEs accounting framework, if land is the sole item of property leased, the lessee accounts for the lease as a capital lease only if the lease transfers ownership of the property at the end of the lease term. • From the point of view of a lessor, some additional criteria must be met to classify the lease as a capital lease. • Under the FRF for SMEs accounting framework, lessors' capital leases are categorized as direct financing leases or sales-types leases (both similar to the finance lease category in IFRS for SMEs).	
Goodwill	• Amortized over the same period as that used for federal income tax purposes or 15 years. • No impairment testing.	• Goodwill is amortized over its useful life. If an entity cannot reliably estimate its useful life, the life is presumed to be 10 years. • Impairment testing is required only when there is an indicator of impairment.
Intangible Assets	• All intangible assets are considered to have a finite useful life and are amortized over their estimated useful lives.	• All intangible assets (including goodwill) are finite-lived and are amortized over their useful lives. If an entity cannot reliably estimate the useful life of an intangible asset, the life is presumed to be 10 years.

FRF-SME

Topic	FRF for SMEs Accounting Framework	IFRS for SMEs
Intangible Assets *(continued)*	• In accounting for expenditures on internally-generated intangible assets during the development phase, management should make an accounting policy choice to either expense such expenditures as incurred or capitalize such expenditures as an intangible asset, provided the criteria are met.	• Expenditures on internally developed intangibles, including research and development costs, are expensed as incurred, unless they are part of the cost of another asset that meets the recognition criteria in IFRS for SMEs.
Statement of Cash Flows	• Cash inflows from interest and dividends received should be classified as cash flows from operating activities. • Cash outflows related to interest paid should be classified as an operating activity, unless capitalized. • Cash outflows related to dividends paid should be classified as cash flows used in financing activities. • Cash outflows from dividends paid by subsidiaries to noncontrolling interests should be presented separately as cash flows used in financing activities.	• An entity may classify interest paid and interest and dividends received as operating cash flows because they are included in profit or loss. • Alternatively, the entity may classify interest paid and interest and dividends received as financing cash flows and investing cash flows, respectively, because they are costs of obtaining financial resources or returns on investments. • An entity may classify dividends paid as a financing cash flow because they are a cost of obtaining financial resources. • Alternatively, the entity may classify dividends paid as a component of cash flows from operating activities because they are paid out of operating cash flows.

(continued)

FRF-SME

Topic	FRF for SMEs Accounting Framework	IFRS for SMEs
Debt Covenant Violation	• Debt covenant violations may be cured after the balance sheet date, eliminating the need to reclassify the debt.	• Curing a debt covenant violation after the balance sheet date may not eliminate the need to reclassify the debt.
Investment Property	• No specific definition of investment property. Investments in land and buildings are accounted for as property, plant, and equipment.	• Separate accounting guidance for investment property. • Investment property is property (land or a building, or part of a building, or both) held by the owner or by the lessee under a finance lease to earn rentals or for capital appreciation or both, rather than for use in the production or supply of goods or services or for administrative purposes, or sale in the ordinary course of business.
Component Depreciation	• No requirement for separate components of an asset (nor is there a prohibition against doing so). • Composite depreciation method may be used.	• If the major components of an item of property, plant, and equipment have significantly different patterns of consumption of economic benefits, an entity shall allocate the initial cost of the asset to its major components and depreciate each such component separately over its useful life.

FRF-SME

Implementation Resources

Topic	*FRF for SMEs Accounting Framework*	*IFRS for SMEs*
Joint Ventures	• A venturer should make an accounting policy choice to account for its interests in joint ventures using one of the following methods: — Equity — Proportionate consolidation • Only applicable to unincorporated entities in which it is an established industry practice	• Investments in jointly controlled entities may be accounted for using one of the following methods: — Cost (if there is no published price quotation) — Equity — Fair-value-through-earnings
Impairment of Long-Lived Assets	• No assessment of impairments for long-lived assets. • A depreciated or amortized cost approach is followed. Assets no longer used are written off.	• Impairment testing is required only when there is an indicator of impairment.
Contingencies	• A contingency is recognized when it is probable that a future event will confirm that the value of an asset has diminished or a liability incurred at the date of the financial statements and the amount of the loss can be reasonably estimable. • *Probable* is defined as likely to occur, a threshold higher than the "more likely than not" threshold used in IFRS for SMEs.	• A contingency is recognized when it is more likely than not that the entity will be required to transfer economic benefits in settlement and the amount of the obligation can be estimated reliably.
Income Taxes	• Policy choice to account for income taxes using either the taxes payable method or the deferred income taxes method. • No evaluation or accrual of uncertain tax positions.	• Income taxes accounted for using a deferred income tax method. • Uncertain income tax positions must be evaluated and accrual made if certain conditions are met.

(continued)

FRF-SME

Topic	FRF for SMEs Accounting Framework	IFRS for SMEs
Borrowing Costs	• An entity can choose to capitalize interest costs related to an item of property, plant, and equipment that is acquired, constructed, or developed over time. • When a financial liability is issued or assumed in an arm's length transaction, an entity should measure it at its exchange amount adjusted by financing fees and transaction costs that are directly attributable to its origination, acquisition, issuance, or assumption. • An entity can choose to capitalize interest costs related to inventories that require a substantial period of time to get them ready for their intended use or sale.	• Borrowing costs are interest and other costs that an entity incurs in connection with the borrowing of funds. An entity should recognize all borrowing costs as an expense in net income in the period in which they are incurred.
Long-Lived Assets Held for Sale	• A long-lived asset to be sold should be classified as held for sale and presented separately in the entity's statement of financial position. The assets and liabilities of a disposal group classified as held for sale should be presented separately in the asset and liability sections, respectively, of the statement of financial position. • A long-lived asset should not be amortized while it is classified as held for sale.	• There is no "held for sale" classification for nonfinancial assets or groups of assets and liabilities and related measurement provisions.

FRF-SME

Presentation and Disclosure Checklist

This presentation and disclosure checklist has been derived from the presentation and disclosure requirements of the FRF for SMEs accounting framework. Disclosure requirements apply to material items. If an item is immaterial, no disclosure is required. This checklist should not be relied upon as a substitute for reading and complying with the presentation and disclosure requirements prescribed in the FRF for SMEs accounting framework. Additional disclosures may be necessary to enable financial statement users to understand a transaction, event, or condition that affect an entity's financial statements.

This financial statement disclosure checklist is organized into sections. Carefully review the topics listed and consider whether they represent potential disclosure items for the entity. Place a check mark by the topics or sections that are applicable and complete those sections of the checklist. Other sections may be marked "N/A" or left blank. For example, if the entity had a change in accounting principle, place a check mark by the section "Accounting Changes" and complete that section of the checklist. On the other hand, if the entity did not have a change in accounting principle, do not place a check mark by "Accounting Changes" and skip that section when completing the checklist.

Note: Paragraph numbers included at the end of each disclosure requirement refer to paragraphs within the *Financial Reporting Framework for Small- and Medium-Sized Entities*. Similarly, chapter numbers refer to chapters within the framework.

Place ✔ by Applicable Sections

I. Presentation
    A. General Principles of Financial Statement Presentation and Accounting Policies [*Financial Reporting Framework for Small- and Medium-Sized Entities* chapters 1–2]
    B. Transition [chapter 3]
    C. Risks and Uncertainties [chapter 10]
    D. Accounting Changes, Changes in Estimates, and Correction of Errors [chapter 9]
    E. Statement of Operations [chapter 7]
    F. Statement of Financial Position [chapter 4]
    G. Statement of Cash Flows [chapter 8]

II. Statement of Financial Position
    A. Current Assets and Current Liabilities [chapter 5]
    B. Inventories [chapter 12]
    C. Equity, Debt, and Other Investments [chapter 11]

(continued)

			Place ✔ by Applicable Sections
	D.	Financial Assets and Liabilities (Except Long-Term Debt) [chapter 6]	_____
	E.	Property, Plant, and Equipment [chapter 14]	_____
	F.	Intangible Assets [chapter 13]	_____
	G.	Commitments [chapter 16]	_____
	H.	Contingencies [chapter 17]	_____
	I.	Long-Term Debt [chapter 6]	_____
	J.	Equity [chapter 18]	_____
III.	Statement of Operations		
	A.	Revenue [chapter 19]	_____
	B.	Retirement and Other Postemployment Benefits [chapter 20]	_____
	C.	Income Taxes [chapter 21]	_____
IV.	Broad Transactions		
	A.	Business Combinations [chapter 28]	_____
	B.	Subsidiaries [chapter 22]	_____
	C.	Consolidated Financial Statements and Noncontrolling Interests [chapter 23]	_____
	D.	Interests in Joint Ventures [chapter 24]	_____
	E.	New Basis (Push-Down) Accounting [chapter 29]	_____
	F.	Foreign Currency Translation [chapter 31]	_____
	G.	Nonmonetary Transactions [chapter 30]	_____
	H.	Leases [chapter 25]	_____
	I.	Subsequent Events [chapter 27]	_____
	J.	Disposal of Long-Lived Assets and Discontinued Operations [chapter 15]	_____
	K.	Related Party Transactions [chapter 26]	_____

I. Presentation

		Yes	No	N/A
A.	**General Principles of Financial Statement Presentation and Accounting Policies** [chapters 1–2]			

Presentation

1. If a statement of financial position and a statement of operations are prepared, has a statement of cash flows also been prepared? [1.04] ____ ____ ____

2. Are material presentation items not netted in the financial statements, unless specifically allowed by the FRF for SMEs accounting framework? [1.06] ____ ____ ____

3. Has management made an assessment of whether the going concern basis of accounting is appropriate, taking into account all known and available information about the future, which is limited to 12 months from the statement of financial position date? [2.07–.08] ____ ____ ____

Disclosure

4. Has the entity described those accounting policies that are significant to its operations, and at a minimum, has disclosure been made of information on areas in which judgment has been exercised? [2.23] ____ ____ ____

5. Has the entity stated prominently in the notes to its financial statements that the financial statements were prepared in accordance with *Financial Reporting Framework for Small- and Medium-Sized Entities* issued by the AICPA, along (if necessary, see paragraph 2.20) with a brief description of the primary differences from generally accepted accounting principles in the United States of America? [2.20] ____ ____ ____

6. Has the entity disclosed information on accounting policies in the following situations:
    a. If its operating cycle is less than or greater than one year, has the entity disclosed that fact, along with the length of the operating cycle? [2.21] ____ ____ ____
    b. If reclassifications of financial statement items to conform to the present year's presentation have been made, has the entity disclosed these reclassifications? [2.22] ____ ____ ____

(continued)

		Yes	No	N/A

    c. When a selection has been made from alternative acceptable accounting principles and methods? [2.24] ____ ____ ____

    d. When accounting principles and methods used are specific to an industry in which an entity operates, even if such accounting principles and methods are predominantly followed in that industry? [2.24] ____ ____ ____

7. Has the summary of accounting policies been disclosed as the first note to the financial statements? [2.25] ____ ____ ____

B. Transition [chapter 3]

Disclosure

1. Has the entity disclosed the amount of each charge or credit to equity at the date of transition to the FRF for SMEs accounting framework resulting from the adoption of these principles and the reason therefor? [3.19] ____ ____ ____

2. If the entity elected to use one or more of the exemptions to the principles in the FRF for SMEs accounting framework allowed at transition, has it disclosed the exemptions used? [3.20] ____ ____ ____

C. Risks and Uncertainties [chapter 10]

Disclosure

1. Has the entity included a description of the major products or services the reporting entity sells or provides and its principal markets, including the locations of those markets? [10.02] ____ ____ ____

2. Has the entity included an explanation that the preparation of financial statements in conformity with the FRF for SMEs accounting framework requires the use of management's estimates? [10.03] ____ ____ ____

3. Has the entity included a discussion of significant estimates when, based on known information available before the financial statements are available to be issued, it is reasonably possible that (*a*) the estimate will change in the near term (a period of time not to exceed one year from the date of the financial statements), and (*b*) the effect of the change will be material? [10.04] ____ ____ ____

Implementation Resources

	Yes	No	N/A

4. Has the entity disclosed the estimate of the effect of a change in a condition, situation, or set of circumstances that existed at the date of the financial statements, based on known information available before the financial statements are available to be issued? [10.04] _____ _____ _____
5. Has the entity disclosed certain concentrations if, based on information known to management before the financial statements are available to be issued, all the following criteria are met? [10.06]
   a. The concentration exists at the date of the financial statements. _____ _____ _____
   b. The concentration makes the entity vulnerable to the risk of a near-term severe impact. _____ _____ _____
   c. It is at least reasonably possible that the events that could cause the severe impact will occur in the near term. _____ _____ _____

D. **Accounting Changes, Changes in Estimates, and Correction of Errors** [chapter 9]
   Disclosure
   1. When initial application of the FRF for SMEs accounting framework or a required change in accounting policy has an effect on the current period or any prior period, or would have such an effect except that it is impracticable to determine the amount of the adjustment, has the entity disclosed [9.29]
      a. when applicable, that the change in accounting policy is made in accordance with its transitional provisions? _____ _____ _____
      b. the nature of the change in accounting policy? _____ _____ _____
      c. when applicable, a description of the transitional provisions? _____ _____ _____
      d. for the current period, to the extent practicable, the amount of the adjustment for each financial statement line item affected? _____ _____ _____
      e. the amount of the adjustment relating to periods before those presented to the extent practicable? _____ _____ _____

(continued)

FRF-SME

	Yes	No	N/A

    f. if retrospective application is impracticable for a particular prior period or for periods before those presented, the circumstances that led to the existence of that condition and a description of how and from when the change in accounting policy has been applied? ____ ____ ____

2. When a voluntary change in accounting policy has an effect on the current period or any prior period or would have an effect on that period, except that it is impracticable to determine the amount of the adjustment, has the entity disclosed [9.30]

    a. the nature of the change in accounting policy? ____ ____ ____

    b. the reasons why applying the new accounting policy provides reliable and more relevant information? ____ ____ ____

    c. for the current period, to the extent practicable, the amount of the adjustment for each financial statement line item affected? ____ ____ ____

    d. the amount of the adjustment relating to periods before those presented to the extent practicable? ____ ____ ____

    e. if retrospective application is impracticable for a particular prior period or for periods before those presented, the circumstances that led to the existence of that condition and a description of how and from when the change in accounting policy has been applied? ____ ____ ____

3. Has the entity disclosed the nature and amount of a change in an accounting estimate that has an effect in the current period? (Disclosure of those effects is not necessary for estimates made each period in the ordinary course of accounting for items such as uncollectible accounts, progress on uncompleted contracts, or inventory obsolescence; however, disclosure is required if the effect of a change in the estimate is material.) [9.31] ____ ____ ____

4. Has the entity disclosed the following, related to prior period errors [9.32]:

    a. The nature of the prior period error? ____ ____ ____

Implementation Resources

	Yes	No	N/A

    b. For each prior period presented, the amount of the correction for each financial statement line item affected?

    c. The amount of the correction at the beginning of the earliest prior period presented?

E. Statement of Operations [chapter 7]

Presentation

1. Does the statement of operations distinguish the following [7.03]:
    - *a.* Income or loss before discontinued operations?
    - *b.* Results of discontinued operations?
    - *c.* Net income or loss for the period?
2. In arriving at the income or loss before discontinued operations, does the statement of operations present major elements, such as revenue, cost of goods sold, operating expenses, other revenues and gains, and other expenses and losses? [7.03]
3. Are the following items distinguished in the statement of operations or included in the notes to the financial statements or in attached schedules [7.04]:
    - *a.* Revenue recognized?
    - *b.* Income from investments, disclosing income from
        - i. nonconsolidated subsidiaries and nonproportionately consolidated joint ventures?
        - ii. all other investments showing separately
            - (1.) investments measured using the cost method?
            - (2.) investments measured using the equity method?
            - (3.) investments measured at market value?
    - *c.* The amount charged for depreciation of property, plant, and equipment?
    - *d.* The amount charged for amortization of intangible assets?
    - *e.* The amount of exchange gain or loss included in net income?

(continued)

FRF-SME

282 Financial Reporting Framework for Small- and Medium-Sized Entities

	Yes	No	N/A

    f. Revenue, expenses, gains, or losses resulting from transactions or events that are not expected to occur frequently over several years or do not typify normal business activities of the entity? ____ ____ ____

    g. Income taxes? ____ ____ ____

F. Statement of Financial Position
[chapter 4]

Presentation

1. If a classified statement of financial position is presented, are the following distinguished [4.03]:
   a. Current assets? ____ ____ ____
   b. Long-term assets? ____ ____ ____
   c. Total assets? ____ ____ ____
   d. Current liabilities? ____ ____ ____
   e. Long-term liabilities? ____ ____ ____
   f. Total liabilities? ____ ____ ____
   g. Equity? ____ ____ ____
   h. Total liabilities and equity? ____ ____ ____

2. Are the following assets presented separately or included in the notes to the financial statements or in attached schedules [4.04]:
   a. Cash and cash equivalents? ____ ____ ____
   b. Trade and other receivables? ____ ____ ____
   c. Prepaid expenses? ____ ____ ____
   d. Other financial assets? ____ ____ ____
   e. Inventories? ____ ____ ____
   f. Investments in nonconsolidated subsidiaries and nonproportionately consolidated joint ventures? ____ ____ ____
   g. All other investments showing separately
      i. investments measured using the cost method? ____ ____ ____
      ii. investments measured using the equity method? ____ ____ ____
      iii. investments measured at market value? ____ ____ ____
   h. Property, plant, and equipment? ____ ____ ____
   i. Intangible assets? ____ ____ ____
   j. Assets for current income taxes? ____ ____ ____
   k. Assets for deferred income taxes? ____ ____ ____
   l. Long-lived assets and disposal groups classified as held for sale? ____ ____ ____
   m. Accrued benefit assets? ____ ____ ____

3. Are the following liabilities separately presented [4.05]:
   a. Main classes of current liabilities? ____ ____ ____

FRF-SME

Implementation Resources 283

		Yes	No	N/A
b.	Liabilities for deferred income taxes?			
c.	Liabilities of disposal groups classified as held for sale?			
d.	Obligations under capital leases?			
e.	Accrued benefit liability?			
f.	Long-term debt?			
g.	Asset retirement obligations?			
h.	Other financial liabilities?			

G. **Statement of Cash Flows** [chapter 8]
Presentation
1. Has the entity excluded from cash and cash equivalents cash subject to restrictions that prevent its use for current purposes, such as compensating balances required in accordance with lending arrangements? [8.05]
2. Has the entity classified an increase (decrease) in bank overdrafts, which represents an increase (decrease) in bank borrowing, as a financing inflow (outflow)? [8.08]
3. Has the net change in overdrafts during the period been classified as a financing activity? [8.08]
4. If the entity with multiple bank accounts (which do not have the right of offset) has one account in an overdraft position at year-end, has the entity presented as cash and cash equivalents on the statement of cash flows only the accounts with the positive balances? [8.08]
5. If the entity used the direct method, are major classes of gross cash receipts and gross cash payments arising from operating activities presented separately? [8.20]
6. If the entity used the direct method, is a separate schedule that reconciles net income to net cash flows from operating activities presented? [8.21]
7. Have cash inflows from interest and dividends received been classified as cash flows from operating activities? [8.27]
8. Have cash outflows related to interest paid been classified as an operating activity, unless capitalized? [8.27]
9. Have cash outflows related to dividends paid been classified as cash flows used in financing activities? [8.27]

(continued)

FRF-SME

	Yes	No	N/A

10. Have cash outflows from dividends paid by subsidiaries to noncontrolling interests been presented separately as cash flows used in financing activities? [8.27] ____ ____ ____

11. Have cash flows arising from income taxes been classified as cash flows from operating activities unless they can be specifically identified with financing and investing activities? [8.30] ____ ____ ____

12. Have the aggregate cash flows arising from each of the business combinations accounted for using the acquisition method and disposals of business units been presented separately and classified as cash flows from investing activities? [8.31] ____ ____ ____

13. Have investing and financing transactions that do not require the use of cash or cash equivalents been excluded from the statement of cash flows? [8.34] ____ ____ ____

Disclosure

14. Has the entity disclosed the policy that it adopts in determining the composition of cash and cash equivalents? [8.36] ____ ____ ____

15. Has the entity disclosed any material restrictions on cash? [8.37] ____ ____ ____

16. Has the entity disclosed the policy for determining components of cash and cash equivalents in circumstances where the entity classified investments that qualify to be treated as cash equivalents as investments? [8.38] ____ ____ ____

17. Has the entity disclosed any change in the policy for determining the components of cash and cash equivalents? [8.38] ____ ____ ____

18. Has the entity disclosed, in aggregate, in respect of both business combinations and disposals of business units during the period [8.39]

    a. the total purchase or disposal consideration? ____ ____ ____

    b. the portion of the purchase or disposal consideration composed of cash and cash equivalents? ____ ____ ____

    c. the amount of cash and cash equivalents acquired or disposed of? ____ ____ ____

    d. the total assets, other than cash or cash equivalents, and total liabilities acquired or disposed of? ____ ____ ____

FRF-SME

| | Yes | No | N/A |

19. For investing and financing transactions that do not require the use of cash or cash equivalents, has the entity either presented these transactions on the face of the statement of cash flows as "noncash investing or financing activities" or disclosed these transactions in the notes to the financial statements in a way that provides all the relevant information about these investing and financing activities? [8.40] ____ ____ ____

II. Statement of Financial Position

A. Current Assets and Current Liabilities
[chapter 5]

Presentation

1. Has the entity included in current assets those assets ordinarily realizable within one year from the date of the statement of financial position or within the normal operating cycle, when that is longer than a year? [5.03] ____ ____ ____
2. Has the entity segregated current assets among the major classes, such as cash, investments, accounts and notes receivable, inventories, prepaid expenses, costs and estimated earnings in excess of billings on uncompleted contracts, and deferred income tax assets? [5.04] ____ ____ ____
3. Has the entity excluded the cash surrender value of life insurance from current assets, unless converted to cash prior to the date the financial statements are available to be issued? [5.05] ____ ____ ____
4. Has the entity included in current liabilities amounts payable within one year from the date of the statement of financial position or within the normal operating cycle, when that is longer than a year? [5.06] ____ ____ ____
5. Has the entity included amounts received or due from customers or clients with respect to goods to be delivered or services to be performed within one year from the date of the statement of financial position in the current liability classification? [5.07] ____ ____ ____
6. Has the entity excluded obligations that would otherwise be classified as current liabilities from the current liability classification to the extent that contractual arrangements have been made for settlement from other than current assets? [5.08] ____ ____ ____

(continued)

		Yes	No	N/A

7. Has the entity segregated current liabilities among the major classes, such as bank loans, trade creditors and accrued liabilities, loans payable, billings in excess of costs and estimated earnings on uncompleted contracts, taxes payable, dividends payable, deferred revenues, current payments on long-term debt, and deferred income tax liabilities? [5.09] _____ _____ _____

8. Has the entity presented amounts owing on loans from directors, officers, and shareholders and amounts owing to parent and other affiliated companies, whether on account of a loan or otherwise, separately? [5.09] _____ _____ _____

9. Has the entity included in the current liability classification only that portion of long-term debt obligations, including sinking-fund requirements, payable within one year from the date of the statement of financial position? [5.10] _____ _____ _____

10. If a creditor has, at the statement of financial position date, or will have within one year [or operating cycle, if longer) from that date, the unilateral right to demand immediate repayment of any portion or all the debt under any provision of the debt agreement, has the entity classified the obligation (or a portion thereof, as appropriate) as a current liability unless

    a. the creditor has waived, in writing, or subsequently lost, the right to demand payment for more than one year (or operating cycle, if longer) from the statement of financial position date? _____ _____ _____

    b. the obligation has been refinanced on a long-term basis before the statement of financial position is available to be issued? _____ _____ _____

    c. the debtor has entered into a noncancellable agreement to refinance the short-term obligation on a long-term basis before the statement of financial position is available to be issued, and there is no impediment to the completion of the refinancing? [5.11] _____ _____ _____

FRF-SME

Implementation Resources

	Yes	No	N/A

11. Has the entity classified long-term debt with a covenant violation as a current liability unless (a) as of the date the financial statements are available to be issued, the creditor has waived, in writing, or subsequently lost, the right, arising from violation of the covenant at the statement of financial position date, to demand repayment for a period of more than one year from the statement of financial position date; or (b) the debt agreement contains a grace period during which the debtor may cure the violation, and contractual arrangements have been made that ensure the violation will be cured within the grace period; and a violation of the debt covenant giving the creditor the right to demand repayment at a future compliance date within one year of the statement of financial position date is remote? [5.12] ____ ____ ____

B. **Inventories** [chapter 12]
   Disclosure
   1. Has the entity disclosed
      a. the accounting policies adopted in measuring inventories, including the cost formula used? ____ ____ ____
      b. the total carrying amount of inventories and the carrying amount in classifications appropriate to the entity? ____ ____ ____
      c. the amount of cost of goods sold during the period? [12.28] ____ ____ ____
   2. Has the entity disclosed information about the carrying amounts held in different classifications of inventories, and the extent of the changes in these assets? (Common classifications of inventories are merchandise, production supplies, materials, works in progress, and finished goods.) [12.29] ____ ____ ____
   3. If material and unusual losses result from measuring inventories at the lower of cost or net realizable value, has the amount of the loss been disclosed in the statement of operations separately identified from the consumed inventory costs described as cost of goods sold? [12.30] ____ ____ ____
   4. Have firm purchase commitments been disclosed? [12.31] ____ ____ ____

(continued)

FRF-SME

	Yes	No	N/A

5. If the contract price of firm purchase commitments exceeds the market value, is the estimated loss disclosed? [12.31] ____ ____ ____

6. If the entity's accounting policy is to capitalize interest costs related to certain items of inventory, are the amounts capitalized disclosed? [12.32] ____ ____ ____

C. Equity, Debt, and Other Investments
[chapter 11]

Presentation

1. Has the entity presented the following separately on the statement of financial position or in the notes to the financial statements:
    a. Investments in companies subject to significant influence accounted for using the equity method? ____ ____ ____
    b. Other investments accounted for at cost? ____ ____ ____
    c. Equity and debt investments held-for-sale? [11.20] ____ ____ ____

2. Has the entity presented separately in the statement of operations or in the notes to the financial statements:
    a. Income from investments in companies subject to significant influence accounted for using the equity method? ____ ____ ____
    b. Income from other investments accounted for at cost? ____ ____ ____
    c. Equity and debt investments held-for-sale? [11.21] ____ ____ ____

3. Has the entity grouped investments reported on the statement of financial position and investment income reported in the statement of operations in the same way? [11.22] ____ ____ ____

4. The FRF for SMEs accounting framework requires that equity method investees normally should follow the same basis of accounting (FRF for SMEs accounting framework) as the investor. Accordingly, have the financial statements of equity-method investees been adjusted, if necessary, to conform with standards in the framework, unless it is impracticable to do so? [11.05] ____ ____ ____

Implementation Resources

	Yes	No	N/A

5. Has the entity's proportionate share of any discontinued operations, changes in accounting policy, corrections of errors relating to prior period financial statements, or capital transactions of an equity-method investee presented and disclosed separately, according to its nature, in the entity's financial statements? [11.13]   _____ _____ _____

Disclosure

6. Has the entity disclosed the basis used to account for investments? [11.23]   _____ _____ _____

7. When the fiscal periods of an investor and an investee are not the same and the equity method is used to account for the investee, has the entity disclosed events relating to, or transactions of, the investee that have occurred during the intervening period and significantly affect the financial position or results of operations of the investor? (This disclosure is not necessary if these events or transactions are recorded in the financial statements.) [11.24]   _____ _____ _____

8. Other than for investments held for sale, has the entity disclosed the name and description of each significant investment, including the carrying amounts, and proportion of ownership interests held in each investment? [11.25]   _____ _____ _____

D. **Financial Assets and Liabilities (Except Long-Term Debt)** [chapter 6]

Presentation

1. Has the entity classified a financial instrument, or its component parts, as a liability or as equity in accordance with the substance of the contractual arrangement on initial recognition and the definitions of a *financial liability* and an *equity instrument*? [6.04]   _____ _____ _____

2. Has the entity offset and reported as a net amount in the statement of financial position a financial asset and a financial liability, only when an entity

    a. currently has a legally enforceable right to set off the recognized amounts?   _____ _____ _____

    b. intends either to settle on a net basis or to realize the asset and settle the liability simultaneously? [6.05]   _____ _____ _____

(continued)

FRF-SME

	Yes	No	N/A

Disclosure

3. Has the entity disclosed the carrying amounts of financial assets either on the face of the statement of financial position or in the notes to the financial statements? [6.11] ____ ____ ____

4. Has the entity segregated accounts and notes receivable to show separately trade accounts, amounts owing by related parties, and other unusual items of significant amount and have the amounts and, when practicable, maturity dates of accounts maturing beyond one year been disclosed separately? [6.12] ____ ____ ____

5. If the entity has transferred financial assets during the period and accounts for the transfer as a sale, has the entity disclosed
   a. the gain or loss from all sales during the period? ____ ____ ____
   b. the accounting policies for
      i. initially measuring any retained interest (including the methodology used in determining its market value)? ____ ____ ____
      ii. subsequently measuring the retained interest? ____ ____ ____
   c. a description of the transferor's continuing involvement with the transferred assets, including, but not limited to, servicing, recourse, and restrictions on retained interests? [6.13] ____ ____ ____

6. If the entity has transferred financial assets in a way that does not qualify for derecognition, has it disclosed
   a. the nature and carrying amount of the assets? ____ ____ ____
   b. the nature of the risks and rewards of ownership to which the entity remains exposed? ____ ____ ____
   c. the carrying amount of the liabilities assumed in the transfer? [6.14] ____ ____ ____

7. For derivatives, has the entity disclosed
   a. the face or contract amount (or notional principal amount if there is no face or contract amount)? ____ ____ ____
   b. the nature and terms, including a discussion of the credit and market risk of those derivatives, and the cash requirements of those derivatives? ____ ____ ____

FRF-SME

			Yes	No	N/A

  c. a description of the entity's objectives for holding the derivatives?

  d. the net settlement amount of the derivative at the statement of financial position date? [6.21]

 8. Has the entity disclosed the following items of income, expense, gains, or losses either on the face of the statements or in the notes to the financial statements:

  a. Net gains or net losses recognized on financial assets and liabilities?

  b. Total interest income?

  c. Total interest expense, separately identifying amortization of premiums, discounts, transaction costs, and financing fees? [6.22]

E. Property, Plant, and Equipment
[chapter 14]

Disclosure

1. For each major category of property, plant, and equipment, has the entity disclosed

 a. cost?

 b. the depreciation method used, including the depreciation period or rate? [14.21]

2. Has the entity disclosed the carrying amount of an item of property, plant, and equipment not being depreciated because it is under construction or development or has been removed from service for an extended period of time? [14.22]

3. Has the entity disclosed the amount of depreciation of property, plant, and equipment charged to income for the period? [14.23]

4. Has the entity disclosed the total accumulated depreciation? [14.23]

5. Has the entity disclosed the following information in the period in which the carrying value of a long-lived asset is reduced (other than for depreciation) due to the cessation of the asset's use or write down in the carrying value of the asset:

 a. A description of the long-lived asset?

 b. A description of the facts and circumstances leading to the reduction in carrying value?

(continued)

FRF-SME

			Yes	No	N/A

      c. If not separately presented on the face of the statement of operations, the amount of the reduction in carrying value and the caption in the statement of operations that includes that amount? [14.25] ___ ___ ___

  6. When the entity's accounting policy is to capitalize interest costs, has disclosure been made of interest costs capitalized? [14.26] ___ ___ ___

F. Intangible Assets [chapter 13]

Presentation

1. Has the entity presented the aggregate amount of goodwill as a separate line item in the entity's statement of financial position? [13.62] ___ ___ ___

2. Has the entity aggregated and presented intangible assets as a separate line item in the entity's statement of financial position? [13.63] ___ ___ ___

Disclosure

3. Has the entity disclosed the following information:

   a. The carrying amount in total and by major intangible asset class? ___ ___ ___

   b. The aggregate amortization expense for the period? ___ ___ ___

   c. The amortization method used, including the amortization period or rate, by major intangible asset class? ___ ___ ___

   d. The accounting policy for internally generated intangible assets, including the treatment of development costs, whether expensed or capitalized? [13.64] ___ ___ ___

4. If the entity has incurred expenditure on start-up costs, has the entity disclosed the policy for accounting for those costs? [13.66] ___ ___ ___

G. Commitments [chapter 16]

Disclosure

1. Has the entity disclosed commitments that are material in relation to the current financial position or future operations? [16.02] ___ ___ ___

H. Contingencies [chapter 17]

Disclosure

1. Has the entity disclosed the existence of a contingent loss at the date of the financial statements when

FRF-SME

Implementation Resources

		Yes	No	N/A

    a. the occurrence of the confirming future event is probable, but the amount of the loss cannot be reasonably estimated?

    b. the occurrence of the confirming future event is probable, and an accrual has been made, but there exists an exposure to loss in excess of the amount accrued?

    c. the occurrence of the confirming future event is reasonably possible? [17.13]

At a minimum, has the entity disclosed

    a. the nature of the contingency?

    b. an estimate of the amount of the contingent loss or a statement that such an estimate cannot be made?

    c. any exposure to loss in excess of the amount accrued? [17.14]

2. When it is probable that a future event will confirm that an asset had been acquired or a liability reduced at the date of the financial statements, has the existence of a contingent gain been disclosed? At a minimum does the disclosure include

    a. the nature of the contingency?

    b. an estimate of the amount of the contingent gain or a statement that such an estimate cannot be made? [17.16–.17]

3. Has the entity disclosed the following information about its asset retirement obligations:

    a. A general description of the asset retirement obligations and the associated long-lived assets?

    b. The amount of the asset retirement obligation at the end of the year?

    c. The total amount paid towards the liability during the year?

    d. The carrying amount of assets legally restricted for purposes of settling asset retirement obligations? [17.37]

4. When a reasonable estimate of the amount of an asset retirement obligation cannot be made, has the entity disclosed that fact, and the reasons therefor? [17.37]

(continued)

FRF-SME

	Yes	No	N/A

5. Has the entity, as a guarantor, disclosed the following information about each guarantee, or each group of similar guarantees, even when the likelihood of the guarantor having to make any payments under the guarantee is remote:

   a. The nature of the guarantee, including the approximate term of the guarantee, how the guarantee arose, and the events or circumstances that require the guarantor to perform under the guarantee? _____ _____ _____

   b. The maximum potential amount of future payments (undiscounted) the guarantor could be required to make under the guarantee before any amounts that may possibly be recovered under recourse or collateralization provisions in the guarantee (see [d] and [e] that follow)? (When the terms of the guarantee provide for no limitation to the maximum potential future payments under the guarantee, that fact should be disclosed. When the guarantor is unable to develop an estimate of the maximum potential amount of future payments under its guarantee, the guarantor should disclose that it cannot make such an estimate.) _____ _____ _____

   c. The current carrying amount of the liability, if any, for the guarantor's obligations under the guarantee, regardless of whether the guarantee is freestanding or embedded in another contract? _____ _____ _____

   d. The nature of any recourse provisions that enable the guarantor to recover from third parties any of the amounts paid under the guarantee? _____ _____ _____

   e. The nature of any assets held as collateral or by third parties that, upon the occurrence of any triggering event or condition under the guarantee, the guarantor can obtain and liquidate to recover all, or a portion of, the amounts paid under the guarantee? [17.39] _____ _____ _____

Implementation Resources

	Yes	No	N/A

I. **Long-Term Debt** [chapter 6]
   Disclosure
   1. For bonds, debentures, and similar securities, mortgages, and other long-term debt, has the entity disclosed
      a. the title or description of the liability?
      b. the interest rate?
      c. the maturity date?
      d. significant terms (for example, covenant details)?
      e. the amount outstanding, separated between principal and accrued interest?
      f. the currency in which the debt is payable if it is not repayable in the currency in which the entity measures items in its financial statements?
      g. the repayment terms, including the existence of sinking fund, redemption, and conversion provisions? [6.15]
   2. Has the entity disclosed the carrying amount of any financial liabilities that are secured? [6.16]
   3. Has the entity disclosed
      a. the carrying amount of assets it has pledged as collateral for liabilities?
      b. the terms and conditions relating to its pledge? [6.16]
   4. Has the entity disclosed the aggregate amount of payments estimated to be required in each of the next five years to meet repayment, sinking fund, or retirement provisions of financial liabilities? [6.17]
   5. For financial liabilities recognized at the statement of financial position date, has the entity disclosed
      a. whether any financial liabilities were in default or in breach of any term or covenant during the period that would permit a lender to demand accelerated repayment?
      b. whether the default was remedied, or the terms of the liability were renegotiated, before the financial statements were available to be issued? [6.18]

(continued)

FRF-SME

		Yes	No	N/A

6. Has the entity disclosed the following items:
   a. Interest capitalized? _____ _____ _____
   b. Unused letters of credit? _____ _____ _____
   c. Long-term debt agreements subject to subjective acceleration clauses, unless the likelihood of the acceleration of the due date is remote? [6.19] _____ _____ _____
7. For an entity that issues any of the following financial liabilities or equity instruments, has the entity disclosed information to enable users of the financial statements to understand the effects of features of the instrument, as follows:
   a. For a financial liability that contains both a liability and an equity element, the following information about the equity element including, when relevant:
      i. The exercise date or dates of the conversion option? _____ _____ _____
      ii. The maturity or expiry date of the option? _____ _____ _____
      iii. The conversion ratio or the strike price? _____ _____ _____
      iv. Conditions precedent to exercising the option? _____ _____ _____
      v. Any other terms that could affect the exercise of the option, such as the existence of covenants that, if contravened, would alter the timing or price of the option? _____ _____ _____
   b. For an instrument that is indexed to the entity's equity or an identified factor, information that enables users of the financial statements to understand the nature, terms, and effects of the indexing feature, the conditions under which a payment will be made, and the expected timing of any payment? [6.20] _____ _____ _____

J. **Equity** [chapter 18]
   Presentation and Disclosure
   1. Has the entity presented separately changes in equity for the period arising from each of the following:

Implementation Resources

		Yes	No	N/A
a.	Net income, showing separately the total amounts attributable to owners of the parent and to noncontrolling interests?	___	___	___
b.	Other changes in retained earnings?	___	___	___
c.	Changes in additional paid-in capital?	___	___	___
d.	Changes in capital stock?	___	___	___
e.	Other changes in equity? [18.17]	___	___	___

2. As applicable, has the entity presented separately the following components of equity either in the body of the financial statements or in the accompanying notes:
   a. Retained earnings? ___ ___ ___
   b. Additional paid-in capital? ___ ___ ___
   c. Capital stock? ___ ___ ___
   d. Noncontrolling interests? ___ ___ ___
   e. Other components of equity? [18.18] ___ ___ ___

3. If the entity is an unincorporated business or partnership, has the entity included a statement setting out the details of the changes in the owners' equity during the period, and does this statement set out separately contributions of capital, income or losses, and withdrawals? [18.19] ___ ___ ___

4. If the entity received a note, rather than cash, for the purchase of its equity, has the note been offset against stock in the equity section? (Such notes may be recorded as an asset if collected in cash before the financial statements are available to be issued.) [18.22] ___ ___ ___

5. Are capital transactions excluded from the determination of net income and shown separately in the statement to which they relate (at least for the year in which the transactions occur)? [18.23] ___ ___ ___

6. Are stock issuance costs recorded as a deduction to equity? [18.23] ___ ___ ___

7. If the entity is an unincorporated business, do the financial statements indicate clearly the name under which the business is conducted? [18.24] ___ ___ ___

(continued)

		Yes	No	N/A

8. If the entity is an unincorporated business, have any salaries, interest, or similar items accruing to owners been clearly indicated by showing such items separately, either in the body of the statement of operations or in a note to the financial statements? (If no such charges are made in the accounts of an unincorporated business, this fact should be disclosed in the financial statements.) [18.25] _____ _____ _____

9. If the entity is a limited liability entity, has the entity presented information related to changes in owners' (members') equity for the period? [18.34] _____ _____ _____

10. Has the equity section in the statement of financial position of a limited liability entity been titled owners' (or members') equity? [18.35] _____ _____ _____

11. If more than one class of members exists in a limited liability entity, each having varying rights, preferences, and privileges, has the entity reported the equity of each class separately within the equity section (encouraged)? [18.35] _____ _____ _____

12. If a limited liability entity records amounts due from owners for capital contributions, have such amounts been presented as deductions from owners' equity? [18.36] _____ _____ _____

Disclosure

13. When there is a condition restricting or affecting the distribution of retained earnings, has the entity disclosed the nature and extent thereof? [18.26] _____ _____ _____

14. If the entity has one or more stock-based compensation plans, has the entity provided a description of the plan(s), including the general terms of awards under the plan(s), such as vesting requirements, and the maximum term of options granted? (An entity that uses equity instruments to acquire goods or services other than employee services should provide disclosures similar to those in accordance with this requirement to the extent that those disclosures are important in understanding the effects of those transactions on the financial statements.) [18.27] _____ _____ _____

FRF-SME

Implementation Resources

		Yes	No	N/A

15. If the entity grants options under multiple stock-based employee compensation plans, has the entity provided information separately for different types of awards to the extent that the differences in the characteristics of the awards make separate disclosure important to an understanding of the entity's use of stock-based compensation? [18.28] _____ _____ _____
16. Has the entity disclosed information about authorized and issued capital stock, including
    a. the number of shares issued and outstanding for each class, giving a brief description and the par value, if any? _____ _____ _____
    b. dividend rates on preference shares and whether or not they are cumulative? _____ _____ _____
    c. the redemption price of redeemable shares? _____ _____ _____
    d. the existence and details of conversion provisions? _____ _____ _____
    e. the number of shares and the amount received or receivable that is attributable to capital for each class (when any shares have not been fully paid, disclosure should be made of the amounts that have not been called and the unpaid amounts that have been called or are otherwise due, as well as the number of shares in each of these categories)? _____ _____ _____
    f. arrears of dividends for cumulative preference shares? [18.29] _____ _____ _____
17. Has the entity disclosed the number of shares of capital stock authorized? [18.30] _____ _____ _____
18. Has the entity disclosed information about commitments to issue or resell shares? [18.31] _____ _____ _____
19. Has the entity disclosed details of transactions during the period, including
    a. the number of shares of each class issued since the date of the last statement of financial position, indicating the value attributed thereto and distinguishing shares issued for cash (showing separately shares issued pursuant to options or warrants), shares issued directly or indirectly for services, and shares issued directly or indirectly for other considerations? _____ _____ _____

(continued)

FRF-SME

	Yes	No	N/A

    b. the number of shares of each class redeemed or acquired since the date of the last statement of financial position and the consideration given and, when the consideration was other than cash, the nature of the consideration given and the value attributed thereto?

    c. the number of shares of each class resold since the date of the last statement of financial position, indicating the value attributed thereto and distinguishing shares resold for cash (showing separately shares resold pursuant to options or warrants), shares resold directly or indirectly for services, and shares resold directly or indirectly for other considerations? [18.32]

20. If the entity is unincorporated, has that fact been disclosed along with the fact that the statements do not include all the assets, liabilities, revenues, and expenses of the owners? [18.33]

21. If a limited liability entity does not report the amount of equity of each class of owners (members) separately within the equity section, has the entity disclosed those amounts in the notes to financial statements? [18.38]

22. If a limited liability entity maintains separate accounts for components of owners' equity (for example, undistributed earnings, earnings available for withdrawal, or unallocated capital), has the entity disclosed those components, either on the face of the statement of financial position or in the notes to financial statements? [18.39]

23. Has the entity disclosed significant differences in the rights, preferences, and privileges of different classes of members in a limited liability entity? [18.40]

III. Statement of Operations

A. **Revenue** [chapter 19]
   Disclosure
   1. Has the entity disclosed its revenue recognition policy? [19.26]

Implementation Resources

	Yes	No	N/A

2. If an entity has different policies for different types of revenue transactions, has the policy for each material type of transaction been disclosed? [19.26] ____ ____ ____

3. If sales transactions have multiple elements, such as a product and service, has the entity clearly stated the accounting policy for each element, as well as how multiple elements are determined and measured? (The policy may contain items such as a description and nature of such an arrangement, including performance, cancellation, termination, or refund-type provisions.) [19.27] ____ ____ ____

4. If the completed contact method is used, has the entity disclosed the reasons why that method, and not the percentage-of-completion method, is not used? [19.28] ____ ____ ____

5. Has the entity disclosed additional revenue from a contract-related claim? [19.29] ____ ____ ____

6. If the entity has claims related to additional contract revenue and the requirements of recognizing that revenue are not met or if those requirements are met but the claim exceeds the recorded contract costs, has a contingent asset been disclosed in accordance with chapter 17? [19.29] ____ ____ ____

7. Has the entity disclosed separately, either on the face of the statement of operations or in the notes to the financial statements, the major categories of revenue recognized during the period? [19.31] ____ ____ ____

8. If the practice of recording revenues from claims only when the amounts have been received or awarded is followed, are the amounts disclosed in the notes to the financial statements? [19.30] ____ ____ ____

B. **Retirement and Other Postemployment Benefits** [chapter 20]

   Disclosure

   1. Has the entity disclosed the following information about defined contribution plans:

      a. A general description of each plan? ____ ____ ____

      b. The amount of cost recognized in the period? [20.09] ____ ____ ____

   2. Has the entity disclosed the following information about significant multiemployer plans:

(continued)

FRF-SME

		Yes	No	N/A

    a. The name of the plan and a description of the type of plan?

    b. If withdrawal from the plan is probable or reasonably possible, whether withdrawal from the plan would give rise to an obligation?

    c. The amount of cost recognized in the period? [20.11]

3. Has the entity disclosed the following information in aggregate about individual deferred compensation contracts:

    a. A general description of the contracts, including expected timing of benefit payments and the discount rate used to determine present value?

    b. The liability at the statement of financial position date and the amount charged to expense in the current period? [20.14]

4. Has the entity disclosed the following information about defined benefit plans:

    a. A description of the plan, including plan participants and the nature of determining benefits?

    b. Information about the funded status of the plan, including benefit obligation, market value of plan assets, and the plan deficit or excess at the end of the reporting period?

    c. The current year's contribution and expected contribution for the subsequent year (under the current contribution payable method only)?

    d. The plan's expected rate of return on plan assets and the discount rate used to determine the accrued benefit obligation? [20.17 and .48]

5. Has the entity disclosed the nature and effect of any termination benefits provided in the period? [20.51]

C. Income Taxes [chapter 21]

Presentation

1. Has the entity presented income tax expense included in the determination of net income or loss before discontinued operations on the face of the statement of operations? [21.54]

Implementation Resources 303

	Yes	No	N/A

2. Has the entity presented income tax liabilities and income tax assets separately from other liabilities and assets? [21.55]

3. Has the entity presented current income tax liabilities and current income tax assets separately from deferred income tax liabilities and deferred income tax assets? [21.55]

4. If the entity segregates assets and liabilities between current and noncurrent assets and liabilities, has the entity also segregated the current and noncurrent portions of deferred income tax liabilities and deferred income tax assets? [21.56]

5. Has the entity offset current income tax liabilities and current income tax assets if they relate to the same taxable entity and the same taxation authority? [21.57]

6. Has the entity offset deferred income tax liabilities and deferred income tax assets if they relate to the same taxable entity and the same taxation authority? [21.57]

Disclosure

7. Has the entity disclosed the accounting policy choice made to account for income taxes, either the taxes payable method or the deferred income taxes method? [21.61]

8. When an entity applies the taxes payable method of accounting for income taxes, has the entity disclosed the following:
   a. Income tax expense (benefit) included in the determination of income or loss before discontinued operations?
   b. A discussion of the differences of income tax rate or expense related to income or loss for the period before discontinued operations to the statutory income tax rate or the dollar amount that would result from its application, including the nature of each significant reconciling item (the entity may include or omit a numerical reconciliation)?
   c. The amount of unused income tax losses carried forward and unused income tax credits?

(continued)

FRF-SME

Financial Reporting Framework for Small- and Medium-Sized Entities

	Yes	No	N/A

    d. The portion of income tax expense (benefit) related to transactions charged (or credited) to equity? [21.62]

9. When an entity applies the deferred income taxes method of accounting for income taxes, has the entity separately disclosed the following:
   - *a.* Current income tax expense (benefit) included in the determination of income or loss before discontinued operations?
   - *b.* Deferred income tax expense (benefit) included in the determination of income or loss before discontinued operations?
   - *c.* The portion of the cost (benefit) of current and deferred income taxes related to capital transactions or other items that are charged or credited to equity?
   - *d.* The total amount of unused tax losses and income tax reductions and the amount of deductible temporary differences for which no deferred income tax asset has been recognized?
   - *e.* A discussion of the differences of income tax rate or expense related to income or loss for the period before discontinued operations to the statutory income tax rate or the dollar amount that would result from its application, including the nature of each significant reconciling item (The entity may include or omit a numerical reconciliation)?
   - *f.* The amount of unused income tax losses carried forward and unused income tax credits? [21.63]

10. If the entity is not subject to income taxes because its income is taxed directly to its owners has the entity disclosed that fact? [21.60]

IV. Broad Transactions

A. Business Combinations [chapter 28]
Disclosure

1. Has the acquirer disclosed the following information for each material business combination:
   - *a.* The name and a description of the acquiree?

			Yes	No	N/A
b.	The acquisition date?		___	___	___
c.	The percentage of voting equity interests acquired?		___	___	___
d.	The acquisition-date market value of the total consideration transferred and the acquisition-date market value of each major class of consideration, such as				
	i.	cash?	___	___	___
	ii.	liabilities incurred (for example, a liability for contingent consideration)?	___	___	___
	iii.	equity interests of the acquirer, including the number of instruments or interests issued or issuable?	___	___	___
e.	A description of the arrangement and the basis for determining the amount of the payment for contingent consideration arrangements and indemnification assets?		___	___	___
f.	A condensed statement of financial position showing the amounts recognized as of the acquisition date for each major class of assets acquired and liabilities assumed?		___	___	___
g.	The amount of any gain recognized in a bargain purchase and the line item in the statement of operations in which the gain is recognized?		___	___	___
h.	The amount of the noncontrolling interest in the acquiree recognized at the acquisition date and the measurement basis for that amount?		___	___	___
i.	The accounting policy related to intangible assets acquired and those intangible assets recognized separately, including their amounts and useful lives?		___	___	___
j.	In a business combination achieved in stages				
	i.	the acquisition-date market value of the equity interest in the acquiree held by the acquirer immediately before the acquisition date?	___	___	___

(continued)

			Yes	No	N/A

    ii. the amount of any gain or loss recognized as a result of remeasuring to market value the equity interest in the acquiree held by the acquirer before the business combination and the line item in the statement of operations in which that gain or loss is recognized? [28.60] _____ _____ _____

2. For individually immaterial business combinations occurring during the reporting period that are material collectively, has the acquirer disclosed the following information:

    a. The number of entities acquired and a brief description of those entities? _____ _____ _____

    b. The acquisition-date market value of the total consideration transferred? _____ _____ _____

    c. The number of equity instruments or interests of the acquirer issued or issuable? _____ _____ _____

    d. A description of the arrangement and the basis for determining the amount of the payment for contingent consideration arrangements and indemnification assets? [28.61] _____ _____ _____

3. If the acquisition date of a business combination is after the end of the reporting period but before the financial statements are available to be issued, has the acquirer disclosed the information in items 1 and 2, unless the initial accounting for the business combination is incomplete at the time the financial statements are available to be issued? (In that situation, the acquirer should describe which disclosures could not be made and the reasons why they cannot be made.) [28.62] _____ _____ _____

4. For combination of entities under common control, has the receiving entity disclosed the following for the period in which the transfer of assets and liabilities or exchange of equity interests occurred:

    a. The name and brief description of the entity included in the reporting entity as a result of the net asset transfer or exchange of equity interests? _____ _____ _____

FRF-SME

Implementation Resources

		Yes	No	N/A

    b. The method of accounting for the transfer of net assets or exchange of equity interests? [28.63]

B. Subsidiaries [chapter 22]

Presentation

1. When an entity consolidates its subsidiaries and prepares consolidated financial statements, has the entity described these financial statements as being prepared on a consolidated basis, and each statement labeled accordingly? [22.05]

2. The FRF for SMEs accounting framework states that a material difference in the basis of accounting between a parent and a subsidiary precludes the preparation of consolidated financial statements and the use of the equity method. If the financial statements of a subsidiary (*a*) are not prepared in accordance with the frameworks (for example, those prepared on a cash or tax basis or using unacceptable accounting principles) or (*b*) otherwise contain errors, have they been revised, or have correcting entries been made to remove any material difference in the basis of accounting? [22.03]

3. When an entity accounts for its subsidiaries using the equity method, has the entity described its financial statements as being prepared on a nonconsolidated basis, and each statement labeled accordingly? [22.10]

4. Have investments in nonconsolidated subsidiaries been presented separately from other investments in the statement of financial position? [22.11]

5. Has income or loss from investments in nonconsolidated subsidiaries been presented as either a gross or net amount in the statement of operations? [22.11]

Disclosure

6. When an entity consolidates its subsidiaries, has the entity provided a listing and description of all subsidiaries, including their names, income from each subsidiary, and the proportion of ownership interests held in each subsidiary? [22.12]

(continued)

FRF-SME

| | Yes | No | N/A |

7. When an entity prepares nonconsolidated financial statements, has the entity disclosed the basis used to account for its subsidiaries? [22.13] _____ _____ _____

8. When an entity prepares nonconsolidated financial statements, has the entity provided a listing and description of all subsidiaries, including their names, carrying amounts, income from each subsidiary, and the proportion of ownership interests held in each subsidiary? [22.14] _____ _____ _____

C. **Consolidated Financial Statements and Noncontrolling Interests** [chapter 23]

Presentation

1. Has the entity included only postacquisition and predisposal income of a subsidiary company in consolidated net income? [22.32] _____ _____ _____

2. If the entity consolidates its subsidiaries, has the entity presented noncontrolling interests in the consolidated statement of financial position within equity, separately from the equity of the owners of the parent? [22.33] _____ _____ _____

3. Has net income been attributed to the owners of the parent and to the noncontrolling interests? [22.34] _____ _____ _____

Disclosure

4. Has the entity disclosed its consolidation policy? [22.35] _____ _____ _____

5. If it is not possible to use financial statements for a period that substantially coincides with that of the investor's financial statements, has the entity disclosed this fact, along with the period covered by the financial statements used? [22.36] _____ _____ _____

6. If the fiscal periods of the parent and a subsidiary, the investment in which is accounted for by the consolidation method, are not the same, has the entity recorded or disclosed events relating to, or transactions of, the subsidiary that have occurred during the intervening period that significantly affect the financial position or results of operations of the group, as appropriate? [22.37] _____ _____ _____

D. **Interests in Joint Ventures** [chapter 24]

Presentation

1. Has the entity presented the following separately in the statement of financial position:

Implementation Resources

	Yes	No	N/A
a. Interests in joint ventures accounted for using the equity method?	___	___	___
b. Assets and liabilities in joint ventures accounted for using the proportionate consolidation method as its share of each asset or liability, such as share of accounts receivable from joint venture activities? [24.19]	___	___	___

2. Has the entity presented income from participation in a joint venture in the following separately in the income statement:
   a. Interests in joint ventures accounted for using the equity method? ___ ___ ___
   b. Interests in joint ventures accounted for using the proportionate consolidation method as a total of its share of the joint venture's revenue, gross profit, and other expenses categories? [24.20] ___ ___ ___

3. Has the entity grouped investments reported in the statement of financial position and investment income reported in the income statement in the same way? [24.21] ___ ___ ___

Disclosure

4. Has the entity disclosed the basis used to account for the entity's interests in joint ventures? [24.22] ___ ___ ___

5. Has the entity provided a listing and description of interests in significant joint ventures, including the names, business purposes, carrying amounts, and proportion of ownership interests held in each joint venture? [24.23] ___ ___ ___

6. Has the entity disclosed its share of any contingencies and commitments of joint ventures and those contingencies that exist when the venturer is contingently liable for the liabilities of the other venturers of the joint ventures? [24.24] ___ ___ ___

7. If investments in common stock of corporate joint ventures are, in the aggregate, material in relation to the statement of financial position or statement of operations of an investor, has the entity presented summarized information about assets, liabilities, and results of operations of the investees to in the notes or in separate statements, either individually or in groups, as appropriate? [24.25] ___ ___ ___

(continued)

310 Financial Reporting Framework for Small- and Medium-Sized Entities

| | | Yes | No | N/A |

8. If the entity guarantees more than its proportionate share of a joint venture's liabilities, has such a guarantee been disclosed? [24.26]
9. If the fiscal periods of the entity and a joint venture are not the same and the proportional consolidation or equity method is used, has the entity disclosed events relating to, or transactions of, the joint venture that have occurred during the intervening period and significantly affect the financial position or results of operations of the entity? (This disclosure is not necessary if these events or transactions are recorded in the financial statements.) [24.27]

E. New Basis (Push-Down) Accounting [chapter 29]
Disclosure
1. In the period that push-down accounting has been first applied, has the entity disclosed the following:
   a. The date push-down accounting was applied and the date or dates of the purchase transaction or transactions that led to the application of push-down accounting?
   b. A description of the situation resulting in the application of push-down accounting?
   c. The amount of the change in each major class of assets, liabilities, and shareholders' equity arising from the application of push-down accounting? [29.17]
2. In the fiscal period that push-down accounting has been applied and the following fiscal period, has the entity disclosed the following:
   a. The date push-down accounting was applied?
   b. The amount of the revaluation adjustment and the shareholders' equity account in which the revaluation adjustment was recorded?
   c. The amount of retained earnings reclassified and the shareholders' equity account to which it was reclassified? [29.18]

		Yes	No	N/A

F. Foreign Currency Translation [chapter 31]
  Disclosure
  1. Has the entity disclosed the amount of an exchange gain or loss included in net income? (An entity may exclude from this amount those exchange gains or losses arising on investments in securities that are measured at market value.) [31.13]

G. Nonmonetary Transactions [chapter 30]
  Disclosure
  1. Has the entity disclosed the following information in the period in which a nonmonetary transaction occurs to enable users of the financial statements to understand the effects of a nonmonetary transaction on the financial statements:
     a. The nature of the transaction?
     b. Its basis of measurement (market value or carrying amount) and the method for determining that amount?
     c. The amount?
     d. Related gains and losses? [30.13]

H. Leases [chapter 25]
  Presentation—Lessee
  1. In order to distinguish between assets that the entity owns and those that it only has the right to use, has the entity presented assets leased under capital leases separately? [25.19]
  2. Has the entity presented obligations related to leased assets separately from other long-term obligations? [25.20]
  3. Has the entity included any portion of lease obligations payable within a year out of current funds in current liabilities? [25.21]
  Presentation—Lessor
  4. Has the entity presented the net investment in the lease separately from other assets? [25.46]
  5. Has the entity presented deferred income taxes, if any, relating to the net investment in the lease separately from the net investment? [25.48]
  6. Has the entity segregated the net investment in direct financing and sales-type leases between current and long-term portions in a classified statement of financial position? [25.49]

(continued)

FRF-SME

| | Yes | No | N/A |

Disclosure
Capital Lease—Lessee
7. For each major category of leased property, plant, and equipment, has the entity disclosed
   a. cost?
   b. accumulated amortization, including the amount of any write-downs?
   c. the amortization method used, including the amortization period or rate? [25.69]
8. For an obligation under a capital lease, has the entity disclosed
   a. the interest rate?
   b. the maturity date?
   c. the amount outstanding?
   d. if the leases are secured, the fact that they are secured? [25.70]
9. Has the entity disclosed interest expense related to lease obligations separately or as part of interest on long-term indebtedness? [25.71]
10. Has the entity disclosed the aggregate amount of payments estimated to be required in each of the next five years to meet repayment, sinking fund, or retirement provisions? [25.72]

Operating Lease—Lessee
11. Has the entity disclosed the future minimum lease payments in the aggregate and for each of the five succeeding years under operating leases? [25.73]
12. Has the entity disclosed rent expense for each period presented in the financial statements? [25.73]
13. Has the entity described the nature of other commitments under such leases? [25.73]

Direct Financing or Sales-Type Lease—Lessor
14. Has the entity disclosed the lessor's net investment in direct financing and sales-type leases along with the interest rates implicit in the leases? [25.74]

Operating Lease—Lessor
15. Has the entity disclosed the cost of property, plant, and equipment held for leasing purposes and the amount of accumulated amortization? [25.75]

FRF-SME

Implementation Resources

	Yes	No	N/A

I. Subsequent Events [chapter 27]
  Disclosure
  1. Has the entity disclosed the date through which subsequent events have been evaluated and the fact that this is the date that the financial statements were available to be issued? [27.10] ____ ____ ____
  2. Has the entity disclosed those events occurring between the date of the financial statements and the date the financial statements are available to be issued that do not relate to conditions that existed at the date of the financial statements but are of such a nature that they should be disclosed to keep the financial statements from being misleading? At a minimum, the disclosure should include a description of the nature of the event and an estimate of the financial effect, when practicable, or a statement that such an estimate cannot be made. [27.11–.12] ____ ____ ____

J. Disposal of Long-Lived Assets and Discontinued Operations [chapter 15]
  Presentation
  1. Has the entity presented long-lived assets classified as held for sale separately in the entity's statement of financial position? [15.14] ____ ____ ____
  2. Has the entity presented the assets and liabilities of a disposal group classified as held for sale separately in the asset and liability sections, respectively, of the statement of financial position? [15.14] ____ ____ ____
  3. Has the entity presented current and long-term assets (and liabilities) separately unless the entity's statement of financial position is unclassified? (Assets and liabilities of a disposal group classified as held for sale are not offset, other than financial assets and liabilities that meet the conditions for offsetting.) [15.15] ____ ____ ____
  4. Has the entity reclassified as current assets long-lived assets classified as held for sale if the entity has sold the assets prior to the date the financial statements are available to be issued, and the proceeds of the sale will be realized within a year of the date of the statement of financial position or within the normal operating cycle if that is longer than a year? [15.16] ____ ____ ____

(continued)

FRF-SME

	Yes	No	N/A

5. If the assets have been classified as current assets due to the subsequent sale, has the entity classified any liabilities to be assumed by the purchaser or required to be discharged on disposal of the assets as current liabilities? [15.16]   ____ ____ ____

6. Has the entity reported the results of discontinued operations, less applicable income taxes, as a separate element of income for both current and prior periods? [15.22]   ____ ____ ____

Disclosure

7. Has the entity disclosed the following information in the period in which a long-lived asset (or disposal group) either has been disposed of by sale or other than by sale, or is classified as held-for-sale:

   a. A description of the facts and circumstances leading to the disposal or expected disposal?   ____ ____ ____

   b. If not separately presented on the face of the statement of operations, the amount of the gain or loss on disposal and the caption in the statement of operations that includes that gain or loss?   ____ ____ ____

   c. If applicable, amounts of revenue and pretax profit or loss reported in discontinued operations? [15.24]   ____ ____ ____

8. In a period in which a decision is made not to sell an asset previously classified as held for sale, has the entity disclosed the change in accounting treatment? [15.25]   ____ ____ ____

K. Related Party Transactions [chapter 26]

Disclosure

1. Has the entity disclosed the following information about its transactions with related parties:

   a. A description of the relationship between the transacting parties?   ____ ____ ____

   b. A description of the transaction(s), including those for which no amount has been recognized?   ____ ____ ____

   c. The recognized amount of the transactions classified by financial statement category?   ____ ____ ____

   d. The measurement basis used?   ____ ____ ____

   e. Amounts due to, or from, related parties and the terms and conditions relating thereto?   ____ ____ ____

FRF-SME

		Yes	No	N/A
f.	Commitments with related parties, separate from other commitments?	____	____	____
g.	Contingencies involving related parties, separate from other contingencies? [26.08]	____	____	____

Illustrations of the Application of Certain Principles and Criteria of the FRF for SMEs Accounting Framework

Introduction

The FRF for SMEs accounting framework is a simplified and intuitive non-GAAP accounting framework. Management and accounting professionals should use its judgment and apply the general principles, concepts, and criteria contained in the framework when developing accounting policies and accounting for transactions and events. As such, extensive examples and illustrations have not been included in the FRF for SMEs accounting framework. However, AICPA staff believes that the illustrations on the following pages may provide helpful guidance to those implementing the framework. These illustrations of the application of certain principles and criteria in the framework are not part of the framework. Management and others should follow the requirements of the FRF for SMEs accounting framework and use their judgment in applying those requirements to particular transactions and events.

Illustrative Example of Transition—Initial Application of the FRF for SMEs Accounting Framework
(This material is illustrative only.)

This example illustrates how the accounting treatment specified in chapter 3, "Transition," of *Financial Reporting Framework for Small- and Medium-Sized Entities*, might be applied in a particular situation. Matters of principle relating to particular situations should be decided in the context of the framework.

Background

ABC Company has a calendar year end. ABC Company's first reporting period using the FRF for SMEs accounting framework is December 31, 2013, and it intends to issue comparative financial statements. Therefore, its date of transition to the framework is the beginning of business on January 1, 2012 (or, equivalently, close of business on December 31, 2011). ABC Company presented financial statements under U.S. GAAP annually to December 31st each year up to, and including, December 31, 2012.

Application of Requirements

ABC Company would apply the FRF for SMEs accounting framework effective for periods ending on December 31, 2013 in

 a. preparing its opening statement of financial position at January 1, 2012; and

 b. preparing and presenting its statement of financial position for December 31, 2013 (including comparative amounts for 2012), statement of operations, statement of retained earnings, and statement of cash flows for the year ending December 31, 2013 (including comparative amounts for 2012), and disclosures (including comparative information for 2012). The disclosures would include the amount of each charge or credit to equity at the date of transition to the FRF for SMEs accounting framework resulting from the adoption of the principles in the framework and the reasons therefor.

Illustrative Example of a Summary of Significant Accounting Policies
(This material is illustrative only.)

This example illustrates how an entity might present its summary of significant accounting policies in the notes to the financial statements.

SUMMARY OF SIGNIFICANT ACCOUNTING POLICIES

Basis of Accounting

The accompanying financial statements have been prepared in accordance with the *Financial Reporting Framework for Small- and Medium-Sized Entities* issued by the American Institute of Certified Public Accountants, which is a special purpose framework and not U.S. generally accepted accounting principles (U.S. GAAP). The accounting principles that compose the framework are appropriate for the preparation and presentation of small- and medium-sized entity financial statements, based on the needs of the financial statement users and cost and benefit considerations. This special purpose framework, unlike U.S. GAAP, does not require the recognition of deferred taxes. We have chosen the option to recognize only current income tax assets and liabilities. [*Other primary differences would be described as necessary.*]

Nature of Business

ABC, Inc. (the Company) is primarily involved in the steel service center and reinforcing bar (rebar) fabrication business. Through the Company's steel service centers located in Virginia, West Virginia, and North Carolina, the Company distributes a full line of hot-rolled and cold-rolled carbon steel and structural steel to industrial accounts.

Principles of Consolidation

The accompanying consolidated financial statements include the accounts of ABC, Inc. and its wholly-owned subsidiary, SubCo, Inc. All significant intercompany transactions have been eliminated.

or

Investments in subsidiaries that the Company controls are accounted for under the equity method. Under the equity method, original investments are recorded at cost and adjusted by the Company's share of undistributed earnings or losses of these entities.

Inventory

Inventory consists of new steel, scrap steel, and hardware supplies and is stated at the lower of cost (determined on a weighted-average basis) or net realizable value.

Cash and Cash Equivalents

For purposes of the statements of cash flows, the Company considers all highly liquid debt instruments purchased with original maturities of three months or less to be cash equivalents.

Accounts Receivable

The Company reports trade receivables at net realizable value. Management determines the allowance for doubtful accounts based on historical losses and current economic conditions. On a continuing basis, management analyzes delinquent receivables and, once these receivables are determined to be uncollectible, they are written off through a charge against the allowance.

Investments

Investments in marketable equity and debt securities held for sale are included in other assets and measured at market value. Accordingly, changes in market value are included in net income in the period incurred. Investments in nonmarketable securities are carried at cost and included in other assets.

Intangible Assets

Intangible assets subject to amortization consist of loan costs. These costs are amortized on a straight-line basis.

Property, Plant, and Equipment

Property, plant, and equipment are recorded at cost. Assets are depreciated over their estimated remaining useful lives using the straight-line method. Maintenance, repairs, and minor renewals are charged against income, when incurred. Additions and significant renewals are capitalized. The cost and accumulated depreciation of assets sold or retired are removed from the respective accounts. Any gain or loss from the sale or retirement of property is reflected in income.

Amortization of assets acquired under a capital lease is computed using the straight-line method over the lesser of the lease term or the useful life of the leased asset.

Use of Estimates in the Preparation of Financial Statements

The preparation of financial statements in conformity with *Financial Reporting Framework for Small and Medium-Sized Entities* requires management to make estimates and assumptions that affect the reported amounts of assets and liabilities and the disclosure of contingencies at the date of the financial statements and revenues and expenses during the reporting period. Actual results could differ from those estimates.

Shipping and Handling

Costs incurred for shipping and handling are included in cost of sales in the statements of income.

Income Taxes

The Company elected under the Internal Revenue Code to be taxed as an S corporation. In lieu of corporation income taxes, the stockholders of an S corporation are generally taxed on their proportionate share of the Company's taxable income. However, certain states require the Company to report income taxes at the corporate level. The provision for income taxes includes taxes on income to those states for which the Company has been required to pay the tax at the corporate level. The Company uses the taxes payable method in accounting for income taxes. Under the taxes payable method, only current income tax assets and liabilities are recognized.

or

The Company elected under the Internal Revenue Code to be taxed as an S corporation. In lieu of corporation income taxes, the stockholders of an S corporation are generally taxed on their proportionate share of the Company's taxable income. However, certain states require the Company to report income taxes at the corporate level. The provision for income taxes includes taxes on income to those states for which the Company has been required to pay the tax at the corporate level. Deferred tax assets and liabilities are recognized for the future tax consequences attributable to differences between the financial statement carrying amounts of existing assets and liabilities and their respective tax bases. Deferred tax assets,

FRF-SME

including tax loss and credit carryforwards and liabilities, are measured using enacted tax rates expected to apply to taxable income in the years in which those temporary differences are expected to be recovered or settled. The effect on deferred tax assets and liabilities of a change in tax rates is recognized in income in the period that includes the enactment date. Deferred income tax expense represents the change during the period in the deferred tax assets and deferred tax liabilities. The components of the deferred tax assets and liabilities are individually classified as current and non-current based on their characteristics. Deferred tax assets are reduced by a valuation allowance when, in the opinion of management, it is more likely than not that some portion or all of the deferred tax assets will not be realized.

Subsequent Events

Management has evaluated subsequent events through May 12, 20X4, which is the date the financial statements were available to be issued.

Start-Up Costs

Start-up costs, consisting of establishment costs, expenditures to open a new facility, and expenditures for starting new operations, are expensed in the year incurred. For 20X2, these costs were $2,050,000, and for 20X1, they were $1,100,000.

or

Start-up costs, consisting of establishment costs, expenditures to open a new facility, and expenditures for starting new operations, are capitalized and amortized over 15 years. For 20X2, these costs were $2,050,000, and for 20X1, they were $1,100,000.

Joint Ventures

From time to time, the Company enters into collaborative arrangements for the research and development (R&D), manufacture or commercialization (or both) of products, and product candidates. These collaborations generally provide for nonrefundable, upfront license fees, R&D, and commercial performance milestone payments, cost sharing, royalty payments, or profit sharing. These collaborative arrangements are accounted for under the equity method. Under the equity method, original investments are recorded at cost and adjusted by the Company's share of undistributed earnings or losses of these entities.

or

From time to time, the Company enters into collaborative arrangements for the research and development (R&D), manufacture or commercialization (or both) of products, and product candidates. These collaborations generally provide for nonrefundable, upfront license fees, R&D, and commercial performance milestone payments, cost sharing, royalty payments, or profit sharing. These collaborative arrangements are accounted for using the proportionate consolidation method. The proportionate consolidation method results in the Company recognizing in its statement of financial position, its share of the assets and liabilities of the jointly controlled joint venture, and in its statement of operations, its share of the revenue and expenses of the joint venture.

Defined Benefit Plans

The Company has two defined benefit retirement plans that cover substantially all of its employees. Defined benefit plans for salaried employees provide benefits based on employees' years of service and five-year final overall base compensation. Defined benefit plans for hourly paid employees, including those covered by multiemployer pension plans under collective bargaining agreements, generally provide benefits of stated amounts for specified periods of service. The Company's policy is to fund, at a minimum, amounts as are necessary on an actuarial basis to provide assets sufficient to meet the benefits to be paid to plan members in accordance with the requirements of the Employee Retirement Income Security Act of 1974. Assets of the plans are administered by an independent trustee and are invested principally in fixed income securities, equity securities, and real estate. The Company accounts for all defined benefit plans using the accrued benefit obligation method. Under this method, the accrued benefit obligation is based on an actuarial valuation report prepared for funding purposes.

or

The Company has two defined benefit retirement plans that cover substantially all of its employees. Defined benefit plans for salaried employees provide benefits based on employees' years of service and five-year final overall base compensation. Defined benefit plans for hourly paid employees, including those covered by multiemployer pension plans under collective bargaining agreements, generally provide benefits of stated amounts for specified periods of service. The Company's policy is to fund, at a minimum, amounts as are necessary on an actuarial basis to provide assets sufficient to meet the benefits to be paid to plan members in accordance with the requirements of the Employee Retirement Income Security Act of 1974. Assets of the plans are administered by an independent trustee and are invested principally in fixed income securities, equity securities, and real estate. The Company accounts for all defined benefit plans using the current contribution payable method. Under this method, only the contribution attributable to the current year is expensed.

Intangibles Acquired in a Business Combination

In connection with its acquisition of XYZ Co., the Company has recognized, separately as identifiable assets, those intangible assets where acquisition-date market value could be measured reliably. These intangible assets are amortized on a straight line basis over their useful lives. Other intangible assets acquired have been subsumed into goodwill.

or

In connection with its acquisition of XYZ Co., the Company has subsumed into goodwill all intangible assets acquired in the transaction.

Illustrative Example—Going Concern

(This material is illustrative only.)

This example provides suggestions on applying the going concern requirements of chapter 2, "General Principles of Financial Statement Presentation and Accounting Policies," of *Financial Reporting Framework for Small- and Medium-Sized Entities*. Matters of principle relating to particular situations should be decided in the context of the framework.

Background

The going concern assumption is a fundamental principle in the preparation of financial statements. When preparing financial statements, management should make an assessment of whether the going concern basis of accounting is appropriate. This assessment involves making a judgment, at a particular point in time (the date of the statement of financial position), about the future outcome of events or conditions that are inherently uncertain.

Under the going concern assumption, an entity is ordinarily viewed as continuing in business for the foreseeable future with neither the intention nor the necessity of liquidation, ceasing trading, or seeking protection from creditors pursuant to laws or regulations. Accordingly, unless the going concern assumption is inappropriate in the circumstances of the entity, assets and liabilities are recorded on the basis that the entity will be able to realize its assets, meet its obligations, and obtain refinancing (if necessary) in the normal course of business.

Management Considerations Related to Going Concern

Management may want to consider the following questions when making an assessment of whether the going concern basis of accounting is appropriate. The questions are not intended to be all-inclusive and neither will all questions be appropriate for every entity.

- Borrowing requirements
  - Are the covenants on current borrowings satisfied as of the date of the statement of financial position?
  - Is interest in arrears on any current borrowings as of the date of the statement of financial position?
  - Have monthly cash flow forecasts been compared to credit facilities available to establish whether or not there are any projected deficits? If so, are there plans in place to cover them; for example, to renegotiate facilities with lenders?
  - Have forecasts been tested against existing covenants to assess whether any violations are expected? If so, are there plans in place to prevent the violations from occurring?
- Contingent liabilities
  - Is the entity exposed to any contingent liabilities; for example, those arising through
    - legal proceedings?
    - guarantees or warranties or both?
    - product liability not covered by insurance?
    - environmental clean-up costs?
- Products and services
  - For each of the main products or services, are any economic, political, or other factors that may cause the market, or the strength of the entity's products within the market, to change?
  - If there is a high risk of losing existing customers, has management considered the likelihood of finding alternative sales markets?
  - Has management considered the robustness of the entity's supply chain and whether there are weak links that could adversely affect the entity's ability to deliver its products and services or increase costs, or both, through the need to seek and use alternative supply sources?

- Financial and operational risk
  - Is there any risk to the entity of
    - adverse movements in interest rates?
    - adverse movements in currency exchange rates?
    - exposure to risk through major fixed-price or fixed-rate contracts?
- Financial adaptability
  - Is there an adequate plan to enable the company to take effective action to alter the amounts and timing of its cash flows so that it can respond to unexpected needs or opportunities?
  - Does the company have the ability to
    - dispose of assets or to postpone the replacement of assets without significantly affecting other cash flows?
    - lease assets rather than to purchase outright?
    - obtain new sources of financing?
    - renew or extend loans?
    - restructure debts?
    - raise additional equity capital?
    - continue business by making limited reductions in the level of operations or by making use of alternative resources?

Illustration

Management may become aware of material uncertainties relating to events or conditions and conclude that a known event or condition is probable of having a severe impact on the entity's ability to realize its assets and discharge its liabilities in the ordinary course of business. The significance of such conditions and events will depend on the circumstances, and some may have significance only when viewed in conjunction with other conditions or events. The following are examples of those conditions and events:

- Negative trends. For example, recurring operating losses, working capital deficiencies, negative cash flows from operating activities, and adverse key financial ratios.
- Other indications of possible financial difficulties. For example, default on loan or similar agreements, arrearages in dividends, denial of usual trade credit from suppliers, restructuring of debt, noncompliance with statutory capital requirements, and a need to seek new sources or methods of financing or to dispose of substantial assets.
- Internal matters. For example, work stoppages or other labor difficulties, substantial dependence on the success of a particular project, uneconomic long-term commitments, and a need to significantly revise operations.
- External matters that have occurred. For example, legal proceedings, legislation, or similar matters that might jeopardize an entity's ability to operate; loss of a key franchise, license, or patent; loss of a principal customer or supplier; and an uninsured or underinsured catastrophe such as a drought, earthquake, or flood.

FRF-SME

Management should consider its plans for dealing with the adverse effects of those conditions and events and whether those plans will mitigate the adverse effects and be effectively implemented. Management's considerations relating to its plans may include the following:

- Plans to dispose of assets
  - Are there restrictions on the disposal of assets, such as covenants limiting such transactions in loan or similar agreements or encumbrances against assets?
  - What is the marketability of assets that the entity plans to sell?
  - What are the possible direct or indirect effects of disposal of assets?
- Plans to borrow money or restructure debt
  - Is debt financing available, such as lines of credit or arrangements for factoring receivables or sale-leaseback of assets?
  - Are there existing or committed arrangements to restructure or subordinate debt or to guarantee loans to the entity?
  - What are the possible effects on the entity's borrowing plans of existing restrictions on additional borrowing or the sufficiency of available collateral?
- Plans to reduce or delay expenditures
  - Is it feasible to reduce overhead or administrative expenditures, to postpone maintenance or research and development projects, or to lease rather than purchase assets?
  - What are the possible direct or indirect effects of reduced or delayed expenditures?
- Plans to increase ownership equity
  - Is it feasible to increase ownership equity, including existing or committed arrangements to raise additional capital?
  - Are there existing or committed arrangements to reduce current dividend requirements or to accelerate cash distributions from affiliates or other investors?

Management should disclose the material uncertainties relating to the events or conditions along with its plans for dealing with the adverse effects of the conditions and events.

Management may conclude that the going concern basis is not appropriate. In that situation, the FRF for SMEs accounting framework should not be used. An entity that is not a going concern should prepare its financial statements on the liquidation basis of accounting.

Illustrative Example—Push-Down Accounting
(This material is illustrative only.)

This example illustrates how the accounting treatment specified in chapter 15, "New Basis (Push-Down) Accounting," of *Financial Reporting Framework for Small- and Medium-Sized Entities* might be applied in particular situations. Matters of principle relating to particular situations should be decided in the context of the framework.

Illustration 1
Push-down accounting is a technique that attributes revised values to the assets and liabilities reported in the entity's financial statements based on a purchase transaction or transactions of its equity interests. Application of the technique results in the acquirer's cost being assigned to the assets and liabilities of the acquired entity. For example, assume ABC Company acquires 100 percent of the equity of XYZ Company for $150 million. ABC Company applies the acquisition method specified in chapter 11, "Business Combinations," of the FRF for SMEs accounting framework to account for this business combination in its consolidated financial statements. Further, assume XYZ Company's net assets equaled $60 million prior to the acquisition. If push-down accounting is applied, XYZ Company would establish a new basis for its net assets equal to $150 million in its separate stand-alone financial statements.

Illustration 2
When an individual or entity already owns an equity interest in an entity, the revaluation or market value is proportionate to that owner's increase in ownership. For example, assume ABC, Inc. is owned by two individuals, A and B. A owns 80 percent of the outstanding equity and B owns 20 percent of the outstanding equity in ABC, Inc. On July 1, 2014, B purchased the 80 percent interest from A for $10 million, after which B owned 100 percent of the outstanding equity in ABC, Inc. For simplicity, assume that the book values of ABC, Inc.'s assets and liabilities equal their market values, with the exception of property, plant, and equipment. The market value of the property, plant, and equipment was determined to be $12 million. Also, for simplicity, the tax effects of the acquisition have been ignored.

Application of Requirements
The following illustrates the application of push-down accounting in illustration 2 and the amounts that would be reflected in ABC, Inc.'s financial statements after push-down accounting is applied.

In millions of dollars

	Book Value	Push-Down Entries	Push-Down Basis
Current assets	$6	—	$6
Property, plant, and equipment	10	Dr. $1.6	11.6
Goodwill	—	Dr. 3.6	3.6
Total assets	$16	Dr. $5.2	$21.2

(continued)

	Book Value	Push-Down Entries	Push-Down Basis
Current liabilities	$6	—	$6
Long-term debt	4	—	4
Common stock	1	Dr. $0.8 Cr. 10.0	10.2
Retained earnings	5	Dr. 4	1
Total liabilities and equity	$16	Cr. $5.2	$21.2

Proportionate step-up:
Step-up in property, plant, and equipment: $2 × 80 percent purchased = $1.6. Premium paid is $5.2, goodwill = $5.2 – 1.6 = $3.6

Illustrative Example—Disclosure of Plain-Vanilla Interest Rate Swap
(This material is illustrative only.)

This example illustrates a "plain-vanilla" interest rate swap and the disclosures required by the FRF for SMEs accounting framework. Matters of principle relating to particular situations should be decided in the context of the framework.

Background
In a *plain-vanilla interest rate swap*, a reporting entity agrees to pay cash flows equal to interest at a predetermined fixed rate on a stated notional principal for a stated period and, in return, the reporting entity receives interest at a floating rate on the same notional principal for the same period of time. Importantly, the reporting entity can be the fixed-rate payer and the floating-rate receiver or vice versa.

The FRF for SMEs accounting framework requires, for derivatives such as an interest rate swap, disclosure of the face or contract amount (or notional principal amount if there is no face or contract amount), the nature and terms, including a discussion of the credit and market risk of those instruments, and the cash requirements of those instruments. In addition, an entity should provide a description of the entity's objectives for holding the derivatives and the net settlement amount of the derivatives at the statement of financial position date.

Illustration
Assume ABC Company has $1,000,000 of nonamortizing variable-rate debt outstanding with interest payments due on a quarterly basis. The note accrues interest at the 3-month London Interbank Offered Rate (LIBOR) plus 2 percent and matures via a balloon payment in 7 years. In order to hedge the Company's interest rate risk, the Company would enter into a 7-year interest rate swap for a notional amount of $1,000,000 at a current swap rate (fixed rate) of 2.85 percent. The Company would pay the fixed rate of 2.85 percent on the $1,000,000 notional amount on a quarterly basis and would receive the 3-month LIBOR rate on a quarterly basis. The LIBOR to be received is determined one quarter prior to payment so the payment is made 3 months in arrears. Accordingly, the Company knows 3 months in advance what the payment will be. Payments are settled on a net basis; so, if the 3-month LIBOR is greater than 2.85 percent, then the Company will receive a payment. Therefore, the Company has effectively converted its variable-rate debt into fixed-rate debt with an effective interest rate of 4.85 percent (2.85 percent fixed + 2 percent spread).

Example Disclosure
The Company sometimes borrows at variable rates and uses interest rate swaps as cash flow hedges of future interest payments, which have the economic effect of converting borrowings from floating rates to fixed rates. The interest rate swaps allow the Company to raise long-term borrowings at floating rates and swap them into fixed rates that are lower than those available if it borrowed at fixed rates directly. Under the interest rate swaps, the Company agrees with other parties to exchange, at specified intervals (mainly quarterly), the difference between fixed contract rates and floating rate interest amounts calculated by reference to the agreed notional principal amounts.

At December 31, 2013, the Company has $1,000,000 of nonamortizing variable-rate debt outstanding with interest payments due on a quarterly basis. The note accrues interest at the 3-month LIBOR plus 2 percent. In order to hedge interest rate risk, the Company entered into an interest rate swap for a notional amount of $1,000,000 at fixed rate of 2.85 percent. Under this swap agreement, the Company pays the fixed rate of 2.85 percent on the $1,000,000 notional amount on a quarterly basis, and receives the 3-month LIBOR rate on a quarterly basis. Payments are settled on a net basis, and the Company has effectively converted its variable-rate debt into fixed-rate debt with an effective interest rate of 4.85 percent (2.85 percent fixed + 2 percent spread). As of December 31, 2013, the net settlement amount of the interest rate swap contact was $6,360.

Illustrative Example—Presentation of Equity-Method Investment on the Statement of Cash Flows
(This material is illustrative only.)

This example illustrates how the accounting treatment specified in chapter 8, "Statement of Cash Flows," of the FRF for SMEs framework might be applied in particular situations. Matters of principle relating to particular situations should be decided in the context of the framework.

Example
The following table presents condensed financial data of ABC Corp. for 2014 and 2013.

ABC Corp.
Statement of Financial Position
as of December 31

	2014	2013
Cash and cash equivalents	$2,200	$600
Receivables	2,250	2,100
Inventory	1,000	600
Plant assets (net)	700	645
Investment in marketable securities	–0–	200
Investment in XYZ Company	800	700
	$6,950	$4,845
Accounts payable	$750	$1,200
Accrued liabilities	330	520
Long-term debt	800	1,000
Capital stock	1,400	1,400
Retained earnings	3,670	725
	$6,950	$4,845

ABC Corp.
Statement of Operations
For the Year Ended December 31, 2014

Sales	$ 15,200
Cost of goods sold	(10,400)
Gross profit	4,800
Selling and administrative expense	(1,455)
Income from operations	3,345

(continued)

FRF-SME

Other revenues and gains

Loss on sale of marketable securities	(50)
Investment income from XYZ Company	250
Net income	$ 3,545

Additional information

- Depreciation expense of $145 is included in the selling and administrative expense in 2014.
- ABC Corp. owns 100 percent of XYZ Company and uses the equity method to account for its investment in XYZ Company.
- During 2014, XYZ Company reported net income of $250 and distributed $150 to ABC Corp.
- ABC Corp. paid cash dividends during 2014 of $600.

Illustration of Indirect Method Statement of Cash Flows

ABC Corp.
Statement of Cash Flows
For the Year Ended December 31, 2014

Cash flows from operating activities:

Net income		$3,545
Adjustments to reconcile by operating activities:		
Depreciation expense	$145	
Loss on sale of marketable securities	50	
Undistributed earnings of XYZ Company	(100)	
Increase in receivables	(150)	
Increase in inventory	(400)	
Decrease in accounts payable	(450)	
Decrease in accrued liabilities	(190)	(1095)
Net cash provided by operating activities		2,450

Cash flows from investing activities:

Sale of marketable securities	150
Purchase of plant assets	(200)
Net cash used by investing activities	(50)

Cash flows from financing activities:

Retirement of long-term debt	(200)
Payment of cash dividends	(600)
Net cash used by financing activities	(800)
Net increase in cash and cash equivalents	1,600
Cash and cash equivalents, December 31, 2013	600
Cash and cash equivalents, December 31, 2014	$2,200

FRF-SME

Illustration of Direct Method Statement of Cash Flows

ABC Corp.
Statement of Cash Flows
For the Year Ended December 31, 2014

Cash flows from operating activities:	
Cash collected from customers	$15,050
Cash paid for inventory	(11,250)
Cash paid for operating expenses	(1,500)
Distribution from XYZ Company	150
Net cash provided by operating activities	2,450
Cash flows from investing activities:	
Sale of marketable securities	150
Purchase of plant assets	(200)
Net cash used by investing activities	(50)
Cash flows from financing activities:	
Retirement of long-term debt	(200)
Payment of cash dividends	(600)
Net cash used by financing activities	(800)
Net increase in cash and cash equivalents	1,600
Cash and cash equivalents, December 31, 2013	600
Cash and cash equivalents, December 31, 2014	$2,200

Illustrative Example—Amortization of Goodwill
(This material is illustrative only.)

This example illustrates how the accounting treatment specified in chapter 13, "Intangible Assets," of *Financial Reporting Framework for Small- and Medium-Sized Entities* might be applied in particular situations. Matters of principle relating to particular situations should be decided in the context of the framework.

Background
Under the FRF for SMEs accounting framework, goodwill should be amortized generally over the same period as that used for federal income tax purposes or, if not amortized for federal income tax purposes, then a period of 15 years.

Illustration
Assume that ABC Company acquires 100 percent of XYZ Company on March 1, 2014, and the acquisition is accounted for using the guidance in chapter 11 of the FRF for SMEs accounting framework. As a result of this acquisition, goodwill in the amount of $750,000 is recognized.

If ABC Company amortizes the goodwill for federal income tax purposes under IRC Section 197 (180 months), the amortization expense reported on ABC Company's statement of operations for the year ending December 31, would be as follows:

2014 (March–December)	$ 41,667
2015–2028	50,000
2029	8,333
Total amortization	$750,000

Illustrative Example—Consolidation When There Is a Material Difference in the Basis of Accounting Between a Parent and a Subsidiary

(This material is illustrative only.)

This example illustrates how the accounting treatment specified in chapter 23, "Consolidated Financial Statements and Noncontrolling Interests," of *Financial Reporting Framework for Small- and Medium-Sized Entities* might be applied in particular situations. Matters of principle relating to particular situations should be decided in the context of the framework.

Background

The FRF for SMEs accounting framework states that "a material difference in the basis of accounting between a parent and a subsidiary precludes the preparation of consolidated financial statements." As such, when the financial statements of a subsidiary (*a*) are not prepared in accordance with the framework (those prepared on a cash or tax basis or using unacceptable accounting principles), or (*b*) otherwise contain errors, they should be revised, or correcting entries should be made in consolidation.

In addition, when the policy choice set out in chapter 22, "Subsidiaries," of *Financial Reporting Framework for Small- and Medium-Sized Entities*, is made to account for its subsidiaries using the equity method, the same revisions or corrections would be required (unless impractical) to properly present the investment in a nonconsolidated subsidiary.

Example

Assume that Parent Corp. owns 100 percent of Subsidiary Company, which prepares its financial statements using U.S. GAAP. The only material difference between the FRF for SMEs accounting framework and U.S. GAAP in Subsidiary Company's financial statements is the treatment of Subsidiary Company's investments in marketable securities. In the U.S. GAAP financial statements, Subsidiary Company's investments in marketable securities are classified as available for sale. Accordingly, unrealized gains and losses are excluded from Subsidiary Company's statements of income and are reported as a separate component in the statements of comprehensive income.

In accordance with chapter 11, "Equity, Debt, and Other Investments," of *Financial Reporting Framework for Small- and Medium-Sized Entities*, an entity should measure investments in equity instruments held for sale at market value with changes in market value being recognized in net income in the period incurred. Therefore, in order to present consolidated financial statements (or to present Subsidiary Company as an investment in a nonconsolidated subsidiary, using the equity method), Parent Corp. would need to make adjustments to Subsidiary Company's U.S. GAAP financial statements so that changes in market value of Subsidiary Company's investments in marketable securities held for sale are included in net income in the period incurred.